John G
Play:

The House of Blue Leaves, Landscape of the Body, Bosoms and Neglect, Six Degrees of Separation

The House of Blue Leaves won two Drama Critics' Circle Awards, as well as the Obie and four Tony Awards: 'Naturally this is a comedy, since Guare knows that nothing is funnier than the clash between American dreams and the American way of death ... a play in touch with darkest intelligence, unsparing in its fundamental concern with public lunacy ... cold-bloodedly accurate.' *Village Voice*
'John Guare's wild, funny and touching American comedy of the sixties ... A witchy brew of distress and absurdity.' *Observer*

Landscape of the Body: 'An important play ... a real find ... Mr Guare's darkly lyric comedy drama about spiritual void and urban overkill ... He appears more interested in delusion versus possibility, enthralling possibility, leaving it to other playwrights to grapple with illusion versus reality.' *New York Times*
'Has power and sting ... a strangely compelling play that skates on dark wit over the macabre.' *Wall Street Journal*

Bosoms and Neglect: 'Emerges as the other (besides *Long Day's Journey Into Night*) terrific American mother–son play ... And it ends with one of the great monologues of the American theater ... a Guare gem.' *New York Post*
'Funny, fizzing and brilliant.' *Observer*

Six Degrees of Separation won the 1992 Olivier Best Play Award:
'Transcendent ... magical ... a masterwork that captures New York as Tom Wolfe did in *Bonfire of the Vanities*. An extraordinary high comedy in which broken connections, mistaken identities, and tragic social, familial, and cultural schisms create an hilarious and finally searing panorama of urban America.' *New York Times*
'A *Volpone* or *The Alchemist* for our American times.' *Herald Tribune*

John Guare, born in New York City, received the Obie and New York Drama Critics' Circle Award for both *House of Blue Leaves* and *Six Degrees of Separation*, which also won the Olivier Award for Best Play in its London Royal Court production. He wrote the lyrics for *Two Gentlemen of Verona* which won the New York Drama Critics' Circle Award and Tony Award for Best Musical. His screenplay for Louis Malle's *Atlantic City* earned him an Oscar nomination. He was elected a member of the American Academy of Arts and Letters, co-edits the *Lincoln Center Theater Review* and is a council member of the Dramatists Guild.

JOHN GUARE

Plays: 1

The House of Blue Leaves
Landscape of the Body
Bosoms and Neglect
Six Degrees of Separation

Introduced by the author

Methuen Drama

METHUEN DRAMA CONTEMPORARY DRAMATISTS

1 3 5 7 9 10 8 6 4 2

This collection first published in Great Britain 1999
by Methuen Publishing Ltd

ISBN 0-413-73040-9

A CIP catalogue record for this book is available from the British Library

Typeset by Deltatype, Birkenhead, Merseyside

The extract from 'Esthétique du mal' by Wallace Stevens from his *Collected Poems* is
quoted by kind permission of Faber and Faber Ltd

Caution
All rights whatsoever in these plays are strictly reserved and application for
performance etc., should be made, before rehearsals begin, as follows: *The House of
Blue Leaves*, Samuel French Ltd, 52 Fitzroy Street, London W1P 6JR; *Landscape of the
Body*, *Bosoms and Neglect* and *Six Degrees of Separation*, Dramatists Play Service, Inc., 440
Park Avenue South, New York NY 10016. No performance may be given unless a
licence has been obtained.

Warning: If permission is obtained to produce *The House of Blue Leaves*, then 'White
Christmas' by Irving Berlin may only be used to the extent indicated herein, unless
special permission for more extensive use is received from Irving Berlin Music
Corporation, 1633 Broadway, New York, New York 10019, USA.

Contents

John Guare
Chronology

1960–63   *Something I'll Tell You Tuesday* and *Did You Write My Name in the Snow?* directed by John Badham, Yale School of Drama

1965   *To Wally Pantoni We Leave a Credenza* directed by Edwin Aldridge, Barr-Wilder-Albee Workshop, New York

The Loveliest Afternoon of the Year directed by John Guare, Caffè Cino, New York

A Day for Surprises directed by John Guare, Theater Genesis, New York

1966   *The House of Blue Leaves*, Act One, directed by Melvin Bernhardt, Eugene O'Neill Theater Center, Waterford, Connecticut

1967   *Muzeeka* directed by Melvin Bernhardt, Eugene O'Neill Theater Center

1968   *Cop-Out* directed by Melvin Bernhardt, Eugene O'Neill Theater Center

Muzeeka directed by Melvin Bernhardt, Provincetown Playhouse, New York

Obie Award for *Muzeeka*

The Exception and the Rule, adaptation of the play by Brecht, in collaboration with Leonard Bernstein, Stephen Sondheim and Jerome Robbins – abandoned

1969   *Cop-Out* directed by Melvin Bernhardt, Cort Theater, New York

Variety Poll of New York Drama Critics Most Promising Playwright of the Season

1970   *Taking Off*, screenplay in collaboration with Milos Forman and Jean-Claude Carrière

Cannes Film Festival Jury Prize

1971   *The House of Blue Leaves* directed by Mel Shapiro, Truck and Warehouse Theater, New York;

New York Drama Critics' Circle Award Best American play; Obie Best Play

Introduction:
The War Against the Kitchen Sink

In 1949, I wrote three plays that the neighborhood kids performed in Bobby Shlomm's garage in East Atlantic Beach on Long Island. Thanks to the photo story the local newspaper ran on the eleven-year-old playwright, my parents gave me a Royal portable typewriter for my twelfth birthday which I would need because I was now officially a playwright. And a playwright it had to be. I had seen *Annie Get Your Gun* and was really impressed by a vivid Indian ceremony that scared the hell out of me along with Ethel Merman. I had seen *Where's Charley* with Ray Bolger leading us, the audience, in a joyous singalong of the show's hit 'Once In Love With Amy'. *Life* magazine, my main connection to the world, showed naked girls waving from giant champagne glasses in *Gentlemen Prefer Blondes*. I got my parents to take me to that. I was going to be in the theater.

In 1950, *Life* magazine covered the opening of a new play called *The Wisteria Trees* by Joshua Logan who did musicals like *South Pacific*. He had taken a Russian play I had never heard of called *The Cherry Orchard* and changed the locale to the Deep South. I understood that move. Every week I saw remarkable actresses like Kim Stanley and Geraldine Page on our Magnavox's 12-inch screen finding brutal truths of loneliness while poised on the brink of wisteria-soaked hysteria. Human emotion could not be rendered true unless it cried out in southern accents which were not easy to come by when you're living in Jackson Heights, Queens. I got a copy of *The Cherry Orchard* out of the library and read it with a Southern accent; it was great but Logan already took it. I looked through other plays by this Chekhov guy to find the one I would set in the South, get produced on Broadway and still be fourteen. By now it was 1952 and I discovered *Three Sisters*. That was the play for me. I could understand those girls being trapped. I was trapped in being fourteen, in hating my life, in wanting life to be splendid which it was not. It was ordinary. I typed out my *Three Sisters* on that proof of my profession, my Royal portable typewriter. Every time the girls cried out for Moscow, I substituted New Orleans. Yes! That was theater! 'Get me to New Orleans!' I could hear Kim Stanley cry it out in that agonized southern voice that she used even when she played Joan of Arc being burned alive at the stake on a surrealistic CBS show called 'You Are There' where every week Walter Cronkite would anchor a 'live' TV pickup of an historical event.

I only got as far as the first act because typing was hard. I couldn't get to New Orleans either. But I could get to the theater. In 1952 I saw – why I wanted to see it I still don't know – Tyrone Guthrie's production of Marlowe's *Tamburlaine the Great*. *Life* must have shown pictures of it. I badgered my parents to take me. Tamburlaine stood on the stage of the Winter Gardens Theater, unrolled an enormous map of the world, and strode across it. That one image so overwhelmed me that I could no longer watch TV miniatures like the original *Marty* set in living rooms like mine. I despised plays with people sitting at kitchen tables pouring their hearts out and the people in the audience oohing when the people in the play turned on the faucet and real water came out. That kitchen sink. That was what I hated most.

We had a wonderful neighbor at East Atlantic Beach named Glendon Allvine who had written a play in 1939 about the life of Gilbert and Sullivan called *Knights of Song* with a cast of 120 that was done on Broadway by Oscar Hammerstein. It may have only lasted a week but Mr Allvine had been there. One week *is* so far ahead of never. In 1954 Glen worked in the press department at the American Shakespeare Festival in Stratford, Connecticut. I went up to visit him and saw Katherine Hepburn and Alfred Drake and Morris Carnovsky do *Much Ado About Nothing*, *Merchant of Venice*, Fritz Weaver do *Hamlet*, June Havoc and Hiram Sherman do *A Midsummer Night's Dream*. Not once, but over and over. Reading the plays made sense after seeing them. What I loved about Shakespeare was he used no stage directions. He didn't use a parenthesis after a character's name to instruct the actor how to say the line, i.e., *(With bitter irony.)* and then have the line be something like 'OK'. Shakespeare packed the emotion into the line of dialogue. He also wrote lots of scene changes. Shakespeare says 'The Sea Coast of Bohemia' and you believe it. I saw if you give audiences an honest crumb of information, they'll build it into an entire Forest of Arden.

Now it was 1957. I couldn't wait to see John Osborne's revolutionary *Look Back in Anger* which was coming to New York. The curtain went up. No! Not a kitchen sink! Where is the revolution?

For me, it didn't come till a couple of years later when Osborne's *The Entertainer* opened, starring Laurence Olivier as the down-at-the-heels comedian. The shock was Olivier played out front to me as if I was not in New York, but in the audience of a shabby theater at a cheesy English seaside resort. And it disturbed me. It was the first time I realized that the audience could play a role in the play. The audience was not a passive witness as it was in realistic, naturalistic plays, barred from the play by a brutal fourth wall.

The other clues I had been collecting started to make sense. I realized that what I loved about musicals was that no fourth wall existed. The clown acknowledged my presence by needing my laughter. Up to then I thought serious plays were the ones with no laughter and plays with lots of laughs were feathers. But *The Entertainer* was a serious play about the death of an Empire that made me roar with laughter. It had songs and girls. I loved it. I ignored *The Entertainer*'s gloomy domestic bits that would alternate with the theater scenes. The kitchen sink in residence was the price to be paid for the dazzle created by Osborne and made manifest by Olivier. I looked at other plays and realized that what I loved about, say, *The Glass Menagerie* was not the emotional authenticity guaranteed by its Southerness. No. I loved the Williams play because Tom was telling me his idea of the truth. In 1957, I saw an Anouilh play called *Time Remembered* that had a full orchestra in the pit but it wasn't a musical. Vernon Duke wrote a score to accompany this play. Between the extravagance of Richard Burton's performance and the lushness of Duke's music, Anouilh's romanticism soared into a realm of lunatic poetry that touched a real pain about loss. The music lulled me into thinking I was seeing a show that was all pleasure and then suddenly took me

somewhere else, some place dark. I was knocked out by
Lorraine Hansberry's *A Raisin in the Sun* which began in the
dreaded living room with a dreaded kitchen sink spouting
water. But suddenly in the second act, in a stroke of madness,
the play moved into an imagined African interior. I was inside
Sidney Poitier's head. I was not simply engaged in watching
these people. In one flash I understood these people. And then
we were back in the kitchen. I began to expand the enemy list
to include the Actor's Studio Strasberg brand of Stanislavski
that sought perfection in the small detail of behavior. That was
great for movies and television. But this was the stage! Let me
see the great gesture delivered by the clowns that I was lucky
to see: Bea Lillie, Nancy Walker, Judy Holliday, Zero Mostel.
Those raunchy boisterous strippers of *Gypsy* warmed me up for
Ethel Merman's blaring out her rage: 'Someone tell me when
is it my turn?' Bert Lahr played six different roles in S. J.
Perelman's *The Beauty Part* and destroyed the idea of a single
coherent human identity for once and for all. Arthur Kopit
(who was my age for God's sake) wrote the outrageous *Oh Dad
Poor Dad* . . . as directed by Jerome Robbins with a great clown
named Barbara Harris. There was a remarkable play called
The Red Eye of Love by Arnold Weinstein, *The Caretaker* by Pinter,
Albee's *Zoo Story* and Beckett's *Krapp's Last Tape*. Arthur Miller?
I wanted everybody in *The Crucible* to go nuts, especially John
Proctor. I didn't want anybody to be spared. I wanted
attention to be paid only to Tamburlaine or his mirror, the
hilarious fools who thought they were Tamburlaine striding
over the map of their own private world.

A remarkable critic and translator Una Ellis-Fermor wrote
there were only two times in the history of the theater where
the unconscious was made palpable, the Greeks and the
Jacobeans.

Putting the unconscious on stage? Unlocking that? Yes,
that's what I responded to in *Three Sisters*. Get me to Moscow.
Get me to New Orleans. Get me some shape to the voices in
my head. Show me the forces moving me. Don't show me a
theater whose prime focus is only creating an illusion of surface
reality, where the play is true because – look – it's a real room
with real water running into the kitchen sink. Ergo it's real.

Zola wrote in the preface to his classic naturalistic play *Therese Raquin* that with the new advances in theatrical scenery 'No one can any longer deny the possibility of producing the reality of environment on the stage.' In the second half of the nineteenth century, the discovery of electricity allowed the theater to replicate the very life of the new ticket-buying audience. The curtain could go up on a mirror of the middle-class audience's lives and for the price of a ticket, the audience could say 'Yes, that is where I live. I believe what I see. So I'll believe what I hear.' Zola could fill his environment with a truth. But the new audience wanted a theater that told them, not only is your life fine, after it deals with this evening's problem, say, divorce or illegitimacy, life is going to go back to being fine and we'll never say anything further to disturb you. We'll lull you and reassure you. How could we lie? Look how artfully we've replicated life. If it looks real, it is real. 'But this is photography . . . This is the misunderstood naturalism which holds that art merely consists of drawing a piece of nature in a natural way; it is not the great naturalism which seeks out the points where the great battles are fought, which loves to see what you do not see every day, which delights in the struggle between natural forces, whether these forces are called love and hate, rebellious or social instincts, which finds the beautiful or ugly unimportant if only it is great.' Strindberg wrote this in 1889, eight years after Zola.

I was learning the difference between the plays of Pinero and the plays of Shaw, the difference between Eugene O'Neill who along with Tennesee Williams showed you the consequences of illusions, as against a representative Broadway playwright such as William Inge. Great White Way Naturalism told you indeed Little Sheba might not Come Back but don't worry, we'll learn from this experience and everything will be all right. I was beginning to see that Great White Way Naturalism is to reality what sentimentality is to feeling. I was beginning to learn that theater has to get into the deepest part of your dreams, has to show you a mirror you might recoil from, but also show you reality so you might know what to do with it. What's the best route to that place of our secret voices? Tennessee Williams wrote two one-act plays called *Slapstick*

Tragedies. I loved that title. He showed one way to that part of our brain or our souls. The part of theater that's vaudeville.

I was in Egypt in 1965 and got a packet of clippings from my parents about the Pope's visit to New York. Imagine! The first time a pope had left Rome to travel overseas to plea for peace. My parents said you might think you're seeing the world but the world has come to us. And they wrote me all about the joy of seeing the Pope on Queens Boulevard. I started writing *The House of Blue Leaves* that day in Cairo. If I had been in New York, I would have discounted that Papal day and sniffed at my parents' response. Being in Egypt allowed me for the first time to look into my life, into the world of my parents and realize that no life is ordinary.

So *The House of Blue Leaves* would take place in a shabby apartment. During the play, one of the characters would try to cook a meal and, to cook a meal, you need a kitchen and if you have a kitchen you have – no! – a sink! Where is Tamburlaine! Does the kitchen sink of a thousand hated modern plays possess a drain so powerful that no modern playwright can escape being sucked down its whirlpool, drowning in its eddies? How to resist the undertow? Luckily, I went into writing *Blue Leaves* armed with the brand new Peter Nichols' *A Day In the Death of Joe Egg* and Shelagh Delaney's *A Taste of Honey*. Those two saints of theater had shown all of us one way to resist the undertow of naturalism. Jazz, direct vaudeville playing to the audience, music – those are the oars against that riptide.

In 1969 a play of mine called *Cop Out* opened to such a brutal reception, I fled New York to find solace – in the Arctic Circle, in Norway. I found in Oslo an English edition of Ibsen and as I traveled further and further north read his last play *When We Dead Awaken*, the journey out of the artist out of the domestic, trying to scale the mountain top and leave the ordinary world behind.

But no matter how far north I travel, all I know is the ordinary world. I live in the ordinary world. I like the ordinary world. I began to realize up there with the midnight sun scalloping nuttily around that bleak horizon that what the playwright does with that icon of naturalism, the kitchen sink, *is* the story of twentieth-century playwrighting. Does the playwright elect to keep that kitchen sink with its real live running water to soothe the audience with familiarity? Does the playwright dismantle the kitchen sink and take the audience into dangerous terrain? New wine in old bottles? Re-invent water. What about new water in new sinks? How the playwright resolves this tension between surface reality and inner reality, how the playwright restores the theater to its true nature as a place of poetry, song, joy, a place where the bright truth is told, that war against the kitchen sink is ultimately the history of our theater.

John Guare

The House of Blue Leaves

Foreword

The House of Blue Leaves takes place in Sunnyside, Queens, one of the five boroughs of New York City. You have to understand Queens. It was never a borough with its own identity like Brooklyn that people clapped for on quiz shows if you said you came from there. Brooklyn had been a city before it became part of New York, so it always had its own identity. And the Bronx originally had been Jacob Bronck's farm, which at least gives it something personal, and Staten Island is out there on the way to the sea, and, of course, Manhattan is what people mean when they say New York.

Queens was built in the twenties in that flush of optimism as a bedroom community for people on their way up who worked in Manhattan but wanted to pretend they had the better things in life until the inevitable break came and they could make the official move to the Scarsdales and the Ryes and the Greenwiches of their dreams, the pay-off that was the birthright of every American. Queens named its communities Forest Hills, Kew Gardens, Elmhurst, Woodside, Sunnyside, Jackson Heights, Corona, Astoria (after the Astors, of all people). The builders built the apartment houses in mock Tudor or Gothic or Colonial and then named them The Chateau, The El Dorado, Linsley Hall, the Alhambra. We lived first in The East Gate, then moved to The West Gate, then to Hampton Court. And the lobbies had Chippendale furniture and Aztec fireplaces, and the elevators had roman numerals on the buttons.

And in the twenties and thirties and forties you'd move there and move out as soon as you could. Your young married days were over, the promotions came. The ads in the magazines were right. Hallelujah. Queens: a comfortable rest stop, a pleasant rung on the ladder of success, a promise we were promised in some secret dream. (The first paid commercial on American radio was Queensboro Management advertising apartments in Jackson Heights in 1922 on WEAF.) And isn't Manhattan, each day the skyline growing denser and more crenellated, always looming up there in the distance?

The elevated subway, the Flushing line, zooms to it, only fourteen minutes from Grand Central Station. Everything you could want you'd find right there in Queens. But the young marrieds become old marrieds, and the children come, but the promotions, the breaks, don't, and you're still there in your bedroom community, your life over the bridge in Manhattan, and the fourteen-minute ride becomes longer every day. Why didn't I get the breaks? I'm right here in the heart of the action, in the bedroom community of the heart of the action, and I live in the El Dorado Apartments and the main street of Jackson Heights has Tudor-topped buildings with pizza slices for sale beneath them and discount radios and discount drugs and discount records and the Chippendale-paneled elevator in my apartment is all carved up with Love to Fuck that no amount of polishing can ever erase. And why do my dreams, which should be the best part of me, why do my dreams, my wants, constantly humiliate me? Why don't I get the breaks? What happened? I'm hip. I'm hep. I'm a New Yorker. The heart of the action. Just a subway ride to the heart of the action. I want to be part of that skyline. I want to blend into those lights. Hey, dreams, I dreamed you. I'm not something you curb a dog for. New York is where it all is. So why aren't I here?

When I was a kid, I wanted to come from Iowa, from New Mexico, to make the final break and leave, say, the flatness of Nebraska and get on that Greyhound and get off that Greyhound at Port Authority and you wave your cardboard suitcase at the sky: I'll Lick You Yet. How do you run away to your dreams when you're already there? I never wanted to be any place in my life but New York. How do you get there when you're there? Fourteen minutes on the Flushing line is a very long distance. And I guess that's what this play is about more than anything else: humiliation. Everyone in the play is constantly being humiliated by their dreams, their loves, their wants, their best parts. People have criticized the play for being cruel or unfeeling. I don't think any play from the *Oresteia* on down has ever reached the cruelty of the smallest moments in our lives, what we have done to others, what others have done to us. I'm not interested so much in how people survive as in how they avoid humiliation. Chekhov says we must never humiliate one another, and I think avoiding humiliation is the core of tragedy and comedy and probably of our lives.

This is how the play got written: I went to Saint Joan of Arc Grammar School in Jackson Heights, Queens, from 1944 to 1952 (wildly pre-Berrigan years). The nuns would say, If only we could get to Rome, to have His Holiness touch us, just to see Him, capital H, the Vicar of Christ on Earth – Vicar, V.I.C.A.R., Vicar, in true spelling-bee style. Oh, dear God, help me get to Rome, the capital of Italy, and go to that special little country in the heart of the capital – V.A.T.I. C.A.N. C.I.T.Y. – and touch the Pope. No sisters ever yearned for Moscow the way those sisters and their pupils yearned for Rome. And in 1965 I finally got to Rome. Sister Carmela! Do you hear me? I got here! It's a new Pope, but they're all the same. Sister Benedict! I'm here! And I looked at the Rome papers, and there on the front page was a picture of the Pope. On Queens Boulevard. I got to Rome on the day a Pope left the Vatican to come to New York for the first time to plead to the United Nations for peace in the world on October 4, 1965. He passed through Queens, because you have to on the way from Kennedy Airport to Manhattan. Like the Borough of Queens itself, that's how much effect the Pope's pleas for peace had. The Pope's no loser. Neither is Artie Shaughnessy, whom *The House of Blue Leaves* is about. They both have big dreams. Lots of possibilities. The Pope's just into more real estate.

My parents wrote me about that day that the Pope came to New York and how thrilled they were, and the letter caught up with me in Cairo because I was hitching from Paris to the Sudan. And I started thinking about my parents and me and why was I in Egypt and what was I doing with my life and what were they doing with theirs, and that's how plays get started. The play is autobiographical in the sense that everything in the play happened in one way or another over a period of years, and some of it happened in dreams and some of it could have happened and some of it, luckily, never happened. But it's autobiographical all the same. My father worked for the New York Stock Exchange, but he called it a zoo and Artie in the play is a zoo-keeper. The Billy in the play is my mother's brother, Billy, a monstrous man who was head of casting at MGM from the thirties through the fifties. The Huckleberry Finn episode that begins Act Two is an exact word-for-word reportage of what happened between Billy and me at our first meeting. The play is a blur of many years that pulled together under the umbrella of the Pope's visit.

In 1966 I wrote the first act of the play, and, like some bizarre revenge or disapproval, on the day I finished it my father died. The first act was performed at the O'Neill Theatre Center in Waterford, Connecticut, and I played Artie. The second act came in a rush after that and all the events in that first draft are the same as you'll find in this version. But in 1966 the steam, the impetus for the play, had gone. I wrote another draft of the second act. Another. A fourth. A fifth. A sixth. A director I had been working with was leading the play into abysmal naturalistic areas with all the traps that a set with a kitchen sink in it can have. I was lost on the play until 1969 in London, when one night at the National Theatre I saw Laurence Olivier do *Dance of Death* and the next night, still reeling from it, saw him in Charon's production of *A Flea in Her Ear*. The savage intensity of the first blended into the maniacal intensity of the second, and somewhere in my head *Dance of Death* became the same play as *A Flea in Her Ear*. Why shouldn't Strindberg and Feydeau get married, at least live together, and *The House of Blue Leaves* be their child? For years my two favorite shows had been *Gypsy* and *The Homecoming*. I think the only playwrighting rule is that you have to learn your craft so that you can put on stage plays you would like to see. So I threw away all the second acts of the play, started in again, and, for the first time, understood what I wanted.

Before I was born, just before, my father wrote a song for my mother:

A stranger's coming to our house.
I hope he likes us.
I hope he stays.
I hope he doesn't go away.

I liked them, loved them, stayed too long, and didn't go away.
This play is for them.

J.G.
1971

The House of Blue Leaves was first presented by Warren Lyons and Betty Ann Besch at the Truck and Warehouse Theatre, New York, on 10 February 1971, directed by Mel Shapiro. It was presented at the Mitzi Newhouse Theater, Lincoln Center, by Gregory Mosher and Bernard Gersten on 19 March 1986, directed by Jerry Zaks, with the following cast:

Artie Shaughnessy	John Mahoney
Ronnie Shaughnessy	Ben Stiller
Bunny Flingus	Stockard Channing
Bananas Shaughnessy	Swoosie Kurtz
Corrinna Stroller	Julie Hagerty
Head Nun	Patricia Falkenhain
Second Nun	Jane Cecil
Little Nun	Ann Talman
Military Policeman	Ian Blackman
White Man	Peter J. Downing
Billy Einhorn	Christopher Walken

The House of Blue Leaves was first produced in the UK at the Sadler's Wells Theatre, London, in October 1988, directed by Nick Hamm, with the following cast:

Artie Shaughnessy	Dennis Quilley
Ronnie Shaughnessy	John Fitzgerald-Jay
Bunny Flingus	Helen Lederer
Bananas Shaughnessy	Nichola McAuliffe
Corrinna Stroller	Kelly Hunter
Billy Einhorn	Harry Towb

Music and lyrics by John Guare

Setting A cold apartment in Sunnyside, Queens, New York City. 4 October 1965

Prologue

The stage of the El Dorado Bar & Grill.

While the house lights are still on, and the audience is still being seated, **Artie Shaughnessy** *comes onstage through the curtains, bows, and sits at the upright piano in front of the curtain. He is forty-five years old. He carries sheet music and an opened bottle of beer. He scowls into the wings and then smiles broadly out front.*

Artie (*out front, nervous*)   My name is Artie Shaughnessy and I'm going to sing you songs I wrote. I wrote all these songs. Words and music. Could I have some quiet, please? (*He sings brightly:*)

> Back together again,
> Back together again.
> Since we split up
> The skies we lit up
> Looked all bit up
> Like Fido chewed them,
> But they're back together again.

> You can say you knew us when
> We were together;
> Now we're apart,
> Thunder and lightning's
> Back in my heart,
> And that's the weather to be
> When you're back together with me.

(*Into the wings.*) Could you please turn the lights down? A spotlight on me? You promised me a spotlight. (*Out front.*) I got a ballad I'm singing and you promised me a blue spotlight.

The house lights remain on. People are still finding their seats.

Artie (*plunges on into a ballad sentimentally*)
> I'm Looking for Something,
> I've searched everywhere,

I'm looking for something
And just when I'm there,
Whenever I'm near it
I can see it and hear it,
I'm almost upon it,
Then it's gone.
It seems I'm looking for Something
But what can it be?
I just need a Someone
To hold close to me.
I'll tell you a secret,
Please keep it entre nous,
That Someone
I thought it was you.

(*Out front.*) Could you please take your seats and listen? I'm going to sing you a song I wrote at work today and I hope you like it as much as I do. (*He plays and sings.*)

Where is the devil in Evelyn?
What's it doing in Angela's eyes?
Evelyn is heavenly,
Angela's in a devil's disguise.
I know about the sin in Cynthia
And the hell in Helen of Troy,
But where is the devil in Evelyn?
What's it doing in Angela's eyes?
Oh boy!
What's it doing in Angela's eyes?

He leaps up from the piano with his sheet music and beer, bows to the audience. Waits for applause. Bows. Waits. Looks. Runs offstage.

The house lights go down.

Act One

The living room of a shabby apartment in Sunnyside, Queens. The room is filled with many lamps and pictures of movie stars and jungle animals. Upstage center is a bay window, the only window in the room. Across the opening of the bay is a crisscross-barred folding gate of the kind jewelers draw across the front of their stores at night. Outside the window is a fire escape. A small window in the side of the bay is close enough to the gate to be opened or closed by reaching through the bars.

It's late at night and a street lamp beams some light into this dark place through the barred window. A piano near the window is covered with hundreds of pieces of sheet music and manuscript paper and beer bottles. A jacket, shirt, and pants — the green uniform of a city employee — are draped over the end of the piano nearest the window.

Artie *is asleep on the couch, zipped tightly into a sleeping bag, snoring fitfully and mumbling:* Pope Ronnie. Pope Ronnie. Pope Ronald the First. Pope Ronald.

There is a pullman kitchen with its doors open far stage right. There are three other doors in the room: a front door with many bolts on it, and two doors that lead to bedrooms. Even though **Artie** *and his family have lived here eighteen years now, there's still an air of transiency to the room as if they had never unpacked from the time they moved in.*

Somebody's at the window, climbing down the fire escape. **Ronnie**, **Artie**'s *eighteen-year-old son, climbs in the window. He gingerly pulls at the folding gate. It's locked. He stands there for a minute, out of breath.*

He's a young eighteen. His hair is cropped close and he wears big glasses. He wears a heavy army overcoat and under that a suit of army fatigue clothes.

He reaches through the bars to his father's trousers, gets the keys out of the pocket, unlocks the lock, comes into the room and relocks the gate behind him, replaces the pants. He tiptoes past his father, who's still snoring and mumbling: Pope Ronnie. Pope Ronnie. Pope Ronnie. **Ronnie** *opens the icebox door, careful not to let the light spill all over the floor. He takes out milk and bread.*

The doorbell buzzes. **Artie** *groans.*

Ronnie *runs into his bedroom. Somebody is knocking on the front door and buzzing quickly, quickly like little mosquito jabs.*

Artie *stirs. He unzips himself from his sleeping bag, runs to the door. He wears ski pajamas. A key fits into the front door. The door shakes.* **Artie** *undoes the six bolts that hold the door locked. He opens the door, dashes back to his bag, and zips himself in.*

Bunny Flingus *throws open the door. The hall behind her is brilliantly lit. She is a pretty, pink, slightly plump, electric woman in her late thirties. She wears a fur-collared coat and plastic booties, and two Brownie cameras on cords clunking against a pair of binoculars.*

At the moment she is freezing, uncomfortable, and furious. She storms to the foot of the couch.

Bunny   You know what your trouble is? You got no sense of history. You know that? Are you aware of that? Lock yourself up against history, get drowned by the whole tide of human events. Sleep it away in your bed. Your bag. Zip yourself in, Artie. The greatest tide in the history of the world is coming in today, so don't get your feet wet.

Artie (*picking up his glow-in-the-dark alarm*)   It's quarter-to-five in the morning, Bunny –

Bunny   Lucky for you I got a sense of history. (*She sits on the edge of the couch, picks up the newspaper on the floor.*) You finished last night's? Oooo, it's freezing out there. Breath's coming out of everybody's mouth like a balloon in a cartoon. (*She rips the paper into long shreds and stuffs it down into the plastic booties she wears.*)

People have been up for hours. Queens Boulevard – lined for blocks already! Steam coming out of everybody's mouth! Cripples laid out in the streets in stretchers with ear muffs on over their bandages. Nuns – you never seen so many nuns in your life! Ordinary people like you and me

in from New Jersey and Connecticut and there's a lady
even drove in from Ohio — Ohio! — just for today! She
drove four of the most crippled people in Toledo. They're
stretched out in the gutter waiting for the sun to come out
so they can start snapping pictures. I haven't seen so many
people, Artie, so excited since the premier of *Cleopatra*. It's
that big. Breathe! There's miracles in the air!

Artie   It's soot, Bunny. Polluted air.

Bunny   All these out-of-staters driving in with cameras
and thermos bottles and you live right here and you're all
zipped in like a turtle. Miss Henshaw, the old lady who's
the check-out girl at the A & P who gyps everybody — her
nephew is a cop and she's saving us two divine places right
by the curb. You're not the only one with connections. But
she can't save them forever. Oh God, Artie, what a
morning! You should see the stars!!! I know all the stars
from the time I worked for that astronomer and you should
see Orion — O'Ryan: the Irish constellation — I haven't
looked up and seen stars in years! I held my autograph
book up and let Jupiter shine on it. Jupiter and Venus and
Mars. They're all out! You got to come see Orion. He's
the hunter and he's pulling his arrow back so tight in the
sky like a Connect-the-Dots picture made up of all these
burning planets. If he ever lets that arrow go, he'll shoot all
the other stars out of the sky. What a welcome for the
Pope!

And right now, the Pope is flying through the star-filled
sky, bumping planets out of the way, and he's asleep
dreaming of the mobs waiting for him. When famous
people go to sleep at night, it's us they dream of, Artie.
The famous ones — they're the real people. We're the
creatures of their dreams. You're the dream. I'm the
dream. We have to be there for the Pope's dream. Look at
the light on the Empire State Building swirling around and
around like a burglar's torch looking all through the sky —
Everybody's waiting, Artie — everybody!

Artie (*angry*)   What I want to know is who the hell is paying for this wop's trip over here anyway –

Bunny (*shocked*)   Artie! (*She reaches through the bars to close the window.*) Ssshhh – they'll hear you –

Artie   I don't put my nickels and dimes in Sunday collections to pay for any dago holiday – flying over here with his robes and gee-gaws and bringing his buddies over when I can't even afford a trip to Staten Island –

Bunny (*puzzled*)   What's in Staten Island?

Artie   Nothing! But I couldn't even afford a nickel ferry-boat ride. I known you two months and can't even afford a present for you – a ring –

Bunny   I don't need a ring –

Artie   At least a friendship ring –

Bunny (*rubbing his head*)   I'd only lose it –

Artie (*pulling away*)   And this guy's flying over here – not tourist – oh no –

Bunny (*suspicious of his bitterness*)   Where'd you go last night?

Artie (*back into his bag*)   You go see the Pope. Tell him hello for me.

Bunny   You went to that amateur night, didn't you –

Artie (*signaling toward the other room*)   Shut up – she's inside –

Bunny   You went to the El Dorado Bar Amateur Night, didn't you. I spent two months building you up to be something and you throw yourself away on that drivel –

Artie   They talked all the way through it –

Bunny   Did you play them 'Where's the Devil in Evelyn?'?

Artie   They talked and walked around all through it –

Bunny   I wish I'd been there with you. You know what I would've said to them? (*To us.*) The first time I heard 'Mairzy Doats' I realized I am listening to a classic. I picked off 'Old Black Magic' and 'I Could've Danced All Night' as classics the minute I heard them. (*She recites:*) 'Where is the devil in Evelyn? What's it doing in Angela's eyes?' I didn't work in Macy's Music Department for nix. I know what I'm talking about. (*To* **Artie**.) That song is a classic. You've written yourself a classic.

Artie   I even had to pay for my own beers.

Bunny   Pearls before swine. Chalk it up to experience.

Artie   The blackboard's getting kind of filled up. I'm too old to be a young talent.

Bunny (*opens the window through the bars*)   Smell the bread –

Artie   Shut the window – it's freezing and you're letting all the dirt in –

Bunny   Miss Henshaw's saving us this divine place right by the cemetery so the Pope will have to slow down –

Artie   Nothing worse than cold dirt –

The other bedroom door opens and **Bananas Shaughnessy**, *a sick woman in a nightgown, looks at them. They don't see her.*

Bunny (*ecstatically*)   And when he passes by in his limousine, I'll call out, 'Your Holiness, marry us – the hell with peace to the world – bring peace to us.' And he won't hear me because bands will be playing and the whole city yelling, but he'll see me because I been eyed by the best of them, and he'll nod and I'll grab your hand and say, 'Marry us, Pope,' and he'll wave his holy hand and all the emeralds and rubies on his fingers will send Yes beams. In a way, today's my wedding day. I should have something white at my throat! Our whole life is beginning – my life – our life – and we'll be married and go out to California and Billy will help you. You'll be out there with the big shots – out where you belong – not in any amateur nights in bars on Queens Boulevard. Billy will get your songs in movies. It's not too late to start. With me behind you! Oh, Artie, the El Dorado Bar will stick up a huge neon sign flashing onto Queens Boulevard in a couple of years flashing 'Artie Shaughnessy Got Started Here'. And nobody'll believe it. Oh, Artie, tables turn.

Bananas *closes the door.*

Artie (*gets out of his bag. He sings thoughtfully:*)
    Bridges are for burning,
    Tables are for turning –

He turns on all the lights. He pulls **Bunny** *over to the kitchen.*

Artie   I'll go see the Pope –

Bunny (*hugging him*)   Oh, I love you!

Artie   I'll come if –

Bunny   You said you'll come. That is tantamount to a promise.

Artie   I will if –

Bunny   Tantamount. Tantamount. You hear that? I didn't work in a law office for nix. I could sue you for breach.

Artie (*seductively*)   Bunny?

Bunny (*near tears*)   I know what you're going to say –

Artie (*opening a ketchup bottle under her nose*)   Cook for me?

Bunny (*in a passionate heat*)   I knew it. I knew it.

Artie   Just breakfast.

Bunny   You bend my arm and twist my heart but I got to be strong.

Artie   I'm not asking any ten-course dinner.

To get away from his plea, **Bunny** *runs over to the piano, where his clothes are draped.*

Bunny   Just put your clothes on over the ski p.j.'s I bought you. It's thirty-eight degrees and I don't want you getting your pneumonia back –

Artie (*holding up two eggs*)   Eggs, baby. Eggs right here.

Bunny (*holding out his jingling trousers*)   Rinse your mouth out to freshen up and come on let's go?

Artie (*seductively*)   You boil the eggs and pour lemon sauce over –

Bunny (*shaking the trousers at him*)   Hollandaise. I know hollandaise. (*She plops down with the weight of the temptation, glum.*) It's really cold out, so dress warm – Look, I stuffed the *New York Post* in my booties. Plastic just ain't as warm as it used to be.

Artie   And you pour the hollandaise over the eggs on English muffins – and then you put the grilled ham on top – I'm making a scrapbook of all the foods you tell me you know how to cook and then I go through the magazines and cut out pictures of what it must look like. (*He gets the scrapbook.*) Look – veal parmagina – eggplant meringue.

Bunny   I cooked that for me last night. It was so good I almost died.

Artie (*sings, as* **Bunny** *takes the book and looks through it with great despair*)
　　If you cooked my words
　　Like they was veal
　　I'd say I love you
　　For every meal.
　　Take my words,
　　Garlic and oil them,
　　Butter and broil them,
　　Sauté and boil them –
　　Bunny, let me eat you!

(*He speaks.*) Cook for me?

Bunny   Not till after we're married.

Artie   You couldn't give me a little sample right now?

Bunny   I'm not that kind of girl. I'll sleep with you anytime you want. Anywhere. In two months I've known you, did I refuse you once? Not once! You want me to climb in the bag with you now? Unzip it – go on – unzip it – Give your fingers a smack and I'm flat on my back. I'll sew those words into a sampler for you in our new home in California. We'll hang it right by the front door. Because, Artie, I'm a rotten lay and I know it and you know it and everybody knows it –

Artie   What do you mean? Everybody knows it –

Bunny   I'm not good in bed. It's no insult. I took that sex test in the *Reader's Digest* two weeks ago and I scored twelve. Twelve, Artie! I ran out of that dentist office with tears gushing out of my face. But I face up to the truth about myself. So if I cooked for you now and said I won't sleep with you till we're married, you'd look forward to sleeping with me so much that by the time we did get to that motel near Hollywood, I'd be such a disappointment, you'd never forgive me. My cooking is the only thing I got to lure you on with and hold you with. Artie, we got to keep some magic for the honeymoon. It's my first honeymoon and I want it to be so good, I'm aiming for two million calories. I want to cook for you so bad I walk by the A & P, I get all hot jabs of chili powder inside my thighs . . . but I can't till we get those tickets to California safe in my purse, till Billy knows we're coming, till I got that ring right on my cooking finger . . . Don't tempt me . . . I love you . . .

Artie (*beaten*)   Two eggs easy over?

Bunny (*shakes her head No*)   And I'm sorry last night went sour . . .

Artie (*sits down, depressed*)   They made me buy my own beers . . .

Bananas (*calling from the bedroom*)   Is it light? Is it daytime already?

Artie *and* **Bunny** *look at each other.*

Bunny   I'll pour you cornflakes.

Artie *(nervous)*   You better leave.

Bunny *(standing her ground)*   A nice bowlful?

Artie   I don't want her to know yet.

Bunny   It'll be like a coming attraction.

Artie *(pushing her into the kitchen)*   You're a tease, Bunny, and that's the worst thing to be. *(He puts on his green shirt and pants over his pajamas.)*

Bananas *comes out of the bedroom. She's lived in her nightgown for the last six months. She's in her early forties and has been crying for as long as she's had her nightgown on. She walks uncertainly, as if hidden barriers lay scattered in her path.*

Bananas   Is it morning?

Artie *(not knowing how to cope with her)*   Go back to bed.

Bananas   You're dressed and it's so dark. Did you get an emergency call? Did the lion have babies yet?

Artie *(checking that the gate is locked)*   The lioness hasn't dropped yet. The jaguar and the cheetah both still waiting. The birds still on their eggs.

Bananas   Are you leaving to get away from me? Tell me? The truth? You hate me. You hate my looks – my face – my clothes – you hate me. You wish I was fatter so there'd be more of me to hate. You hate me. Don't say that! You love me. I know you love me. You love me. Well, I don't love you. How does that grab you? *(She is shaking violently.)*

Artie *takes pills from the piano and holds her, forcing the pills in her mouth. He's accepted this as one of the natural facts of his life. There is no violence in the action. Her body shakes. The spasms stop. She's quiet for a long time. He walks over to the kitchen.* **Bunny** *kisses the palm of his hand.*

Bananas   For once could you let my emotions come out?
If I laugh, you give me a pill. If I cry, you give me a pill
. . . no more pills . . . I'm quiet now . . .

*Artie comes out of the kitchen and pours two pills into his hand. He
doesn't like to do this.*

Bananas (*smiles*)   No! No more -- look at me – I'm a
peaceful forest, but I can feel all the animals have gone
back into hiding and now I'm very quiet. All the wild
animals have gone back into hiding. But once – once let
me have an emotion? Let the animals come out? I don't
like being still, Artie. It makes me afraid . . .

(*Brightly.*) How are you this morning? Sleep well? You were
out late last night. I heard you come in and moved over in
the bed. Go back to bed and rest. It's still early . . . come
back to bed. . . .

Artie (*finishing dressing*)   The Pope is coming today and I'm
going to see him.

Bananas   The Pope is coming here?

Artie   Yes, he's coming here. We're going to kick off our
shoes and have a few beers and kick the piano around.
(*Gently, as if to a child.*) The Pope is talking to the UN about
Vietnam. He's coming over to stop the war so Ronnie
won't have to go to Vietnam.

Bananas   Three weeks he's been gone. How can twenty-
one days be a hundred years?

Artie (*to the audience*)   This woman doesn't understand. My
kid is charmed. He gets greetings to go to basic training for
Vietnam and the Pope does something never done before.
He flies out of Italy for the first time *ever* to stop the war.
Ronnie'll be home before you can say Jake Rabinowitz.
Ronnie – what a kid – a charmed life . . .

Bananas   I can't go out of the house . . . my fingernails
are all different lengths. I couldn't leave the house. . . .
Look – I cut this one just yesterday and look how long it is
already . . . but this one . . . I cut it months ago right down

to the quick and it hasn't moved that much. I don't understand that . . . I couldn't see the Pope. I'd embarrass him. My nails are all different. I can feel them growing . . . they're connected to my veins and heart and pulling my insides out my fingers. (*She is getting hysterical.*)

Artie *forces pills down her mouth. She's quiet. She smiles at him.* **Artie**'s *exhausted, upset. He paces up and down in front of her, loathing her.*

Artie   The Pope takes one look at you standing on Queens Boulevard, he'll make the biggest U-turn you ever saw right back to Rome. (*Angry.*) I dreamed last night Ronnie was the Pope and he came today and all the streets were lined with everybody waiting to meet him – and I felt like Joseph P. Kennedy, only bigger, because the Pope is a bigger draw than any President. And it was raining everywhere but on him and when he saw you and me on Queens Boulevard, he stopped his glass limo and I stepped into the bubble, but you didn't. He wouldn't take you.

Bananas   He would take me!

Artie (*triumphant*)   Your own son denied you. Slammed the door in your face and you had open-toe shoes on and the water ran in the heels and out the toes like two Rin Tin Tins taking a leak – and Ronnie and I drove off to the UN and the war in Vietnam stopped and he took me back to Rome and canonized me – made me a Saint of the Church and in charge of writing all the hymns for the Church. A hymn couldn't be played unless it was mine and the whole congregation sang 'Where Is the Devil in Evelyn?' only they made it sound like monks singing it – You weren't invited, Bananas. Ronnie loved only me . . . (*He finds himself in front of the kitchen. He smiles at* **Bunny**.) What a dream . . . it's awful to have to wake up. For my dreams, I need a passport and shots. I travel the whole world.

Bunny (*whispering*)   I dreamed once I met Abraham Lincoln.

Artie   Did you like him?

Bunny   He was all right. (*She opens a jar of pickles and begins eating them.*)

Bananas *sees* **Bunny**'s *fur coat by* **Ronnie**'s *room. She opens the front door and throws the coat into the hall. She closes the door behind her.*

Bananas   You know what I dream? I dream I'm just waking up and I roam around the house all day crying because of the way my life turned out. And then I do wake up and what do I do? Roam around the house all day crying about the way my life turned out.

An idea comes to **Artie**. *He goes to the piano and sings.*

Artie
   The Day that the Pope came to New York
   The Day that the Pope came to New York,
   It really was comical
   The Pope wore a yarmulke
   The Day that the Pope came to New York.

Bananas   Don't be disrespectful.

She gets up to go to the kitchen. **Artie** *rushes in front of her and blocks her way.* **Bunny** *pushes herself against the icebox trying to hide; she's eating a bowl of cornflakes.*

Artie   Stay out of the kitchen. I'll get your food –

Bananas   Chop it up in small pieces . . .

Bunny (*in a loud, fierce whisper*)   Miss Henshaw cannot reserve our places indefinitely. Tantamount to theft is holding a place other people could use. Tantamount. Her nephew the cop could lock us right up. Make her go back to bed.

Artie *fixes* **Bananas**'s *food on a plate.* **Bananas** *sits up on her haunches and puts her hands, palm downward, under her chin.*

Bananas   Hello, Artie!

Artie   You're going to eat like a human being.

Bananas   Woof? Woof?

Artie   Work all day in a zoo. Come home to a zoo.

He takes a deep breath. He throws her the food. She catches it in her mouth. She rolls on her back.

Bananas   I like being animals. You know why? I never heard of a famous animal. Oh, a couple of Lassies – an occasional Trigger – but, by and large, animals weren't meant to be famous.

Artie *storms into the kitchen.*

Bunny   What a work of art is a dog. How noble in its thought – how gentle in its dignity –

Artie *buries his head against the icebox.*

Bananas (*smiling out front*)   Hello. I haven't had a chance to welcome you. This is my home and I'm your hostess and I should welcome you. I wanted to say Hello and I'm glad you could come. I was very sick a few months ago. I tried to slash my wrists with spoons. But I'm better now and glad to see people. In the house. I couldn't go out. Not yet. Hello. (*She walks the length of the stage, smiling at the audience, at us. She has a beautiful smile.*)

Bunny *comes out of the kitchen down to the edge of the stage.*

Bunny (*to us*)   You know what my wish is? The priest told us last Sunday to make a wish when the Pope rides by. When the Pope rides by, the wish in my heart is gonna knock the Pope's eye out. It is braided in tall letters, all my veins and arteries and aortas are braided into the wish that she dies pretty soon. (*She goes back to the kitchen.*)

Bananas (*who has put a red mask on her head*)   I had a vision – a nightmare – I saw you talking to a terrible fat woman with newspapers for feet – and she was talking about hunters up in the sky and that she was a dream and you were a dream . . . (*She crosses to the kitchen, pulls the mask down over her eyes, and comes up behind **Bunny**.*) Hah!!!

Bunny *screams in terror and runs into the living room.*

Bunny I am not taking insults from a sick person. A healthy person can call me anything they want. But insults from a sickie – a sicksicksickie – I don't like to be degraded. A sick person has fumes in their head – you release poison fumes and it makes me sick – dizzy – like riding the back of a bus. No wonder Negroes are fighting so hard to be freed, riding in the back of buses all those years. I'm amazed they even got enough strength to stand up straight . . . Where's my coat? Artie, where's my coat? My binox and my camera? (*To* **Bananas**.) What did you do with my coat, Looney Tunes?

Artie *has retrieved the coat from the hallway.*

Bunny You soiled my coat! This coat is soiled! Arthur, are you dressed warm? Are you coming?

Artie (*embarrassed*) Bananas, I'd like to present – I'd like you to meet – this is Bunny Flingus.

Bunny You got the ski p.j.'s I bought you on underneath? You used to go around freezing till I met you. I'll teach you how to dress warm. I didn't work at ski lodges for nothing. I worked at Aspen.

Bananas (*thinks it over a moment*) I'm glad you're making friends, Artie. I'm no good for you.

Bunny (*taking folders out of her purse, to* **Bananas**) I might as well give these to you now. Travel folders to Juarez. It's a simple procedure – you fly down to Mexico – wet-back lawyer meets you – sign a paper – jet back to little old NY.

Artie Bunny's more than a friend, Bananas.

Bunny Play a little music – 'South of the Border' – divorce Meheeco style! –

Artie Would you get out of here, Bunny. I'll take care of this.

Bananas *sings hysterically, without words, 'South of the Border'.*

Bunny I didn't work in a travel agency for nix, Arthur.

Artie   Bunny!

Bunny   I know my way around.

Bananas *stops singing.*

Artie (*taking the folders from* **Bunny**)   She can't even go to the incinerator alone. You're talking about Mexico –

Bunny   I know these sick wives. I've seen a dozen like you in movies. I wasn't an usher for nothing. You live in wheelchairs just to hold your husband and the minute your husband's out of the room, you're hopped out of your wheelchair doing the Charleston and making a general spectacle of yourself. I see right through you. Tell her, Artie. Tell her what we're going to do.

Artie   We're going to California, Bananas.

Bunny   Bananas! What a name!

Bananas   A trip would be nice for you . . .

Bunny   What a banana –

Bananas   You could see Billy . . . I couldn't see Billy . . . (*Almost laughing.*) I can't see anything . . .

Artie   Not a trip.

Bunny   To live. To live forever.

Bananas   Remember the time we rode up in the elevator with Bob Hope? He's such a wonderful man.

Artie   I didn't tell you this, Bunny. Last week, I rode out to Long Island. (*To* **Bananas**, *taking her hand.*) You need help. We – *I* found a nice hosp . . . By the sea . . . by the beautiful sea . . . It's an old estate and you can walk from the train station and it was raining and the roads aren't paved so it's muddy, but by the road where you turn into the estate, there was a tree with blue leaves in the rain – I walked under it to get out of the rain and also because I had never seen a tree with blue leaves and I walked under the tree and all the leaves flew away in one big round bunch – just lifted up, leaving a bare tree. Whoosh . . . It

was birds. Not blue leaves but birds, waiting to go to
Florida or California ... and all the birds flew to another
tree a couple of hundred feet off and that bare tree
blossomed – snap! like that – with all these blue very quiet
leaves ... You'll like the place, Bananas. I talked to the
doctor. He had a mustache. You like mustaches. And the
Blue Cross will handle a lot of it, so we won't have to
worry about expense ... You'll like the place ... a lot of
famous people have had crackdowns there, so you'll be
running in good company.

Bananas   Shock treatments?

Artie   No. No shock treatments.

Bananas   You swear?

Bunny   If she needs them, she'll get them.

Artie   I'm handling this my way.

Bunny   I'm sick of you kowtowing to her. Those poison
fumes that come out of her head make me dizzy –
suffering – look at her – what does she know about
suffering ...

Bananas   Did you read in the paper about the bull in
Madrid who fought so well they didn't let him die? They
healed him, let him rest before they put him back in the
ring, again and again and again. I don't like the shock
treatments, Artie. At least the concentration camps – I was
reading about them, Artie – they put the people in the
ovens and never took them out – but the shock treatments
– they put you in the oven and then they take you out and
then they put you in and then they take you out ...

Bunny   Did you read *Modern Screen* two months ago? I am
usually not a reader of film magazines, but the cover on it
reached right up and seduced my eye in the health club. It
was a picture like this – (*She clutches her head.*) – and it was
called 'Sandra Dee's Night of Hell'. Did you read that by
any happenstance? Of course you wouldn't read it. You
can't see anything. You're ignorant. Not you. Her. The

story told of the night before Sandra Dee was to make her first movie and her mother said, 'Sandra, do you have everything you need?' And she said – snapped back, real fresh-like – 'Leave me alone, Mother. I'm a big girl now and don't need any help from you.' So her mother said, 'All right, Sandra, but remember I'm always here.' Well, her mother closed the door and Sandra could not find her hair curlers anywhere and she was too proud to go to her mom and ask her where they were –

Artie   Bunny, I don't understand.

Bunny   Shut up, I'm not finished yet – and she tore through the house having to look her best for the set tomorrow because it was her first picture and her hair curlers were nowhere! Finally at four in the a.m., her best friend, Annette Funicello, the former Mouseketeer, came over and took the hair curlers out of her very own hair and gave them to Sandra. Thus ended her night of hell, but she had learned a lesson. Suffering – you don't even know the meaning of suffering. You're a nobody and you suffer like a nobody. I'm taking Artie out of this environment and bringing him to California while Billy can still do him some good. Get Artie's songs – his music– into the movies.

Artie   I feel I only got about this much life left in me, Bananas. I got to use it. These are my peak years. I got to take this chance. You stay in your room. You're crying. All the time. Ronnie's gone now. This is not a creative atmosphere . . . Bananas, I'm too old to be a young talent.

Bananas   I never stopped you all these years . . .

Bunny   Be proud to admit it, Artie. You were afraid till I came on the scene. Admit it with pride.

Artie   I was never afraid. What're you talking about?

Bunny   No man takes a job feeding animals in the Central Park Zoo unless he's afraid to deal with humans.

Artie   I walk right into the cage! What do you mean?

Bunny   Arthur, I'm trying to talk to your wife. Bananas, I want to be sincere to you and kind.

Artie   I'm not afraid of nothing! Put my hand right in the cage –

Bunny (*sitting down beside* **Bananas**, *speaks to her as to a child*)   There's a beautiful book of poems by Robert Graves. I never read the book because the title is so beautiful there's no need to read the book: *Man Does. Woman Is.* Look around this apartment. Look at Artie. Look at him.

Artie (*muttering*)   I been with panthers.

Bunny (*with great kindness*)   I've never met your son, but – no insult to you, Artie – but I don't want to. Man does. What does Artie do? He plays the piano. He creates. What are you? What is Bananas? Like he said before when you said you've been having nightmares. Artie said, 'You been looking in the mirror?' Because that's what you are, Bananas. Look in the mirror.

Artie *is playing the piano – 'Where Is the Devil in Evelyn?'*

Bunny   *Man Does. Woman Is.* I didn't work in a lending library for nothing.

Artie   I got panthers licking out of my hands like goddam pussycats.

Bunny   Then why don't you ever call Billy?

Artie (*stops playing*)   I got family obligations.

Bananas (*at the window*)   You could take these bars down. I'm not going to jump.

Bunny   You're afraid to call Billy and tell him we're coming out.

Bananas   I'd like to jump out right in front of the Pope's car.

Artie   Panthers lay right on their backs and I tickle their armpits. You call me afraid? Hah!

Bananas He'd take me in his arms and bless me.

Bunny Then call Billy now.

Artie It's the middle of the night!

Bunny It's only two in the morning out there now.

Artie Two in the morning is the middle of the night!

Bunny In Hollywood! Come off it, he's probably not even in yet – they're out there frigging and frugging and swinging and eating and dancing. Since Georgina died, he's probably got a brace of nude starlets splashing in the pool.

Artie I can't call him. He's probably not even in yet –

Bunny I don't even think you know him.

Artie Don't know him!

Bunny You've been giving me a line – your best friend – big Hollywood big shot – you don't even know him –

Artie Best friends stay your best friends precisely because you don't go calling them in the middle of the night.

Bunny You been using him – dangling him over my head – big Hollywood big-shot friend, just to take advantage of me – just to get in bed with me – Casting couches! I heard about them –

Artie That's not true!

Bunny And you want me to cook for you! I know the score, baby. I didn't work in a theatrical furniture store for nothing!

She tries to put her coat on to leave. He pulls it off her.

If you can't call your best friends in the middle of the night, then who can you call – taking advantage of me in a steam bath –

Bananas (*picking up the phone*) You want me to get Billy on the phone?

Artie You stay out of this!

Bananas   He was always my much better friend than yours, Artie.

Artie   Your friend! Billy and I only went to kindergarten together, grammar school together, high school together till his family moved away. Fate always kept an eye out to keep us friends. (*He sings.*)

If you're ever in a jam, here I am.

Bananas (*sings*)
   Friendship.

Artie (*sings*)
   If you're ever up a tree, just phone me.

(*Turns to us exuberantly.*) He got stationed making training movies and off each reel there's what they call leader – undeveloped film – and he started snipping that leader off, so by the time we all got discharged, he had enough film spliced up to film Twenty Commandments. He made his movie right here on the streets of New York and Rossellini was making his movies in Italy, only Billy was making them here in America and better. He sold everything he had and he made *Conduct of Life* and it's still playing in museums. It's at the Museum of Modern Art next week – and Twentieth-Century Fox signed him and MGM signed him – they both signed him to full contracts – the first time anybody ever got signed by two studios at once . . . You only knew him about six months' worth, Bananas, when he was making the picture. And everybody in that picture became a star and Billy is still making great pictures.

Bunny   In his latest one, will you ever forget that moment when Doris Day comes down that flight of stairs in that bathrobe and thinks Rock Hudson is the plumber to fix her bathtub and in reality he's an atomic scientist.

Bananas   I didn't see that . . .

Artie (*mocking*)   Bananas doesn't go out of the house . . .

Bunny (*stars in her eyes*)   Call him, Artie.

Artie   He gets up early to be on the set. I don't want to
wake him up –

Bunny   Within the next two years, you could be out there
in a black tie waiting for the lady – Greer Garson – to
open the envelope and say as the world holds its breath –
'And the winner of the Oscar for this year's Best Song is –'
(*She rips a travel folder very slowly.*)

Artie (*leaning forward*)   Who is it? Who won?

Bunny   And now Miss Mitzi Gaynor and Mr Franco
Corelli of the Metropolitan Opera will sing the winning
song for you from the picture of the same name made by
his good friend and genius, Billy Einhorn. The winner is of
course Mr Arthur M. Shaughnessy.

Artie (*goes to the telephone. He dials once, then*)   Operator, I
want to call in Bel Air, Los Angeles –

Bunny   You got the number?

Artie   Tattooed, baby. Tattooed. Your heart and his
telephone number right on my chest like a sailor. Not you,
operator. I want and fast I want in Los Angeles in Bel Air
GR 2-4129 and I will not dial it because I want to speak
personally to my good friend and genius, Mr Billy Einhorn
. . . E-I-N – don't you know how to spell it? The name of
only Hollywood's leading director my friend and you better
not give this number to any of your friends and call him
up and bother him asking for screen tests.

Bunny   When I was an operator, they made us take
oaths. I had Marlon Brando's number for years and pistols
couldn't've dragged it out of my head – they make you
raise your right hand –

Artie   My number is Ravenswood 1-2276 and don't go
giving that number away and I want a good connection . . .
hang on, Bunny – (*She takes his extended hand.*) – you can
hear the beepbeepbeeps – we're traveling across the
country – hang on! Ring. It's ringing. Ring.

Bunny (*his palm and her palm forming one praying hand*)   Oh

God, please –

Artie (*pulling away from her*)   Ring. It's up. Hello? Billy?
Yes, operator, get off – that's Billy. Will you get off – (*To*
Bunny.) I should've called station-to-station. He picked it
right up and everything. Billy! This is Ramon Navarro! . . .
No, Billy, it's Artie Shaughnessy. Artie. No, New York! Did
I wake you up! Can you hear me! Billy, hello. I got to tell
you something – first of all, I got to tell you how bad I
feel about Georgina dying – the good die young – what
can I say – and second, since you, you old bum, never
come back to your old stomping grounds – your happy
hunting grounds, I'm thinking of coming out to see you.
. . . I know you can fix up a tour of the studios and that'd
be great . . . and you can get us hotel reservations – that's
just fine . . . But, Billy, I'm thinking I got to get away –
not just a vacation – but make a change, get a break, if
you know what I'm getting at . . . Bananas is fine. She's
right here. We were just thinking about you – no, it's not
fine. Billy, this sounds cruel to say but Bananas is as dead
for me as Georgina is for you. I'm in love with a
remarkable wonderful girl – yeah, she's here too – who I
should've married years ago – no, we didn't know her
years ago – I only met her two months ago – yeah . . .

(*Secretively, pulling the phone off to the corner.*) It's kind of funny,
a chimpanzee knocked me in the back and kinked my back
out of whack and I went to this health club to work it out
and in the steam section with all the steam I got lost and I
went into this steam room and there was Bunny – yeah,
just towels – I mean you could make a movie out of this, it
was so romantic – She couldn't see me and she started
talking about the weight she had to take off and the food
she had to give up and she started talking about duckling
with orange sauce and oysters baked with spinach and
shrimps baked in the juice of melted sturgeon eyes which
caviar comes from – well, you know me and food and I
got so excited and the steam's getting thicker and thicker
and I ripped off my towel and kind of raped her . . . and
she was quiet for a long time and then she finally said one

of the greatest lines of all time . . . She said, 'There's a man in here.' . . . And she was in her sheet like a toga and I was all toga'd up and I swear, Billy, we were gods and goddesses and the steam bubbled up and swirled and it was Mount Olympus. I'm a new man, Billy – a new man – and I got to make a start before it's too late and I'm calling you, crawling on my hands and knees – no, not like that, I'm standing up straight and talking to my best buddy and saying Can I come see you and bring Bunny and talk over old times . . . I'll pay my own way. I'm not asking you for nothing. Just your friendship. I think about you so much and I read about you in the columns and *Conduct of Life* is playing at the Museum of Modern Art next week and I get nervous calling you and that Doris Day pic – well, Bunny and I fell out of our loge seats – no, Bananas couldn't see it – she don't go out of the house much . . . I get nervous about calling you because, well, you know, and I'm not asking for any Auld Lang Syne treatment, but it must be kind of lonely with Georgina gone and we sent five dollars in to the Damon Runyon Cancer Fund like Walter Winchell said to do and we're gonna send more and it must be kind of lonely and the three of us – Bunny and you and me – could have some laughs. What do you say? You write me and let me know your schedule and we can come any time. But soon. Okay, buddy? Okay? No, this is my call. I'm paying for this call so you don't have to worry – talking to you I get all opened up. You still drinking rye? Jack Daniels! Set out the glasses – open the bottle – no, I'll bring the bottle – we'll see you soon. Good night, Billy. (*The call is over.*)

Soon, Billy. Soon. Soon. (*He hangs up.*)

Bunny (*dances and sings*)
    The Day that the Pope came to New York
    The Day that the Pope came to New York,
    It really was comical
    The Pope wore a yarmulke
    The Day that the Pope came to New York.

Artie (*stunned*)   Did you hear me!

Bunny   You made me sound like the Moon Coming Over the Mountain! So fat!

Artie   He said to say hello to you, Bananas.

Bananas   Hello . . .

Artie (*to* **Bunny**)   Get the copy of *Life* magazine with the story on his house . . .

Bunny *gets the magazine off the top of the piano.*

Bunny (*thrilled*)   You made me sound so fat! So Kate Smith!

Artie (*taking the magazine and opening it*)   Look at his house – on the highest part of all Los Angeles –

Bunny (*devouring the pictures*)   It's Bel Air! I know Bel Air! I mean, I don't know Bel Air, but, I mean, I know Bel Air!

Artie *and* **Bunny** *flop on the sofa.* **Bananas**, *in the kitchen behind them, throws rice at them.*

Bunny   Let's get out of here. She gives me the weeping willies.

Bananas   Oh, no, I'm all right. I was just thinking how lucky we all are. You going off to California and me going off to the loony bin –

Artie (*correcting her*)   It's a rest place –

Bananas   With beautiful blue trees?

Artie   Birds – waiting to go to Florida or California –

Bananas   Maybe it was a flock of insane bluebirds that got committed –

Artie (*to* **Bunny**)   I'm gonna take a shower. My shirt's all damp from the telephone call.

Bunny (*putting her coat on*)   Artie, I'll be at the corner of Forty-Sixth Street near the cemetery by the TV repair store . . . Hello, John the Baptist. That's who you are. John the Baptist. You called Billy and prepared the way – the

way for yourself. Oh, Christ, the dinners I'm gonna cook
for you. (*She sings.*)

It really was comical
The Pope wore a yarmulke
The Day that the Pope came to New York.

She blows a kiss and exits. **Artie** *yelps triumphantly. He comes
downstage.*

Artie   Hello, Billy. I'm here. I got all my music. (*He sings.*)

I'm here with bells on,
Ringing out how I feel.
I'll ring,
I'll roar,
I'll sing
Encore!
I'm here with bells on.
Ring! Ring! Ring!

Bananas   The people downstairs . . . they'll be pumping
broomsticks on the ceiling . . .

Artie (*jubilant*)   For once the people downstairs is Bunny!
(*He sings.*)

For once the people downstairs is Bunny!

(*He jumps up and down on the floor.*) Whenever the
conversation gets around to something you don't like, you
start ringing bells of concern for the people downstairs. For
once in my life, the people downstairs is Bunny and I am a
free man! (*He bangs all over the keys of the piano.*) And that's a
symphony for the people upstairs!

Bananas   There's just the roof upstairs . . .

Artie   Yeah, and you know roofs well. I give up six
months of my life taking care of you and one morning I
wake up and you're gone and all you got on is a
nightgown and your bare feet – the corns of your bare feet
for slippers. And it's snowing out, snowing a blizzard, and
you're out in it. Twenty-four hours you're gone and the

police are up here and long since gone and you're being
broadcasted for in thirteen states all covered with snow –
and I look out that window and I see a gray smudge in a
nightgown standing on the edge of the roof over there in
a snowbank and I'm praying to God and I run out of this
place, across the street. And I grab you down and you're
so cold, your nightgown cuts into me like glass breaking
and I carried you back here and you didn't even catch a
cold – not even a sniffle. If you had just a sniffle, I
could've forgiven you ... You just look at me with that
dead look you got right now ... You stay out twenty-four
hours in a blizzard hopping from roof to roof without even
a pair of drawers on – and *I* get the pneumonia.

Bananas   Can I have my song?

Artie   You're tone-deaf. (*He hits two bad notes on the piano.*)
Like that.

Bananas   So I won't sing it ... My troubles all began a
year ago – two years ago today – two days ago today?
Today.

Artie *plays 'The Anniversary Waltz'.*

Bananas (*to us*)   We used to have a beautiful old green
Buick. The Green Latrine! ... I'm not allowed to drive it
any more ... but when I could drive it ... the last time I
drove it, I drove into Manhattan.

Artie *plays 'In My Merry Oldsmobile'.*

Bananas   And I drive down Broadway – to the
Crossroads of the World.

Artie *plays 'Forty-Second Street'.*

Bananas   I see a scene that you wouldn't see in your
wildest dreams. Forty-Second Street. Broadway. Four
corners. Four people. One on each corner. All waving for
taxis. Cardinal Spellman. Jackie Kennedy. Bob Hope.
President Johnson. All carrying suitcases. Taxi! Taxi! I stop
in the middle of the street – the middle of Broadway – and
I get out of my Green Latrine and yell, 'Get in. I'm a

gypsy. A gypsy cab. Get in. I'll take you where you want to go. Don't you all know each other? Get in! Get in!'

They keep waving for cabs. I run over to President Johnson and grab him by the arm. 'Get in.' And pull Jackie Kennedy into my car and John-John, who I didn't see, starts crying and Jackie hits me and I hit her and I grab Bob Hope and push Cardinal Spellman into the back seat, crying and laughing, 'I'll take you where you want to go. Get in! Give me your suitcases' – and the suitcases spill open and Jackie Kennedy's wigs blow down Forty-Second Street and Cardinal Spellman hits me and Johnson screams and I hit him. I hit them all. And then the Green Latrine blew four flat tires and sinks and I run to protect the car and four cabs appear and all my friends run into four different cabs. And cars are honking at me to move.

I push the car over the bridge back to Queens. You're asleep. I turn on Johnny Carson to get my mind off and there's Cardinal Spellman and Bob Hope, whose ski-nose is still bleeding, and they tell the story of what happened to them and everybody laughs. Thirty million people watch Johnny Carson and they all laugh. At me. At me. I'm nobody. I knew all those people better than me. You. Ronnie. I know everything about them. Why can't they love me?

And then it began to snow and I went up on the roof . . .

Artie (*after a long pause*) Come see the Pope. Pray. Miracles happen. He'll bless you. *Reader's Digest* has an article this month on how prayer answers things. Pray? Kneel down in the street? The Pope can cure you. The *Reader's Digest* don't afford to crap around.

Bananas My fingernails are all different lengths. Everybody'd laugh . . .

Artie We used to have fun. Sometimes I miss you so much . . .

Bananas (*smiling nervously*) If I had gloves to put on my hands . . .

Artie The Pope must be landing now. I'm going to turn on the television. I want you to see him. (*He turns on the television.*) Here he is. He's getting off the plane. Bananas, look. Look at the screen. (*He pulls her to the screen. He makes her kneel in front of it.*) Oh God, help Bananas. Please God? Say a prayer, Bananas. Say, 'Make me better, God . . .'

Bananas Make me better, God . . .

Artie 'So Artie can go away in peace.' . . . Here's the Pope. (*He speaks to the screen.*) Get out of the way! Let a sick woman see! There he is! Kiss him? Kiss his hem, Bananas. He'll cure you! Kiss him.

Bananas *leans forward to kiss the screen. She looks up and laughs at her husband.*

Bananas The screen is so cold . . .

Artie (*leaping*) Get out of the way, you goddam newsman! (*He pushes* **Bananas** *aside and kisses the screen.*) Help me – help me – Your Holiness . . .

While he hugs the set, **Bananas** *leaves the room to go into her bedroom.*

The front door flies open. **Bunny** *bursts in, flushed, bubbling. She has an enormous 'I Love Paul' button on her coat.*

Bunny He's landed! He's landed! It's on everybody's transistors and you're still here! And the school kids! The Pope drives by, he sees all those school kids, he's gonna come out for birth control today!! Churches will be selling Holy Diaphragms with pictures of Saint Christopher and all the saints on them. You mark my words. (*To us, indicating her button.*) They ran out of 'Welcome Pope' buttons so I ran downstairs and got my leftover from when the Beatles were here! I am famished. What a day! (*She goes to the icebox and downs a bottle of soda.*)

Bananas *comes out of the bedroom. She wears a coat over her nightgown, and two different shoes, one higher than the other, and a hat cocked on her head. She is smiling. She is pulling on gloves.*

Artie *turns off the TV.* **Bunny** *gapes. Band music plays joyously in the distance.* **Artie** *goes to* **Bananas** *and takes her arm.*

Bunny   Now wait one minute. Miss Henshaw is going to be mighty pissed off.

Artie   Just for today.

Bananas   Hold me tight . . .

Artie *(grabbing his coat)*   Over the threshold . . . *(They go out.)*

Bunny   Artie, are you dressed warm? Are you dressed warm? Your music! You forgot your music! You gotta get it blessed by the Pope!!

Bananas *appears in the doorway and grabs the music from* **Bunny**.

Bananas *(sings)*
   It really was comical
   The Pope wore a yarmulke
   The Day that the Pope came to New York.

Bunny   You witch! You'll be in Bellevue tonight with enough shock treatments they can plug Times Square into your ear. I didn't work for Con Edison for nothing! *(She storms out after them and slams the door behind her.)*

The bedroom door **Ronnie** *went into at the beginning of the act opens. He comes out carrying a large gift box.*

He comes downstage and stares at us.

Curtain.

Act Two

Scene One

Ronnie *is standing in the same position, staring at us. Out of the pocket of his fatigues he first takes two hand grenades, then wire, then his father's alarm clock. He wires them together, setting the alarm on the clock at a special time. He puts the whole device into the gift box.*

He is very young – looks barely seventeen – his hair is cropped close all over; he is tall, skinny. He speaks with deep, suffocated religious fervor; his eyes bulge with a strange mixture of terrifying innocence and diabolism. You can't figure out whether he'd be a gargoyle on some Gothic cathedral or a skinny cherub on some altar.

Ronnie My father tell you all about me? Pope Ronnie? Charmed life? How great I am? That's how he is with you. You should hear him with me, you'd sing a different tune pretty quick, and it wouldn't be 'Where Is the Devil in Evelyn?'

He goes into his room and returns carrying a large, dusty box. He opens it and takes out an altar boy's bright red cassock and white surplice that used to fit him when he was twelve. As he puts them on, he speaks to us:

I was twelve years old and all the newspapers had headlines on my twelfth birthday that Billy was coming to town. And *Life* was doing stories on him and *Look* and the newsreels, because Billy was searching America to find the Ideal American Boy to play Huckleberry Finn. And Billy came to New York and called my father and asked him if he could stay here – Billy needed a hide-out. In Waldorf-Astorias all over the country, chambermaids would wheel in silver carts to change the sheets. And out of the sheets would hop little boys saying, 'Hello, I'm Huckleberry Finn.' All over the country, little boys dressed in blue jeans and straw hats would be sent to him in crates, be under the silver cover covering his dinner, in his medicine cabinet in

all his hotel rooms, his suitcase – 'Hello, hello, I'm
Huckleberry Finn.' And he was coming here to hide out.
Here – Billy coming here – I asked the nun in school who
was Huckleberry Finn –

The nun in Queen of Martyrs knew. She told me. The
Ideal American Boy. And coming home, all the store
windows reflected me and the mirror in the tailor shop
said, 'Hello, Huck.' The butcher shop window said, 'Hello,
Huck. Huckleberry Finn. All America Wants to Meet Billy
and He'll Be hiding Out in Your House.' I came home –
went in there – into my room and packed my bag . . . I
knew Billy would see me and take me back to California
with him that very day. This room smelled of ammonia
and air freshener and these slipcovers were new that day
and my parents were filling up the icebox in their brand-
new clothes, filling up the icebox with food and liquor as
excited as if the Pope was coming – and nervous because
they hadn't seen him in a long while – Billy. They told me
my new clothes were on my bed. To go get dressed. I
didn't want to tell them I'd be leaving shortly to start a
new life. That I'd be flying out to California with Billy on
the HMS *Huckleberry*. I didn't want tears from them – only
trails of envy . . . I went to my room and packed my bag
and waited.

The doorbell rang. (*He starts hitting two notes on the piano.*) If
you listen close, you can still hear the echoes of those wet
kisses and handshakes and tears and backs getting hit and
Hello, Billys, Hello. They talked for a long time about
people from their past. And then my father called out,
'Ronnie, guess who? Billy, we named him after your father.
Ronnie, guess who?'

I picked up my bag and said goodbye to myself in the
mirror. Came out. Billy there. Smiling.

It suddenly dawned on me. You had to do things to get
parts.

I began dancing. And singing. Immediately. Things I have
never done in my life – before or since. I stood on my

head and skipped and whirled – (*He cartwheels across the stage.*) – spectacular leaps in the air so I could see veins in the ceiling – ran up and down the keys of the piano and sang and began laughing and crying soft and loud to show off all my emotions. And I heard music and drums that I couldn't even keep up with. And then cut off all my emotions just like that. Instantly. And took a deep bow like the Dying Swan I saw on Ed Sullivan. (*He bows deeply.*) I picked up my suitcase and waited by the door.

Billy turned to my parents, whose jaws were down to about there, and Billy said, 'You never told me you had a mentally retarded child.'

'You never told me I had an idiot for a godchild,' and I picked up my bag and went into my room and shut the door and never came out the whole time he was here.

My only triumph was he could never find a Huckleberry Finn. Another company made the picture a few years later, but it flopped.

My father thinks I'm nothing. Billy. My sergeant. They laugh at me. You laughing at me? I'm going to fool you all. By tonight, I'll be on headlines all over the world. Cover of *Time*. *Life*. TV specials. (*He shows a picture of himself on the wall.*) I hope they use this picture of me – I look better with hair – Go ahead – laugh. Because you know what I think of you? (*He gives us hesitant Bronx cheers.*) I'm sorry you had to hear that – pay popular prices to hear that. But I don't care. I'll show you all. I'll be too big for any of you.

The sound of a key in the door. **Artie** *is heard singing 'The Day That the Pope Came to New York'.* **Ronnie** *exits to his room, carrying the gift box containing the bomb.* **Artie** *runs in and begins grabbing up sheet music.*

Artie   Bunny says, 'Arthur, I am not talking to you but I'll say it to the breeze: Arthur, get your music. "Bring On the Girls." Hold up your music for when the Pope His Holiness rides by.' (*To us.*) You heard these songs. They don't need blessings. I hate to get all kissy-ass, you know? But it can't hurt. 'Bring On the Girls.' Where is it? Whenever Bunny cleans up in here you never can find anything. You should see the two girls holding each other up like two sisters and they're not even speaking which makes them even more like sisters. Wouldn't it be great if they fell in love and we all could stay . . .

A beautiful girl in a fur coat stands hesitantly in the doorway. She carries flowers and liquor in her arms. She is **Corrinna Stroller**.

Corrinna   Mr Shaughnessy?

Artie   Did I win something? Where'd I put those sweepstake tickets – I'll get them –

Corrinna   Oh oh oh ohhhhh – it's just like Billy said. Oh God, it's like walking into a photo album. Norman Rockwell. Grandma Moses. Let me look at you. Oh, I was afraid with the Pope, you'd be out, but it's just like Billy said. You're here!

Artie   Billy? We talked this morning . . .

Corrinna   Billy called me just as I was checking out and told me to stop by on my way to the airport.

Artie   A friend of Billy's and you stay in a hotel? Don't you know any friend of Billy's has a permanent address right here . . . Don't tell me . . .

Corrinna   What?

Artie   I know your name.

Corrinna   (*very pleased*)   Oh, how could you . . .

Artie   You're Corrinna Stroller.

Corrinna   (*modestly*)   Oh . . .

Artie   I knew it. I saw that one movie you made for Billy . . .

Corrinna   That's how we met.

Artie   And then you retired –

Corrinna (*a sore point*)   Well . . .

Artie   You were fantastic.

Corrinna   Well . . .

Artie   Why did you quit?

Corrinna   Well . . .

Artie   Will you sit down for a few minutes? Just let me get my girls. If you left without seeing them . . . (*He comes down to us.*) You call Billy and he sends stars. Stars! (*To* **Corrinna**.) The icebox is yours. I'll be right back. Corrinna Stroller! (*He exits.*)

Corrinna *is alone. There is a high, loud whine. Her hands go to her ears. The whine becomes very electronic. The sound is almost painful. She pulls a hearing aid from each ear. The sound suddenly stops. She reaches into her dress and removes a receiver that the aids are wired to. She sits on the couch and replaces the dead transistors with fresh transistors. She looks up.*

Corrinna (*to us*)   Don't tell – please? I don't want them to know I'm deaf. I don't want them to think Billy's going around with some deaf girl. There was an accident on a set – a set of Billy's . . . I can hear with my transistors. (*She shows us a vial containing new transistors.*) I want them to know me first. So please, don't tell. Please.

Bunny *enters with* **Artie** *close behind.*

Bunny   Where is she? Where is she? Oh – (**Corrinna** *hastily puts her hearing aids away.*) – Corrinna Stroller! Limos in the streets. Oh, Miss Stroller, I only saw your one movie, *Warmonger*, but it is permanently enshrined in the Loew's of my heart. (*To us.*) That scene where she blows up in the landmine – so realistic. (*To* **Corrinna**.) And then you never made another picture. What happened?

Corrinna   I just dropped in to say hi –

Bunny   Hi! Oh, Corrinna Stroller! (*To* **Artie**.) You know that phoney Mrs Binard in 4-C who wouldn't give you the time of day – she says, 'Oh Miss Flingus, is this limo connected to you?' I'd like to put my fist through her dimple. (*She takes the newspapers out of her booties. To* **Corrinna**.) Hi, I'm Bunny, the future His. You want some snacks?

Corrinna   I've got to catch a plane –

Bunny   Should I send some down to the chauffeur? Oh, stay, have some snacks –

Artie   Are you gonna cook?

Bunny   Just short-order snacks, while you audition . . .

Artie   Audition?

Bunny   You get your ass on those tunes while the Pope's blessing is still hot on them. Artie, the Pope looked right at me! We're in solid. (*To* **Corrinna**, *with a tray of celery*.) Ta Ta!! That's a trumpet. Look, before we start chattering about hellos and how-are-yous and who we all are and old times and new times, bite into a celery for some quick energy and I'll get you a soda and Arthur here writes songs that could be perfect for Oscar-winning medleys and love themes of important motion-picture presentations and you should tell Billy about it. Artie being the Webster's Dictionary Definition for Mr Shy. *Gone with the Wind. The Wizard of Oz.* That is the calibre of film that I am talking about. And his Holiness the Very Same Pope has seen these songs and given them his blessings. (*She shows the sheet music to* **Corrinna**.)

Corrinna   I'd love to, but I have a very slight post-nasal drip.

Bunny   Isn't she wonderful! Go on, Artie, while Mister Magic still shimmers!

Artie   (*at the piano, sings*)
    Back together again,
    Back together again.

Three **Nuns** *appear at the window.* **Corrinna** *sees them and screams. Her transistors fall on the floor.*

Corrinna My transistors!! (*She is down on her knees, searching for them.*)

Bunny Get away from here! Scat! Get away! Go! Go!

Head Nun We got locked out on your roof! Please, it's fifty below and our fingers are icicles and our lips are the color of Mary –

Second Nun The doorknob came right off in our hands –

Artie I'm sorry, Sisters, but these are secret auditions . . .

Head Nun But we missed the Pope! And we came all the way from Ridgewood! Let us see it on television!

All Three Nuns Please! Please! On television!

Artie (*opening the gate*) Oh, all right . . .

Bunny Don't do it, Arthur. (*She sees* **Corrinna** *on the floor.*) What's the matter, honey, did you drop something? It's like a regular Vatican here.

During the scene **Corrinna** *will pick up her transistors at any moment she feels she is not being observed. She keeps them in a small vial for safety.*

The **Nuns** *are now inside.*

Second Nun We stole Monsignor Boyle's binoculars!

Second Nun We couldn't see the Pope, the crowds were so thick, so we climbed up onto your roof . . .

Second Nun And I put the binoculars up to my eyes and got the Pope in focus and the pressure of Him against my eyes, oh God, the binoculars flew out of my hands like a miracle in reverse . . .

Head Nun We'll be quiet.

Little Nun (*in the kitchen*) Look! Peanut butter! They have peanut butter! (*To us.*) We're not allowed peanut butter!

Artie Put that away!

Head Nun (*a sergeant*)   You! Get over here.

The **Little Nun** *obeys.* **Artie** *turns on the TV.*

Second Nun   Oh, color. They don't have color!

Head Nun   Would you have some beers? To warm us up? We will pray for you many years for your kindness today.

Bananas (*offstage, in the hall, terrified*)   Artie? Artie, are you there? Is this my home? Artie?

Artie   Oh God, Bananas. Bunny, get the beers, would you?

Bunny   What do I look like?

Artie *runs into the hall to retrieve* **Bananas**.

Bunny (*to* **Corrinna**)   Excuse the interruption; we're not religious as such, but his heart is the Sistine Chapel. (*She goes to the kitchen for beers.*)

Bananas (*entering with* **Artie**)   I didn't know where home was. Miss Henshaw showed me. And then your fat girlfriend ran away. I had to ask directions how to get back.

Bunny *plunks the beers on the TV set.*

Second Nun   Oh, imported! They don't have imported! We could've stayed back in Ridgewood and watched color and had imported, but no, she's got to see everything in the flesh –

Head Nun   You were the one who dropped the binoculars –

Second Nun   You were the one who stole them –

Bananas   Artie, did you bring work home from the office?

Artie   They're nuns, Bananas, nuns.

Head Nun   We got locked out on the upstairs roof. Hi!

Bananas   Hi!

Artie   This is Corrinna Stroller, Billy's girlfriend. Corrinna, this is Bananas.

The Nuns   Corrinna Stroller! The movie star!

Bananas   Hello, Billy's girlfriend. God, Billy's girlfriends always make me feel so shabby!

Bunny (*to* **Corrinna**)   Arthur believes in keeping family skeletons out in the open like pets. Heel, Bananas, heel!

Little Nun (*to* **Corrinna**)   I saw *The Sound of Music* thirty-one times. It changed my entire life.

Corrinna   Unitarian.

Artie   All right now, where were we?

Bunny   Ta Ta! The trumpet.

Artie (*at the piano, sings*)
  Back together again,
  Back together again . . .

Head Nun (*screams*)   There's Jackie Kennedy!!! Get me with Jackie Kennedy!!! (*She puts her arm around the TV.*)

The **Little Nun** *takes out her Brownie with flash and takes a picture of the* **Head Nun** *posing with Jackie on TV.*

Second Nun   There's Mayor Lindsay! Get me with him! Mayor Lindsay dreamboat! Mayor Wagner ugh!

There is a scream from the kitchen. **Bananas** *has burned herself.*

Artie (*running into the kitchen*)   What do you think you're doing?

Bananas   Cooking for our guests. I'm some good, Artie. I can cook.

Artie   What is it?

Bananas   Hamburgers. I felt for them and I cooked them.

Artie   Brillo pads. You want to feed our guests Brillo pads? (*To the* **Nuns**.) Sisters, please, you're going to have to go into the other room. You're upsetting my wife. (*He unplugs the TV and hustles the* **Nuns** *off into* **Ronnie**'s *bedroom*.)

Second Nun   Go on with what you're doing. Don't bother about us. We're nothing. We've just given our lives up praying for you. I'm going to start picking who I pray for. (*She exits*.)

The **Little Nun** *crosses to the kitchen to retrieve the peanut butter.*

Bunny (*to* **Corrinna**)   That man is a saint. That woman is a devil.

Bananas   I'm burned.

Bunny   Put some vinegar on it. Some salt. Take the sting out.

Head Nun (*coming out of the bedroom, very pleased*)   There is an altar boy in here. (*She exits*.)

Bananas   My son was an altar boy. He kept us in good with God. But then he grew up. He isn't an altar boy any more. (*She exits into her room*.)

Bunny (*to* **Corrinna**)   Sometimes I think the whole world has gone cuckoo, don't you?

Corrinna   For two days.

The **Little Nun** *goes into* **Ronnie**'s *room as* **Artie** *comes out and downstage.*

Artie (*to us*)   My son Ronnie's in there! He's been picked to be the Pope's altar boy at Yankee Stadium – out of all the boys at Fort Dix! I tell you – miracles tumble down on this family. I don't want you to meet him yet. If his mother sees him, her head will go all over the wall like Spanish omelettes. (*To* **Corrinna**.) Are you comfortable?

Bunny   She's adorable! And so down to earth! (*She takes* **Corrinna**'s *bejeweled hands*.)

Corrinna   It's five carats. It's something, isn't it?

Bunny (*to* **Corrinna**)   Sit right up here with Mister Maestro – (*She seats* **Corrinna** *next to* **Artie** *at the piano.*)

Artie   Where was I –

Bunny   'Like Fido chewed them.' You left off there –

Artie *sings as* **Bunny** *dances.* **Bananas** *enters and watches them.*

Artie
   ... Like Fido chewed them,
   But we're
   Back together again.
   You can say you knew us when
   We were together;
   Now we're apart,
   Thunder and lightning's
   Back in my heart,
   And that's the weather to be
   When you're back together with me.

Bunny *claps wildly.* **Corrinna** *follows suit.* **Bananas** *claps slowly.*

Bunny   Encore! Encore!

Artie (*happy now*)   What should I play next?

Bunny   Oh God, how do you pick a branch from a whole Redwood Forest?

Bananas (*licking her hand*)   'I Love You So I Keep Dreaming.'

Bunny (*picks up the phone, but doesn't dial*)   Come and get her!

Bananas   Play 'I Love You So I Keep Dreaming'.

Artie (*pleased*)   You really remember that?

Bananas   How could I forget it . . .

Bunny   I'm not used to being Queen of the Outsiders. What song is this?

Artie I almost forgot it. It must have been like Number One that I ever wrote. The one that showed me I should go on.

Bunny Well, let me hear it.

Artie You really surprise me, Bananas. Sometimes I miss you so much . . .

Bunny (*warning*) Arthur, I still haven't forgiven you for this morning.

Artie (*sings*)
  I love you so I keep dreaming
  Of all the lovely times we shared . . .

Bunny Heaven. That is unadulterated heaven.

Bananas (*interrupting*) Now play 'White Christmas'?

Bunny Shocks for sure.

Bananas (*banging the keys of the piano*) Play 'White Christmas'?

Artie (*to* **Corrinna**) She's . . . not feeling too . . . hot . . .

Bunny (*to* **Corrinna**) In case you haven't noticed . . .

Artie She keeps crawling under the weather . . . (*He plays a run on the piano.*)

Bananas 'White Christmas'???????

Artie *groans, then plays and sings 'White Christmas'.*

Bunny (*to* **Corrinna**) It really burns me up all these years The Telephone Hour doing salutes to fakers like Richard Rodgers. Just listen to that. Blaaaagh.

Artie *stops playing.*

Bananas Don't you hear it?

Artie (*plays and sings slowly*)
  I'm dreaming of a . . .
  I love you so I . . .

They are the same tune.

Artie   Oh God. Oh God.

Bananas (*sings desperately*)
   I love you so I keep dreaming –

Are you tone-deaf? Can't you hear it? (*She bangs the keys on the piano.*)

Artie *slams the lid shut on her hand. She yells and licks her fingers to get the pain off them.*

Artie   Oh, you have had it, Little Missy. All these years you knew that and made me play it. She's always trying to do that, Corrinna. Always trying to embarrass me. You have had it, Little Missy. Did Shakespeare ever write one original plot? You tell me that?

He drags **Bananas** *down to the edge of the stage.*

(*To us.*) In front of all of you, I am sorry. But you are looking at someone who has had it.

Bananas   I am just saying your song sounds an awful lot like 'White –

Artie   Then they can sing my song in the summertime. (*He pushes her away and picks up the phone.*)

Bananas   Who are you calling?

Bunny   Do it, Arthur.

Bananas (*terrified*)   Artie, who are you calling??????

Bunny   Do you have a little suitcase? I'll start you packing.

Bananas (*to* **Corrinna**)   Billy's friend? Help me? Billy wouldn't want them to do this. Not to me. He'd be mad. (*Whispering desperately, grabbing* **Corrinna**'s *hands.*) Help me? Bluebirds. He'll tell you all about it. Me walking on the roof. Can't you say anything? You want bribes? Here – take these flowers. They're for you. Take this liquor. For you. (*She is hysterical.*)

Bunny *pulls her away and slaps her.*

Bananas   I'll be quiet. I'll take my pills. (*She reaches for the vial containing* **Corrinna***'s transistors and swallows them.*)

Corrinna (*to us*)   My transistors?

Artie (*on the telephone*)   This is Mr Shaughnessy. Arthur M. . . . I was out there last week and talked about my wife.

Bananas   That's why my ears were burning . . .

Artie   I forgot which doctor I talked to.

Bananas   He had a mustache.

Artie   He had a mustache. (*To his wife.*) Thank you. (*Into the phone.*) Doctor? Hello? That's right, Doctor, could you come and . . . all that we talked about. The room over the garage is fine. Yes, Doctor. Now. Today . . . Really? That soon? She'll be all ready . . . (*He hangs up the phone.*)

Bunny   Arthur, give me your hand. Like I said, today's my wedding day. I wanted something white at my throat. Look, downstairs in a pink cookie jar, I got a thousand dollars saved up and we are flying out to California with Corrinna. As soon as Bananas here is carted off, we'll step off the plane and Billy and you and I and Corrinna here will eat and dance and drink and love until the middle of the next full moon. (*To* **Bananas**.) Bananas, honey, it's not just a hospital. They got dances. (*To* **Corrinna**.) Corrinna, I'll be right back with my suitcase. (*To* **Artie**.) Artie, start packing. All my life I been treated like an old shoe. You turned me into a glass slipper. (*She sings.*)

I'm here with bells on.
Ring! Ring! Ring! Ring! Ring!

She exits.

Artie   I'm sorry. I'm sorry.

Bananas *runs into her bedroom.* **Corrinna** *edges toward the front door.*

Artie   Well, Corrinna, now you know everything. Dirty

laundry out in the open. I'll be different out West. I'm great at a party. I never took a plane trip before. I guess that's why my stomach is all queasied up . . . Hey, I'd better start packing . . . (*He exits.*)

Corrinna *heads for the door. The* **Nuns** *enter.*

Head Nun   Miss Stroller! Miss Stroller! He told us all about Hollywood and Billy and Huckleberry Finn –

Second Nun   You tell Billy he ought to be ashamed treating a boy like that –

Little Nun (*with paper and pen*)   Miss Stroller, may I have your autograph?

Corrinna   Sisters, pray for me? Pray my ears come out all right. I'm leaving for Australia –

The Nuns   Australia?!?

Corrinna   For a very major ear operation and I need all the prayers I can get. (*To us.*) South Africa's where they do the heart work, but Australia's the place for ears. So pray for me. Pray my operation's a success.

Artie *enters with his suitcase half-packed.*

Artie   Australia?

Corrinna   I'm so glad I made a new friend my last day in America.

The Nuns   She's going to Australia!

Corrinna   Perhaps you'll bring me luck.

Artie   Your last day in America? Sisters, please.

Corrinna   I'll be Mrs Einhorn the next time you see me . . . Billy and I are off to Australia tomorrow for two fabulous years. Billy's making a new film that is an absolute breakthrough for him – *Kangaroo* – and you must – all of you – come to California.

The Nuns   *Kangaroo*! California!

Corrinna And we'll be back in two years.

Artie But we're coming with you today . . .

*The **Nuns** are praying for **Corrinna**.*

Little Nun Our Father, Who art in heaven . . .

Second Nun You shut up. I want to pray for her. Our Father –

Head Nun (*blows a whistle*) I'll pray for her. (*She sings.*) Ave Maria –

*The three **Nuns** sing 'Ave Maria'.*

Ronnie *enters wearing his army overcoat over the altar boy's cassock and carrying the box with the bomb. He speaks over the singing.*

Ronnie Pop! Pop! I'm going!

Artie Ronnie! Corrinna, this is the boy. (*To us.*) He's been down to Fort Dix studying to be a general –

Ronnie Pop, I'm going to blow up the Pope.

Artie See how nice you look with your hair all cut –

*The **Nuns** have finished singing 'Ave Maria' and take flash pictures of themselves posing with **Corrinna**.*

Ronnie Pop, I'm going to blow up the Pope and when *Time* interviews me tonight, I won't even mention you. I'll say I was an orphan.

Artie Ronnie, why didn't you write and let me know you were coming home? I might've been in California – It's great to see you –

Corrinna (*runs to the front door, then stops*) Oh, wait a minute. The Pope's Mass at Yankee Stadium! I have two tickets for the Pope's Mass at Yankee Stadium. Would anybody like them?

*The **Nuns** and **Ronnie** rush **Corrinna** for the tickets, forcing her back against the door. **Ronnie** wins the tickets and comes downstage to retrieve his gift-wrapped bomb. When he turns around to* *leave, the three* **Nuns** *are advancing threateningly on him. They will not let him pass. They lunge at him. He runs into the bedroom for protection. The* **Nuns** *follow.*

Artie (*at the front door*)   Miss Stroller, two years? Let's get this Australia part straight. Two years?

A **Military Policeman** *steps between* **Artie** *and* **Corrinna** *and marches into the room. The* **M.P.** *searches the room.*

Artie   Who are you? What are you doing here? Can I help you?

Corrinna   Oh! This must be Ronnie! The son in the Army! I can't *wait* to hear all about you! (*She embraces the* **M.P.**)

The **M.P.** *hears the noises and fighting from* **Ronnie**'s *room and runs in there.*

Corrinna (*to* **Artie**)   He looks just like you!

Artie (*following the* **M.P.**)   You can't barge into a house like this – where are you going?

The **Little Nun** *runs out of the bedroom, triumphantly waving the tickets, almost knocking* **Artie** *over.*

Little Nun   I got 'em! I got 'em!

Ronnie *runs out after her. The other two* **Nuns** *run after him. The* **M.P.** *runs after them.* **Ronnie** *runs into the kitchen after the* **Little Nun**, *who leaps over the couch.* **Ronnie** *leaps after her. He lands on top of her. He grabs the tickets.*

Head Nun (*to the* **M.P.**)   Make him give us back our tickets.

M.P. (*takes a deep breath and then*)   Ronald-V.-Shaughnessy.-You-are-under-arrest-for-being-absent-without-leave.-You-have-the-right-to-remain-silent.-I-must-warn-you-that-anything-you-say-may-be-used-against-you-in-a-military-court-of-law.-You-have-the-right-to-counsel.-Do-you-wish-to-call-counsel?

Ronnie *attempts to escape. The* **Head Nun** *bears down on him.*

Head Nun   That altar boy stole our tickets!

Second Nun   Make him give them back to us!

Ronnie *throws the tickets down. The* **Head Nun** *grabs them.*

Head Nun (*to the* **Little Nun**)   You! Back to Ridgewood! Yahoo! (*She exits.*)

Second Nun (*to* **Corrinna**)   Good luck with your ear operation. (*She exits.*)

Corrinna   This is an invitation – come to California.

Ronnie (*tossing the bomb to* **Corrinna**)   From me to Billy –

Corrinna   Oh, how sweet. I can't wait to open it. Hold the elevator!! (*She runs out.*)

Artie (*to the* **M.P.**, *who is struggling with* **Ronnie**)   Hey, what are you doing to my boy?!?

A **Man** *dressed in medical whites enters.*

White Man   I got a radio message to pick up a Mrs Arthur M. Shaughnessy.

Artie   Bananas! (*He runs to her bedroom.*)

Bunny (*dancing in through the front door, beaming and dressed like a million bucks*)   Ta Ta! Announcing Mrs Arthur M. Shaughnessy!

White Man   That's the name. Come along.

Bunny (*to us, sings*)
  I'm here with bells on,
  Ringing out how I feel . . .

The **White Man** *slips the straitjacket on* **Bunny**. *She struggles. He drags her out. She's fighting wildly.* **Artie** *returns.*

Artie   Wait. Stop.

Ronnie *pulls him from the door as there is a terrible explosion. Pictures fly off the wall. Smoke pours in from the hall.*

Bunny (*entering through the smoke*)   Artie? Where's Corrinna?

Where's Corrinna?

Artie   Corrinna?

Artie *runs out into the hall with* **Bunny**. *The lights dim as* **Ronnie** *and the* **M.P.** *grapple in slow motion, the* **Little Nun** *trying to pull the* **M.P.** *off* **Ronnie**.

Bananas *comes downstage into the light. An unattached vacuum hose is wrapped around her shoulders. She cleans the floor with the metallic end of the hose. She smiles at us.*

Bananas (*to us*)   My house is a mess ... Let me straighten up ... I can do that ... I'm a housewife ... I'm good for something ... (*She sings as she vacuums.*)

I love you so I keep dream ...

(*She closes her eyes.*) Artie, you could salvage that song. You really could.

Curtain.

Scene Two

In the darkness after the curtain we hear the **Pope** *from Yankee Stadium. He gives his speech in heavily accented English. An announcer provides simultaneous translation in unaccented English.*

Voice of the Pope   We feel, too, that the entire American people is here present with its noblest and most characteristic traits: a people basing its conception of life on spiritual values, on a religious sense, on freedom, on loyalty, on work, on the respect of duty, on family affection, on generosity and courage –

The curtain goes up. It is later that night, and the only illumination in the room is the light from the television.

The house is vaguely picked up but not repaired, and everything is askew: neat – things are picked up off the floor, for instance – but lampshades are just tilted enough, pictures on the wall just slanted enough, and we see that everything that had been on the floor – the clothes, the suitcases – has been jammed into corners.

Artie *is watching the television. Another person is sitting in the easy chair in front of the TV.*

– safeguarding the American spirit from those dangers which prosperity itself can entail and which the materialism of our day can make even more menacing . . . From its brief but heroic history, this young and flourishing country can derive lofty and convincing examples to encourage us all in its future progress.

From the easy chair, we hear sobbing. The deep sobbing of a man.

Artie *clicks off the television and clicks on the lights. He has put a coat and tie over his green park clothes. He's very uncomfortable and is trying to be very cheery. The man in the chair keeps sobbing.*

Artie   I'm glad he said that. That Pope up at Yankee Stadium – some guy. Boy, isn't that Pope some guy. You ever met him in your travels? . . . You watch. That gang war in Vietnam – over tomorrow . . .

(*Brightly.*) People always talking about a certain part of the anatomy of a turkey like every Thanksgiving you say give me the Pope's nose. But that Pope is a handsome guy. Not as good-looking as you and me, but clean. Businesslike.

(*To us.*) This is the one. The only. You guessed it: this is Billy. He got here just before the eleven o'clock news. He had to identify Corrinna's body, so he's a little upset. You forgive him, okay?

Billy, come on – don't take it so hard . . . You want to take off your shoes? . . . You want to get comfortable? . . . You want a beer? . . . (*He sits at the piano and plays and sings.*)

    If there's a broken heart
    For every light on Broadway,
    Screw in another bulb . . .

You like that? . . . Look, Billy, I'm sorry as hell we had to get together this way . . . Look at it this way. It was quick. No pain. Pain is awful, but she was one of the luckies, Bill.

She just went. And the apartment is all insured. They'll give us a new elevator and everything.

Billy   The one thing she wanted was . . .

Artie   Come on, boy. Together. Cry, cry, get it all out.

Billy   She wanted her footprints in Grauman's Chinese. I'm going to have her shoes set in wet cement. A ceremony. A tribute. God knows she'd hate it.

Artie   Hate it?

Billy   Ahh, ever since the ears went, she stopped having the push, like she couldn't hear her different drummer any more, drumming up all that push to get her to the top. She just stopped. (*He cries. Deep sobs.*)

Artie (*uncomfortable*)   She could've been one of the big ones. A lady Biggie. Boy. Stardust. Handfuls of it. All over her. Come on, boy . . . easy . . . easy . . . (*Impatient.*) Bill, that's enough.

Billy   Do you have any tea bags?

Artie   You want a drink? Got the bourbon here – the Jack Daniels –

Billy   No. Tea bags. Two. One for each eye.

Artie (*puzzled*)   Coming right up . . . (*He goes into the kitchen and opens the cabinets.*)

Billy   Could you wet them? My future is all ashes, Artie. In the morning, I'll fly back with Corrinna's body, fly back to L.A. and stay there. I can't work. Not for a long, long time, if ever again. I was supposed to go to Australia, but no . . . all ashes . . . (*He puts one wet tea bag over each eye.*) God, it's good to see you again, Artie.

Artie   Billy, you can't! You owe it – golly, Billy, the world – Bunny and me – we fell out of our loge seats – I'd be crazy if it wasn't for the laughs, for the romance you bring. You can't let this death stand in the way. Look what's happened to your old buddy. I've become this Dreaming

Boy. I make all these Fatimas out of the future. Lourdes and Fatima. All these shrines out of the future and I keep crawling to them. Don't let that happen to you. Health. Health. You should make a musical. Listen to this. (*He goes to the piano and plays and sings.*)

Back together again,
Back together again . . .

Bananas *appears in the bedroom doorway dressed in clothes that must have been very stylish and elegant ten years earlier.*

Billy (*starts*) Georgina!!

Artie *stops playing.*

Bananas No, Billy . . .

Billy (*stands up*) Oh God – for a minute I thought it was . . .

Artie Don't she look terrific . . .

Billy Let me look at you. Turn around. (*She does.*) Jesus, didn't Georgina have good taste.

Bananas (*turning*) I used to read *Vogue* on the newsstands to see what I'd be wearing in three years.

Billy Georgina took that dress right off her back and gave it to you. What a woman *she* was . . . (**Billy** *is crying again.*)

Bananas I put it on to make you happy, Billy.

Artie Easy, Billy, easy . . .

Bananas It's a shame it's 1965. I'm like the best-dressed woman of 1954.

Billy (*starting to laugh and cheer up*) You got the best of them all, Artie. Hello, Bananas!

Bananas Sometimes I curse you for giving me that name, Billy.

Billy A little Irish girl. What else was I going to call her?

The **Little Nun** *rushes in from the bedroom, her habit wet.*

Little Nun   Mr Shaughnessy! Quick – the bathtub – the shower – the hot water is steaming – running over – I can't turn it – there's nothing to turn –

Artie *runs into the bedroom. The* **Little Nun** *looks at* **Billy**. **Billy** *smiles back at her. The* **Little Nun** *runs into the bedroom.* **Bananas** *shows him a spigot.*

Bananas   I did it to burn her.

Billy   Burn who?

Bananas   Burn her downstairs. Have the hot water run through the ceiling and give her blisters. He won't like her so much when she's covered with blisters. Hot water can do that. It's one of the nicest properties of hot water.

Billy   Burn who???

Bananas   Kate Smith!! (*She holds the spigot behind her back.*)

Artie (*running in from the bedroom to the kitchen*)   Wrench. Wrench. Screwdriver. (*He rattles through drawers. Brightly, to* **Billy**.) God, don't seem possible. Twenty years ago. All started right on this block. Didn't we have some times? The Rainbow Room. Leon and Eddie's. I got the pictures right here.

The pictures are framed on the wall by the front door. **Billy** *comes up to them.*

Billy   Leon and Eddie's!

Artie (*indicating another picture*)   The Village Barn.

Bananas   The Village Barn. God, I loved the Village Barn.

Artie   It's closed, Bananas. Finished. Like you.

Little Nun   Mr Shaughnessy – please?

Artie *runs into the bedroom.*

Little Nun Mr Einhorn?

Billy Hello?

Little Nun I was an usher before I went in and your name always meant quality. (*She runs into the bedroom.*)

Billy Why – Thank you . . .

Bananas Help me, Billy? They're coming again to make me leave. Let me stay here? They'll listen to you. You see, they give me pills so I won't feel anything. Now I don't mind not feeling anything so long as I can remember feeling. You see? And this apartment, you see, here, right here, I stand in this corner and I remember laughing so hard. Doubled up. At something Ronnie did. Artie said. And I stand over here where I used to iron. When I could iron, I'd iron right here, and even then, the buttons, say, on button-down shirts could make me sob, cry . . . and that window, I'd stand right here and mix me a rye-and-ginger pick-me-up and watch the lights go on in the Empire State Building and feel so tender . . . unprotected . . . I don't mind not feeling so long as I can be in a place I remember feeling. You get me? You get me? Don't look at me dead. I'm no Georgina. I'm no Corrinna. Help me? Help Ronnie?

Billy Ronnie's in jail.

Bananas I don't mind the bars. But he can't take them. He's not strong like his mom. Come closer to me? Don't let them hear. (*She strokes his eyebrows.*) Oh, you kept your mustache. Nothing's changed. (*She sings.*)

Should auld acquaintance be forgot . . .

Artie (*comes out of the bedroom, soaking wet*)   Those are eyebrows, Bananas. Eyebrows. Come on, where is it? (*He reaches behind **Bananas**'s back and pulls the silver faucet handle from her clenched fist.*) Billy, you see the wall I'm climbing? (*He goes back into the bedroom with it.*)

*The **Little Nun** looks out into the living room.*

Little Nun (*to* **Billy**)   We never got introduced.

Billy   Do I know you?

Little Nun (*coming into the room*)   No, but my two friends died with your friend today.

Billy   I'm very sorry for you.

Little Nun   No, it's all right. All they ever wanted to do was die and go to heaven and meet Jesus. The convent was very depressing. Pray a while. Scream a while. Well, they got their wish, so I'm happy.

Billy   If your friends died with my friend, then that makes us – oh God! Bananas! That makes us all friends! You friends and me friends and we're all friends!

Bananas   Help Ronnie. Help him. (*She hands* **Billy** *the phone.*)

Billy (*on the phone*)   Operator – my friend the operator – get me person-to-person my friend General Buckley Revere in the Pentagon – 202 Lincoln 5-5600.

Artie (*coming out of the bedroom*)   No, Billy . . . no favors for Ronnie. The kid went AWOL, M.P.s dragging him out of the house. You think I like that? (*To* **Bananas**.) That kid's your kid, Bananas. You got the crazy monopoly on all the screwball chromosomes in that kid.

Billy   Buck? Bill.

Artie (*to* **Bananas**)   Let him learn responsibility. Let him learn to be a man.

Billy   Buck, just one favor: my godchild, Ron Shaughnessy. He's in the brig at Fort Dix. He wanted to see the Pope.

Artie (*to* **Bananas**)   Billy and me served our country. You think Billy could call up generals like that if he wasn't a veteran! (*To us.*) I feel I got to apologize for the kid . . . I tried to give him good strong things . . .

Billy Buck, has the Army lost such heart that it won't let a simple soldier get a glimpse of His Holiness . . .

The front door opens. **Bunny** *enters. She looks swell and great and all the* Webster Dictionary *synonyms for terrific. She's all exclamation points: pink and white!!! She carries an open umbrella and a steaming casserole in her potholder-covered hands.*

Bunny Arthur, are you aware *The Rains of Ranchipur* are currently appearing on my ceiling?

Artie Ssshhhhhhh . . . (*Indicating her pot.*) Is that the veal and oranges?

Bunny That's right, Arthur. I'm downstairs making veal and oranges and what do I get from you? Boiling drips.

Artie That's Billy . . . Billy's here. (*He takes the umbrella from her.*)

Bunny Billy Einhorn here? And you didn't call me? Oh, Mr Einhorn. (*She steps into the room. She is beaming. She poses.*) And that's why the word Voilà was invented. Excuse my rudeness. Hi, Artie. Hi, Bananas.

Billy (*on the phone*) Thank you, Buck. Yes, Yes, Terrific, Great. Talk to you tomorrow. Love ya. Thank you. (*He hangs up.*) Ronnie'll be all right. Buck will have him stationed in Rome with NATO. He'll do two weeks in the brig just to clear the records . . .

Artie Then off to Rome? Won't that be interesting. And educational. Thank you, Billy. Thank you.

Billy Ronnie's lucky. Buck said everybody at Dix is skedded for Vietnam.

Bunny I wouldn't mind that. I love Chinese food.

Artie That's the little girl from the steambath . . .

Billy *notices* **Bunny**. *They laugh.*

Bunny Hi! I'm Bunny from right down below.

Billy *kisses her hand.*

Bunny   Oohhhh ... Artie, perhaps our grief-stricken visitor from Movieland would join us in a Snack à la Petite.

Billy   No, no.

Artie   Come on, Bill.

Bunny   Flying in on such short notice you must have all the starving people of Armenia in your tumtum, begging, 'Feed me, feed me.'

Billy   Just a bite would be –

Bananas (*comes down to us with* **Artie**'s *scrapbook*)   What they do is they make a scrapbook of all the things she can cook, then they paste them in the book – veal parmagina, eggplant meringue ...

Artie *grabs it from her.*

Bananas   Yughh ...

Artie (*to* **Billy**)   We make a scrapbook of all the things Bunny can cook, you see, then we paste them in the book.

Bunny *serves.* **Artie** *takes a deep breath. He tastes.*

Artie (*to us*)   I wish I had spoons enough for all of you.

They eat.

Bunny   Mr Einhorn, I met your friend today before Hiroshima Mon Amour happened out there and all I got to say is I hope when I go I got two Sisters of Charity with me. I don't know your persuasion God-wise, but your friend Corrinna, whether she likes it or not, is right up there in heaven tonight.

Billy   Artie, you were right. We are what our women make us. Corrinna: how easily deaf becomes dead. It was her sickness that held us together. Health. Health. You were always healthy. You married a wonderful little Irish girl. You have a son. Where am I?

Bunny   Deaf starlets. That's no life.

Billy   So how come she's dead? Who blew her up?

Bananas   It was on the eleven o'clock news.

Bunny   Crying and explanations won't bring her back.
Mr Einhorn, if it took all this to get you here, I kiss the
calendar for today. Grief puts erasers in my ears. My world
is kept a beautiful place. Artie . . . I feel a song coming on.

Artie   How about a lovely tune, Bill, to go with that food.
(*He goes to the piano and plays.*)

Bunny (*opens the umbrella and does a dance with it, as she sings*)
    Where is the devil in Evelyn?
    What's it doing in Angela's eyes?
    Evelyn is heavenly,
    Angela's in a devil's disguise.
    I know about the sin in Cynthia
    And the hell in Helen of Troy,
    But where is the devil in Evelyn?
    What's it doing in Angela's eyes?
    Oh boy!
    What's it doing in Angela's eyes?

Billy   My God!

Artie (*up from the piano*)   What!

Billy   Suddenly!

Bananas   Was it the veal?

Billy   I see future tenses! I see I can go on! Health! I
have an extra ticket. Corrinna's ticket. For Australia.

Artie   God, Billy, I'd love to. I have all my music . . .
(**Artie** *races to* **Billy**.)

Billy (*coming to* **Bunny**)   Cook for me a while? Stay with
me a while? In two hours a plane leaves from Kennedy
and on to a whole new world. Los Angeles. We drop off
Corrinna's body. Then on to Hawaii. Samoa. Nonstop to
Melbourne. Someone who listens. That's what I need.

Bunny   But my whole life is here . . .

Billy   Chekhov was right. Work. Work. That's the only answer. All aboard??????

Bunny   My my my my my my my . . .

Artie   Are you out of your head? Leaving in two hours? It takes about six months to get shots and passports –

Bunny   Luckily two years ago I got shots and a passport in case I got lucky with a raffle ticket to Paree. (*To us.*) I'm in raffles all over the place.

Artie   Bunny –

Bunny   Leave me alone, Arthur. I have to think. I don't know what to say. It's all so sudden.

*The **Little Nun** comes out of the bedroom. She is in civvies. As a matter of fact, she has on one of Georgina's dresses, off the shoulder, all covered with artificial cherries. It is too big for her. She carries her wet habit.*

Little Nun   I was catching a cold so I put on one of your dresses, Mrs Shaughnessy. I have to go now. I want to thank you for the loveliest day I've ever had. You people are so lucky. You have so much. (*She is near tears.*) And your son is so cute. Maybe when I take my final vows I can cross my fingers and they won't count.

Billy   How would you like to stay here?

Artie   Stay here?

Billy   There'll be an empty apartment right down below and you could come up and take care of Bananas. (*He takes out his wallet and gives a number of hundred-dollar bills to the **Little Nun**.*) How's this for a few months' salary?

Artie   What's all that money?

Billy   Artie, don't send Bananas away. Love. That's all she needs.

Bananas   It is? (*The telephone rings. She answers it.*) Yes? Yes? (*To **Artie**, who is on his knees, trying to reason with **Bunny**.*) It's the Zoo.

Artie   Tell them I'll call – what are they calling this late for?

Bananas   The animals are all giving birth! Everything's having a baby. The leopards and the raccoons and the gorillas and the panthers and the . . .

Artie   (*taking the phone*)   Who is this? Al? Look, this is what you have to do. Heat the water. Lock the male elephants out. They get testy. The leopardess tends to eat her children. Watch her careful . . .

As he talks on the phone so we can't hear him, **Bunny** *comes downstage and talks to us.*

Bunny   The Pope saw my wish today. He looked me right in the eye and he winked. Hey! Smell – the bread is starting again and there's miracles in the air! The Pope is flying back through the night-time sky and all the planets fall back into place and Orion the Hunter relaxes his bow . . . and the gang war in Vietnam will be over and all those crippled people can now stand up and walk back to Toledo. And, Billy, in front of all these people, I vow to you I'll be the best housekeeper money can buy . . . and I'll cook for you and clean and, who knows, maybe there'll be a development . . . And, Bananas, honey, when I get to California, I'll send you some of my clothes. I'll keep up Georgina's traditions. Sister, here are the keys to my apartment downstairs. You can write a book, *I Jump Over the Wall*, and, Billy, you could film it.

Artie   (*on the phone*)   Yes! I'll be right down. I'll be right on the subway. Yes. (*He hangs up.*) I . . . have to go to work . . . Billy? Bun? Would you like to come? See life starting? It's beautiful.

Bunny   (*in the kitchen*)   Bananas, honey, could I have this copper pot? I've always had my eye on this pot.

Bananas   Take it.

Artie   Listen, Bill.

Bunny   Well, I'm packed.

Artie   I write songs, Bill. (*He starts playing and singing 'Back Together Again'.*)

Bananas (*to* **Billy**, *who is on his way out*)   Thank you, Billy.

Billy (*coming back and sitting alongside* **Artie**)   Artie, can I tell you a secret?

Artie *stops playing.*

Billy   Do you know who I make my pictures for? Money? No. Prestige? No. I make them for you.

Artie   Me?

Billy   I sit on the set and before every scene I say, 'Would this make Artie laugh? Would this make Artie cry?'

Artie   I could come on the set and tell you personal!

Billy   Oh no, Artie. If I ever thought you and Bananas weren't here in Sunnyside, seeing my work, loving my work, I could never work again. You're my touch with reality. (*He goes to* **Bananas**.) Bananas, do you know what the greatest talent in the world is? To be an audience. Anybody can create. But to be an audience . . . be an audience . . .

Artie (*runs back to the piano. He sings desperately*)
   I'm looking for something,
   I've searched everywhere . . .

Bunny   Artie, I mean this in the best possible sense: You've been a wonderful neighbor.

Billy (*to* **Artie**)   I just saved your life.

Billy *takes* **Bunny**'s *hand and leads her out.*

Artie *plays 'Where Is the Devil in Evelyn?' hysterically, then runs after them, carrying his sheet music.*

Artie (*shouting*)   Bill! Bill! I'm too old to be a young talent!!!

The **Little Nun** *comes downstage, her hands filled with money.*

Little Nun (*to us*)   Life is this orchard and we walk
beneath it and apples and grapes and cherries and
mangoes all tumble down on us. Ask and you shall receive.
I didn't even ask and look how much I have. Thank you.
Thank you all. (*She kisses the television.*) A shrine . . . I wanted
to be a Bride of Christ but I guess now I'm a young
divorcee. I'll go downstairs and call up the convent.
Goodbye. Thank you. (*She wrings out her wet habit, then throws
it up in the air and runs out.*)

Bananas *turns off all the lights in the room.* **Artie** *returns. He
stands in the doorway.* **Bananas** *sits on the edge of the armchair.
She is serene and peaceful and beautiful in the dim light.* **Artie**
comes into the room slowly. He lets his music slip to the floor.

Bananas   I don't blame you for that lady, Artie. I really
don't. But I'm going to be good to you now. Cooking. I
didn't know you liked cooking. All these years and I didn't
know you liked cooking. See, you can live with a person
. . . Oh God, Artie, it's like we're finally alone for the first
time in our life. Like it's taken us eighteen years to get
from the church to the hotel room and we're finally alone.
I promise you I'll be different. I promise you . . .

He smiles at her, hopefully.

Hello, Artie.

She sits on her haunches like a little dog smiling for food. She sings:

Back together again,
Back together again.
Since we split up
The skies we lit up
Looked all bit up
Like Fido chewed them,
But they're
Back together again.
You can say you knew us when . . .

*She barks. She sits up, begging, her hands tucked under her chin. She
rubs her face into* **Artie**'*s legs. He pats her head. She is thrilled. He
kneels down in front of her. He touches her face. She beams. She licks*

his hand. He kisses her. He strokes her throat. He looks away. He holds her. He kisses her fully. She kisses him. He leans into her. As his hands go softly on her throat, she looks up at him with a beautiful smile as if she had always been waiting for this. He kisses her temples, her cheeks. His hands tighten around her throat. Their bodies blend as he moves on top of her. She smiles radiantly at him. He squeezes the breath out of her throat. She falls.

Soft piano music plays.

The stage begins to change. Blue leaves begin to filter all over the room until it looks like **Artie** *is standing in a forest of leaves that are blue. A blue spotlight appears downstage and he steps into it. He is very happy and smiles at us.*

Artie   Hello. My name is Artie Shaughnessy and I'd like to thank you for that blue spot and to sing you some songs from the pen of. (*He sings.*)

I'm here with bells on,
Ringing out how I feel.
I'll ring,
I'll roar,
I'll sing
Encore!
I'm here with bells on.
Ring! Ring! Ring!

The stage is filled with blue leaves.

Curtain.

Landscape of the Body

This play is for
Adele Chatfield-Taylor

Landscape of the Body was first produced by William Gardner at the Academy Festival Theater, in Lake Forest, Illinois, in July 1977, directed by John Pasquin with the following cast:

Betty	Shirley Knight
Captain Marvin Holahan	F. Murray Abraham
Rosalie	Peg Murray
Raulito	Richard Bauer
Bert	Paul McCrane
Donny	Anthony Marciona
Joanne	Alexa Kenin
Margie	Bonnie Deroski
Masked Man	Jay Sanders
Durwood Peach	Rex Robbins
Dope King of Providence	Jay Sanders
Bank Teller	Jay Sanders

Sets by John Wulp
Costumes by Laura Crow
Lighting by Jennifer Tipton

It was then presented by Joseph Papp at the Public Theater, New York (New York Shakespeare Festival) on 12 October 1977, directed by John Pasquin.

Music and lyrics for all songs by John Guare

Setting On a ferry to Nantucket and in Greenwich Village

Act One

The deck of a ferry boat sailing from Hyannisport to Nantucket.

A woman sits writing notes on the deck. She is bundled up in layers of clothes against the cool. She has shopping bags around her feet. When she finishes one note, she rolls it into a cylinder and inserts it into a bottle she takes out of the shopping bags. She seals the bottle and tosses it overboard. She watches it go. She begins another.

A man is watching her. He is heavily disguised. Comic false eyeglasses and nose with mustache dangling beneath. Muffler wrapped high. Hat pulled down. He carries a little suitcase.

Man   That's the Kennedy compound over there. I bought a postcard at the bus station in Hyannisport and the postcard tells you whose house is who.

He proffers it. She looks at it briefly, looks at the shore, and resumes her note writing.

Man   That house is Teddy Kennedy's and that house was where Jack lived and that house is where the parents lived and that house is where the sister Eunice lived and that house is where the sister Jean lived and that house – the postcard seems not to match up to reality. I get them all mixed up now, it's been so long. Empty rooms. Open windows. White curtains blowing out.

She looks up, tosses another bottle over, and watches it go.

Man   I won a contest in grammar school knowing the names of the Dionne Quintuplets. I could rattle them off. Emilie. Annette. See I can't even remember. Yvonne. And the worst is nobody remembers the Dionne Quintuplets. You tell young people, younger than we are, about the Dionne Quintuplets and they don't know who you're talking about.

Woman   Emilie was the left-handed one. Emilie was the only left-handed Dionne Quintuplet. What was the name of the doctor who delivered the Dionne Quintuplets?

Man   Dr Dafoe.

Woman   Dr Dafoe.

Man   We could have a marriage made in heaven sharing information like that.

Woman   I'm not in the market.

Man   I went down to Washington in 1960 for Kennedy's inauguration. They were selling at the Union Station an entire set of dishes of china and every plate was a different Kennedy. The big meat platter was Poppa Joe. The other cake platter had Momma Rose on it. John-John and Caroline were on little bread-and-butter plates. You're so open to talk to. Generally on trips of this nature – two-hour ferry trips from the mainland to an island – you begin talking to your fellow shipmates desperately leaping into conversational gambits, reduced to buying dusty postcards of abandoned compounds of families who once made all the difference in America. I begin talking and you pick right up on it. We could have a marriage made in heaven. We can talk. I think that's why marriages fail. People can't talk. People fight to have something to talk about. People kill each other, say, because the words won't come into place. I think of murder, say, as a sentence that did not make it through the computer up here in the head. If people had a better grasp of language, of syntax, of the right word, of being understood, you'd hear that crime rate, you'd see that homicide rate plunge like those bottles you're tossing over . . . would they be sentences you'd be writing on that piece of paper?

She tosses another bottle over.

Man   What attracted you to me first? My confidence-inspiring voice? My ability to select the proper word out of the autumn air? A poll said what women notice most in men was their butts. Is that it? You liked my ass? Is that what attracted you to me? Are the polls right? My confidence is in bad disrepair and needs all the propping up it can beg, borrow, or infer.

Woman I saw you getting on the boat. I wondered if you were in disguise. I said to myself, is this a masquerade cruise? Then I thought, this is a man with a facial cancer and his face has been removed and replaced by a necessary false nose to disguise the two gaping holes under there. A false mustache to cover the missing upper lip. False eyebrows to cover the grafted skin around the eyeballs which still function or he'd be tapping a white cane around this deck. He walks with a steady stride. No, I won't have to be yelling Man Overboard. It's a disguise.

Man You recognized me?

Woman Captain Marvin Holahan. Sixth Precinct Homicide.

*The **Man** pulls off his disguise.*

Holahan What did you write in that note? A confession?

She throws sheets of small papers into the wind. They blow away. She pours bottles overboard.

Woman A confession. A full confession. I wrote down everything that happened. And it's all gone. There it goes! There's your case.

They face each other. The lights go down on them. They each take off their coats. The light is harsh in this interrogation room. She sits down in a chair. He circles her. He shines a desk lamp in her eyes.

Voice Flashback. Five months before. Marvin Holahan. Betty Yearn. Sixth Precinct. New York City. A spring day. Easter Sunday. Vernal equinoxes. The sun and moon cross each other's path.

Betty I don't see how you can ask me these questions.

Holahan Easy.

Betty At this point in my life in history you could ask me these questions.

Holahan The kid is dead.

Betty   I cannot cannot cannot – draw underlines under
the cannot -- cannot cannot cannot – six negatives make a
positive – cannot understand –

Holahan   How I can ask you these questions?

Betty   How you can ask me these questions –

Holahan   Lady, I'm not talking simple child-battering.

Betty   The kid is dead. The kid is dead. You leave out
the fact it's my kid.

Holahan   Decapitation, Betty.

Betty   My son is dead. My boy is dead. My kid killed.
Not *the* kid. My kid.

Holahan   The head chopped off, Betty. That's not Family
Court. Chopped-off heads are not referrals to Family
Counseling. That goes beyond child-battering.

Betty   Not *the* kid. *My* kid. *My* kid.

Holahan   You and your boyfriend didn't say my kid
when you got out the hacksaw. You must've said, oh, let
me guess: you little bastard.

Betty   I'm not going to throw up.

Holahan   What did your kid see, Betty, that you had to
chop his head off?

Betty   If I throw up, it's like you win. You're not going
to win.

Holahan   Where's the boy's father?

Betty   I haven't seen him in years.

Holahan   Maybe the boy's father did it in revenge
against you?

Betty   Strangers don't do revenge. The father didn't even
know where we live. I feel like I'm standing in that corner
over there watching me, and if I try hard enough I can
switch the dial and I'll see me on another channel. I'd like

a laugh track around my life. I'd like a funny theme
introducing my life. I'm standing right over there in that
corner watching me.

Holahan   Was your boy homosexual?

Betty   He's fourteen, for God's sake.

Holahan   Lady, we got bodies coming in here don't even
live to be fourteen. Their ages never get off the fingers of
two hands.

Betty   There's a whole series of homosexual murders
going on down there at Christopher Street. Maybe the kid
was into something. I don't think so. Don't those murders
involve decap – the heads off . . .

Holahan   How do you know about that?

Betty   Is that the clue that gives myself away? I read the
papers. I hear on the street. Did you follow up that clue?
Why did you drag me in here? I'm supposed to be out
there, mourning, weeping –

Holahan   Betty, I'm trying to be kind. If you're
embarrassed confessing to such a heinous crime, you want
me to get Sergeant Lorraine Dean down here? There ain't
nothing Lorraine hasn't heard. She's a good woman, a
good listener, heavy in the ankles, platinum blonde, a nice
soft bosom that I swear she keeps Seconal and Libriums in.
She'd hold you and rock you in the cradle of the deep and
she'll sing 'I'm confessing that I love you . . .' She'll sing
that and make it easy for you to talk about what you did
and get you help. She's got a nice voice Lorraine does. She
could've made it big in the show biz department were it
not for her tragedy in the ankle department. Should I get
Lorraine down here and you can tell her all? You want
Lorraine? 'I just found joy. I'm as happy as a baby boy.
With another brand new choo-choo toy when I marry my
Lorraine!' Betty? You could tell me too? There's nothing
hasn't been poured into these ears. I'm taking courses at
NYU nights in psychology. Things like you did happen all
the time. We even had a spot quiz last week on a woman,

went into a deep depression, drowned her two kids. Two! You just did one. Imagine how she feels. But they were infants. And she drowned them. I can't wait to ask my teacher about decapitation. You might help me get an honors. I might do a paper on you. Most infanticides are drownings or smotherings or an occasional throwing off a bridge . . .

Betty   I remember when I was a little kid at the end of the McCarthy hearings when Joe McCarthy was destroying human lives, this great lawyer –

Holahan   Welch. Joseph Welch.

Betty   Stood up and said to McCarthy Is there no such thing as human decency? And that question shocked everybody and destroyed Joe McCarthy.

Holahan   I'll tell you that great lawyer Welch after that made a film for Otto Preminger called *Anatomy of a Murder* starring James Stewart and Lee Remick. Is there no such thing as human decency left?

Betty   Is there no such thing as human decency left?

Holahan   A damn good little question.

Betty   Will I get off to go to my son's funeral?

Holahan   Is Otto Preminger filming it?

Betty   Am I booked? What's up? Do I go to my son's funeral?

Holahan   Did you kill him?

Betty   Do I get off for the funeral?

Holahan   Say yes, beautiful Betty, and there's no place you can't go.

Betty   I want my boy buried in Bangor, Maine, with his grandparents and his aunts and his uncles. I want him buried in Bangor with my father, with my sister Rosalie. Where I'll be buried when I die. I want him there. I want him out of New York.

Holahan   You think 't's fair to be at the funeral when you caused the funeral?

Betty   I'm sorry, Your Honor, Mr Kangaroo Court. I missed his death.

Holahan   I keep thinking you were there.

Betty   What is my motive? I cannot believe I am a suspect in my own son's death. I am supposed to be comforted. I am supposed to be held and allowed to cry and not made to feel . . . there's no insurance. I am no beneficiary. I cannot believe. I don't kill my own flesh and blood. I don't kill me. If I wanted to kill him, I would've killed me along with him. I don't kill me. I am here. Am I a car? A car you have to pull over to the side of the road and give a ticket to? You have to torture a certain number of people a day? Is this torture a routine formality? My boy is dead. I would like to grieve.

Holahan   When did you come to New York?

Betty   Two years ago.

Holahan   Why?

Betty   To get my sister.

Holahan   Where is your sister now?

Betty   My sister's dead.

Holahan   Let me get this straight. You came to New York two years ago to get your dead sister.

Betty   She was not dead at the time.

Holahan   You came to New York two years ago alone to get your sister.

Betty   Not alone. With Bert.

Holahan   Bert? Bert?

Betty   My kid.

Holahan   The one you killed. Ah, yes, *that* Bert.

A redhead appears out of the dark. She's very tough, very blowsy. A good sport. Her name is **Rosalie**.

Rosalie   They're getting you for your life style, kid. They can't stand it that you got the life style of the future and they're stuck here in their little precincts.

Betty   I'm being prosecuted for my life style. You can't stand it that I got the life style of the future and you're stuck here in your little precinct.

Rosalie *embraces* **Betty** *and comforts her.* **Rosalie** *goes back into the dark.*

Holahan   Bert's body was found yesterday afternoon floating off an abandoned pier at the bottom of Charles Street in a particularly seedy part of Greenwich Village. The boy's head was found floating close by. No signs of sexual molestation. But the boy was not killed there. The murder took place someplace else. The body was taken and dumped off this abandoned pier notorious for sexual pick-ups between members shall we say of the same sex and for the exchange of narcotic goods exchanged between people so spaced out they don't know what sex they are. From the boy's school pass, we find where he lives on Christopher Street, a notorious street in the self-same Greenwich Village. We find evidence in the boy's apartment where he lives with his mother, we find evidences of blood in his own home. In the bathroom. The boy was murdered and decapitated in the bathroom of his own legal abode. The mother lived there with the boy. The mother is a hotsy-totsy we find out. The mother works in porno films.

Betty   Soft core.

Holahan   *Do Me Do Me Do Me Till It Falls Off* does not sound soft core to me. *Leather Sheets* does not sound soft core to me. Vaginal penetration recorded in medical detail by a sixteen-millimeter camera owned by Mafia people does not sound soft core to me.

Betty   That wasn't me in all of them. My sister worked in porno films. I was finishing up a contract she had made shortly before her death.

Holahan   And when you appear on *What's My Line?* how do you sign in, please?

Betty   I work for a travel agency.

Holahan   A fake travel agency.

Raulito, *a Cuban in a trench coat, appears out of the dark.*

Raulito   Honeymoon Holidays was not fake.

Holahan   Closed down for selling fraudulent trips –

Raulito   It don't harm nobody to start off a marriage with a good honeymoon.

Raulito *goes back into the dark.* **Betty** *takes pills out of her pocket.* **Holahan** *knocks them out.*

Holahan   No junkie shit here, baby.

Betty   They're Tums for the tummy, asshole. I don't want to throw up. If I do not throw up, it will somehow prove to me that I am not on your level, that I possess a strength, am the proud possessor of a dignity –

Holahan   And yet Miss Dignity seems to appear in these loops. We raided Dirty Mort's on Forty-Second Street. We ran the loops. I remembered your face from the loops when they brought you in. I had long said to myself what kind of person would allow another human being to urinate on her while a Mafia-run camera was whirring away. Little did I think, Miss Life Style of the Future, I would have the honor of having met you. As you see, I am a movie buff. Those films. These films. This doesn't look like anybody's sister to me. This looks coincidentally like you. Or maybe it's Gene Kelly in outtakes from *Singin' in the Rain?* What kind of human being allows herself to be treated in this way? I hate you, baby.

Betty   No shit, Dick Tracy. I thought this was a love story.

Holahan   When I was a kid my parents chained me to

the piano so I'd play. I was a fat kid, too, so the chains had a double purpose. The pressure of them would stop me eating and force me to play. I eat, baby. I eat the right amounts and I am thin and I play the piano very well. And I also know all about family hatred. I know that families are there to learn your deepest secrets and betray you with their intimacy. Your kid must've found out too much about you. Your kid, I'm beginning to see, cramped your style. Of course! Every kid thinks his mother is the Virgin Mary, for Christ's sake, and one day your kid sees the films you work in when you're not in the fake travel agency. I get it! And I find it a fantastic fact that a woman who gives head in twenty-five-cent loops should be in here for taking head. To get rid of the son's head that contained the eyes that saw her life.

Betty   Are you nuts?

Holahan   Because his eyes turned into these Mason jars preserving the disgust at what you had become.

Betty   I want out of here! (*She bangs on doors.*) That's not me in those films. That's my sister.

Holahan   Oh sure. Your sister. Bring her in here. Testify for you.

Betty   She's dead.

Holahan   When?

Betty   A year ago, last October.

Raulito *appears.*

Raulito   Is that what happened to you?

Rosalie *appears.*

Betty   She was walking on Hudson Street.

Rosalie   I was just walking on Hudson Street.

Betty   A cyclist hit her.

Holahan   And Raulito?

Betty   He's dead.

Raulito *and* **Rosalie** *go in the black.*

Holahan   You're a terrific dame to know. All the people connected to you via the avenue of blood die in one year. Maybe I'll go to Bangor, Maine, and dig your sister up.

Betty   I'm really grateful to you.

Holahan   The Grateful Dead. The noted rock group.

Betty   I am alive, detective. Because I am, I *was* going crazy from my kid's murder. When they came and told me the kid was dead, they could've fit me for a straitjacket at the same time they were fitting him for a shroud. You have actually taken my mind off it. My loathing for you replaces my grief. I mean, my fury is real. You're nuts.

Holahan   Do you deny you made golden shower films where people urinated on you?

Betty   That was my sister.

Holahan   Oh, this is one of those movies where there's a good twin and an evil twin.

Betty   You got movies on the brain. It must make life easy for you. You can just put anything you want into a movie and that explains everything.

Holahan   One good twin. One bad twin. Was it the good twin or the bad twin who made those animal films? *Barnyard Bimbo. Six With a Pig.* An alleged human being has sex with a German Shepherd. Is that the sister? It looks a hell of a lot like the good twin sitting right here in her little Mary Janes and golden braids.

Betty   I did it for the money.

Holahan   Of all the motives, that still has to be my favorite motive. I did it for the money.

Betty   My sister was in the hands of the mob. She owed them money. She was a junkie. They forced me to make the films to work off the bread she owed them for smack.

Holahan   After 'I did it for the money' my next favorite
motive is the Mob made me do it. Get the Mob. The Mob
did this, the Mob did that. The Mob must be pretty busy.
That's some pretty busy Mob. My heart goes out to the
Mob more and more every day. Nothing better than
having a convenient fall guy. I'm sorry, Betty. I look to the
family. I go right to the scene of the crime between those
shapely gams. The family, Betty.

Betty   You're a class act, detective. Detective Marvin
Holahan. *Detective That's Entertainment Parts One and Two and
Three and Four.* What are you? Some faggot out to get me
because –

Holahan   I know everything about you.

Betty   You don't know nothing about me except I posed
for some sleazy pictures and who cares. But I know about
you. They chained you to a piano so you wouldn't eat and
you would play. And you do both and you're a good boy.
A lot of things happened to me, but nobody ever chained
me to a piano and you know what? I didn't throw up. I
can look you right in the eye. I didn't throw up. I won.

The interrogation room goes dark. Lights come up on **Rosalie**. *A
piano swings into view. Music plays at the piano.* **Rosalie** *sings to
us in the audience. She's really good-natured, has a swell voice, moves
like a stripper.*

Rosalie
　　Hey Stay a While
　　In the crook of my arms
　　All you got to do is
　　Look in my arms
　　And you'll see Home Sweet Home
　　I'll invest in a doormat
　　Hey Home Sweet Home
　　We'll test the mattress
　　Our arms are sinuous
　　All performances are continuous
　　Hey Stay a While
　　Feel the smile in my arms

And the smile's in my arms
All for you
Sit back/Relax
Cool brow/Tension slacks
Hey Stay a While
My arms are filled with
What the whole world lacks
Hey Stay a While

Being dead is not the worst thing in the world. Is there life
after death? I dare ask the question: Is there life before
death? The good thing about being dead is at least you
know where you stand. You have one piece of information
in life and you think life means this. Then you get a new
piece of info and everything you knew means something
else. The scary thing about death is how comfortable it is.
Finally giving in to the drowning. Life was always wriggling
out of my hands like a fish you thought you had all
hooked and ready to pop in the pan. Was there ever a day
I didn't at one point say, 'Hey, when will life end?'
Flashback! A new scene starring the boy who would soon
be murdered.

Bert, *a fourteen-year-old kid, swaggers on, wearing earphones. He
dances to silent music.*

Rosalie   This scene you are about to see contains
information completely unknown to the boy's mother, my
sister. Information unknown to Captain Marvin Holahan of
the Sixth Precinct Homicide. Those two people in the
course of their lives never learned the information you are
about to receive right now. This scene takes place in the
Parthenon. Not the one in Greece that's the cradle of all
civilization. Hell, baby, I'm talking the Parthenon
Luncheonette on West Eleventh Street and Bleecker in
Greenwich Village. This scene takes place four weeks
before this boy, my nephew, will be murdered.

A booth and table and chairs come in. **Bert** *sits in the booth, his
arm around one of the girls. Another boy,* **Donny**, *has his sleeves
rolled up and is wearing a lot of wristwatches. The girls lean*

forward. The kids are roughly twelve, thirteen, fourteen.

Bert   It's so easy.

Donny   Easy he says.

Bert   You stand on Christopher Street.

Donny   I got to wait in the tub.

Bert   Pretty soon the guy stops.

Donny   The tub gets cold. You get a cold ass waiting in the tub.

Bert   You noticed him cause he's walked back and forth a few times looking at you.

Donny   All the things a tub can be. A coffin. I pretend I'm in a coffin.

Joanne   Does he look at you like you're a girl?

Donny   I pretend I'm in a boat.

Joanne   Do they really look fruity?

Bert   Sometimes they're in cars. Not fruity cars, but Pontiacs. Oldsmobiles.

Joanne   Fruits driving Pontiacs?

Donny   I pretend I'm in a car.

Margie   I could see a Chevrolet. Chevrolets are fruity.

Bert   Not the '65 Chevy, Joanne. Holy shit, Joanne, I look at you sometimes and I say –

Joanne   It was Margie who said it.

Bert   You were looking at her, agreeing with her.

Joanne   Don't get mad at me. I'm sorry, Bert?

Bert   I don't like the two of you hanging around together. She's dragging you down. We all got to protect each other. Make each other better. Margie's dragging you down.

Joanne   She's not cheap.

Margie   I only felt cheap once in my life. Charlie
Ebbermann said he'd give me ten cents to let him touch
me in the cloakroom. This is the fifth grade. The sixth
grade. So I do. Big deal. Then I hear later, Charlie
Ebbermann is paying a girl from the public school a
quarter to take out her glass eye and let him look in. I saw
him and I said Look, Ebbermann, you can take your dime
back and I threw it at him.

Bert (*calls*)   Hey, could we get a Coke or something? A
toasted bran?

Donny   Bert brings the fruit upstairs. His mother's away.
He leads them into the bathroom. I'm happy cause I can
finally get out of the fucking tub. I hear the voices behind
the shower curtain. I make sure the shower curtain's shut. I
see the fruit's shadow on the shower curtain. I leap out of
the tub and bang the guy on the head with the monkey
wrench. He don't know what hit him.

Bert   I pull the watch off. Take the wallet. We roll 'em to
the door. Push 'em out in the hall. We piss in the corner.

Donny   Piss on the guy.

Bert   Then I knock on the door next door. Mrs Pantoni,
I tell her, there's another drunk broke in. He peed on the
floor. I spill some wine on him. She calls the cops. The
cops come and clear the guy out.

Margie   They don't ever report you?

Bert   You don't have big ears, but you're a real dumbo,
Margie. I don't want you hanging around with her, Joanne.

Joanne   I got to have some friends, Bert.

Bert   You got me.

Joanne   You swear?

Bert (*with his arm around* **Joanne**)   Who they gonna report?
Some fairy tries to pick up a fourteen-year-old?

Joanne   All that ticking. Your arm is so noisy.

Donny   You have all the fun. I got to stick in the tub.
You wait in the tub for a while. You see how much fun it
is in a fucking tub.

Bert   Some fairy in a Chevrolet with Jersey plates is
gonna pick you up? I want to make some money, not scare
'em away.

Donny   That's right. I'd scare 'em away. (*He makes a face.*)

Joanne   Let me wind your watches? You read in the
papers today about the lady in Forest Hills who died and
they couldn't figure out how she died? She was healthy.
Well, you know how she died?

Bert   Donny hit her over the head with his monkey.

Donny   That's right. I hit her over the head with my
monkey.

Margie   Would you let her tell her story?

Bert (*calls*)   You burning that bran muffin?

Joanne   She had this beautiful beehive hairdo that she
wore. Really intricate. Curls. Upswept. Spit curls. And she
didn't want to damage it because her hairdo was really a
work of art. *Hairdo Magazine* was considering her for a
feature. And she kept spraying her hairdo with hair spray
so her hairdo wouldn't get hurt when she went to sleep at
night and you know what happened? In Forest Hills,
Queens, they traced black widow spiders escaped and hid
in her hair. Somehow they ended up in her hair because
they like dark places and the hair spray made this shield
like *Gardol* on the toothpaste commercial where the decay
can't get through the toothpaste. And the black widow
spiders got trapped within her hairdo in this wall of hair
spray and got panicked and couldn't get out and ate their
way through her skull. Bit her in the skull to get out and
that's how she died.

Bert *and* **Joanne** *neck.*

Donny   Bert?

Margie   Can I have a bite of that bran muffin?

Donny   Bert? Is your mother at work?

Joanne   Bran is supposed to be the secret of life.

Bert   You feel like getting another wrist watch?

Margie   How'd that woman do her hair?

Bert *and* **Donny** *get up and go.* **Joanne** *begins demonstrating.*
The lights come down on the luncheonette . . . a fanfare of music. The
lights come up on **Rosalie**, *by her piano. She prepares herself for*
the next scene, putting on a red kimono.

Rosalie   Flashback. Eighteen months ago. I was still
among the living. How my sister and nephew came to New
York in the first place.

The lights come up on **Rosalie**'s *apartment.* **Rosalie** *moves into*
the scene. The apartment contains a sink, a table, a chair, a day-bed
strewn with clothes, a vanity. **Rosalie**'s *waking up and putting on*
make-up and drinking coffee and looking in the mirror. **Betty** *looks*
different from what we have seen before. Two years ago, she was very
plain. Very nervous.

Betty   Rosalie, you got to come home. You're growing up
not knowing your family. Your nephew. Our mother. (**Bert**
shyly looks out from under his mother's arm.)

Rosalie   Hiya, kid. Want a snort?

Betty   Tell her, Bert.

Bert   Bangor, Maine, is about the greatest place I know.
It's not like the old days when nothing was there. Bangor,
Maine, is the home of one of the world's busiest airports.
(*He holds out a pennant marked 'Bangor'.*)

Rosalie   He's great.

Bert   Bangor, Maine, is the center of the chartered jet
service that takes Americans to all parts of the globe on
budget flights.

Rosalie   You done good, Betty.

Betty   Rosalie, Bangor is so interesting. You meet people
from all over the world who are laying over. Lots of times
they're fogged in and you get to hear about their travels
and I sell souvenirs and there's an opening in the cocktail
lounge. You could sing. You'd meet such interesting people.
I pray for snow. I pray for fog. All the things that used to
make life so dismal in Bangor are now the exact things
that make it so interesting.

Rosalie   Honeybunch, you're hearing about the world.
But hearing about don't put no notches on anyone's pistol.
I'm doing. Bert, would you go out onto Christopher Street
to the Li-Lac Chocolate store and request about a pound
of kisses?

She gives **Bert** *money.* **Bert** *goes.*

Betty   Bert, you be careful. Is it safe out there?

Rosalie   Honeybunch, I get this call last week, would I
be interested appearing in a film. Sure, why not.

Betty   He's never been to a city before.

Rosalie   I report to a motel in Forty-Second Street and
Eleventh Avenue. Way west. Take elevator to the sixth
floor. Knock. Go in. Floodlights. A camera. Workmen
setting up. The real thing! A man said, 'You the girl? Get
your duds off. Sink into the feathers and go to it.' Holy
shit, they're loading the cameras and I'm naked and
nobody's really paying attention. They say, 'You all set?'
Sure, why not. Lights. Camera. Action. And a door I
thought was a closet opens up and it's from another room
and a gorilla leaps out with a slit in his suit and this
enormous erection and the gorilla jumps on me.
Honeybunch, there's no surprises like that in Maine. And
we're going at it and I can't believe it and after about five
minooties, the director yells, 'Cut!' and the gorilla rolls off
me, takes off his gorilla head and it's Harry Reems from
Deep Throat and *The Devil in Miss Jones*. What an honor to
meet you, sir, I said. Christ! Go back to Bangor, Maine!
Honey, you should move in with me. Get yourself

unsaddled from Momma and that house and airports.

Betty It's our family.

Rosalie Honeybaby, start your own family. I started my own family. I've got a family motto. She Travels Fastest Who Travels Alone. I live here on Christopher Street. A lovely building. Lovely neighbors. Leave you alone. Nobody knows me. I don't know anybody. I'm flying high. I'm working for a travel agency. Dawn's Promising Star Travel Agency. Founder and sponsor of Honeymoon Holidays. No charter jets for me. When I travel, which shall be soon, I'll be traveling first class not out of Bangor, but right out of old JFK. Wait till you meet my boss, Raulito. Take it back. Erase those tapes. You'll never meet him. I'd show you my life, you'd get so jealous, you'd want to move right in and take me over. You can't have me. You can have yourself but you can't have me. Ditch the kid. He comes from a whole other rotten period of your life. Erase those tapes. Get rid of him. I got a pull out sofa. Move in. We can have some laughs.

Betty I've got lots of laughs in Bangor. When it isn't raining, it's snowing. I meet boys at the airport, but they end up taking planes. Momma sits by the TV singing 'Rosalie, My Darling'. Aside from that, everything's okay.

Rosalie Listen, send the kid back. There's an extra key.

Betty Momma sent me down here to bring you back.

Rosalie You just wire a little wire to Momma. Hey, Momma, send me a change-of-address card. I get lonely, Honeybunch. We could have some laughs. I'm proud of my life and I'd like to show it off to you. We're young.

Bert *enters with a box of chocolates.*

Rosalie Hiya, kid. We were just talking about you.

Bert Kisses!

The lights go out on **Bert** *and* **Betty** *in* **Rosalie**'s *apartment.*
Rosalie *whips off her bathrobe and steps in time to the very jazzy*

*piano music. Behind the stage is bare, black. A cyclist wearing a
mask, goggles, helmet, and shorts appears upstage, holding a bicycle
over his head. As* **Rosalie** *speaks to us, he advances slowly,
threateningly, toward her.*

Rosalie   So I walk out on Christopher, cut down on
Bleecker to walk to work and I'm just jazzing along
Hudson Street, and you know where that Ristorante
Rigoletto is that the papers gave eighteen tureens to and
they got limousines parked out front and I happen to
know the chef sprays fresh herbs on the canned Boyardee,
but, what the hell, it's over-priced, out of the way, they
treat you like shit, and Uptown loves it. Well, I'm being so
specific because it's just at that very location that a ten-
speed yellow Raleigh bike bears down on me. I apparently
splattered up against the window of the Ristorante
Rigoletto like a pizza that suddenly appeared on the menu.
My last thoughts were of Betty moving down to New York.
I won her. Revenge on our Momma. I was feeling very
happy.

The sound of a crash. **Rosalie** *shrugs her shoulders and goes into
the dark. The* **Masked Man** *glares at us, never lowering his
bicycle.*

Masked Man   I don't give a shit if she's dead! Who's
gonna fix my bike? The chain is off my bike! Who's gonna
pay for that? Give me her bag. She owes me money. Life
belongs to the living. I don't give a shit if she just died.
She should've looked. I am traveling. I am moving. Who's
gonna pay for my bike? Chocolate? That's all she's got in
the fucking bag? Chocolate kisses? How am I supposed to
fix my bike with chocolate kisses? She deserves to die. (*He
walks off into the black.*)

The lights come up on **Rosalie**, *who sits by the piano and sings.*

Rosalie
  Was that Mister Right?
  If it was, I'll let it pass.
  The right Mister Right
  That funky looking skunk put me kerplunk on my ass

I thought Mister Right
Would have a little more couth.
He'd come on a white charger
Say Hi-de-hi to my charm
And Vo-de-oh to my youth.

The bright jazz tune plays.

Rosalie   So Betty Yearn, newly arrived from Bangor,
Maine, stays in New York to settle my estate along with
my hash. She moves into my apartment, she takes over my
job. I'm not even cool in the grave yet, and she's got my
job. She moves into my life. Betty Yearn's first day
eighteen months ago in the Dawn's Promising Star Travel
Agency. A division of Honeymoon Holidays.

*The jazz music turns Latin. The lights come up on the travel agency:
a desk, a telephone, lots of telephone books, a cassette recorder that
contains tapes of cheering and applause.* **Betty** *is dressed in a pretty
outfit for her first day at work. And if she can wear pants and look
pretty,* **Raulito** *can wear what appears to be – is it? – a gold lamé
evening gown over his business suit, and still look mucho macho.
Raulito is very handsome, like a 1940s Latin leading man with a
pompadour and diamond rings. He carries an armful of Sunday's
papers. He is sexually very threatening.* **Betty** *is unnerved.*

Raulito   You take the *Daily News*. You take the *Sunday
Times*. Not the financial section. Not the sports section.

Betty   There's so many sections.

Raulito   The engagement section.

Betty   The society page.

Raulito   You look up the name of the father, the man
who is paying for the wedding.

Betty   Mr and Mrs Bernard Culkin of Corona and Point
Lookout announce the engagement of their daughter,
Lillibet –

Raulito   Stop right there. You look in the phone book.
Not the Manhattan phone book.

Betty   So I look up Corona in . . . there are so many phone books. I've only been here a few days.

Raulito   Corona is in Queens.

Betty   Culkin. BBBBBB Bernard.

Raulito   Don't *show* it to me. Copy the phone number down on the pad.

Betty   I swear to you, I'm generally very good at writing numbers.

Raulito   Check the bride-to-be's name.

Betty   Lillibet.

Raulito   See what Lillibet does? Where Lillibet is employed.

Betty   Educated at St John's University.

Raulito   Your sister was like streaks of lightning here.

Betty   Is employed as a researcher at Mutual Life.

Raulito   So she should be home at five thirty. Mark down to call her at?

Betty   Five forty-five?

Raulito   Five thirty-one!

Betty   Nice to have a few minutes to get your coat off.

Raulito   Your late and more and more lamented sister would have that phone ringing off the hook the instant Lillibet Culkin Corona Queens stuck her key in the door.

Betty   Fine.

Raulito   If I may be so bold, petals on a pool drifting, you want a travel brochure back to Bangor?

Betty   No! I feel my sister wanted me to have this job.

Raulito   No hard feelings. We can be friends. If I'm ever in Bangor, God forbid, I'll look you up. Is the job too hard for you?

Betty   I can do it.

Raulito   Then, honey through the comb sifting, you must be prepared to play Follow-the-Leader. Miss Lisa Staminelli to wed law student. Bayside, Queens. Father Frank Staminelli. Presented to society the Gotham Ball. You have the Queens phone book. Zut zut zut zut *zutt* you have the number. You dial it. (*He accomplishes this task in a brilliant quick stroke.*) This is where my Rosalie was brilliant. (*He talks into the phone.*) Miss Lisa Staminelli. Is she there? Is this she? This is she? The noted debutante? I am talking to her. Ohhhhh, Miss Staminelli, this is *Bride's Magazine* calling. Of course I'm breathless. Are you sitting down? Miss Staminelli, you've won our lottery. An all-expense-paid honeymoon for two to Paradise Cove. Two weeks!

Betty   Two weeks?

Raulito   Yes! For you and Mr Right – (*He checks the paper.*) Bruce Mandrake. How did I know? Darling, we here at *Bride's Magazine* know *tout!* If we didn't know who was getting married, we wouldn't know if the world would keep spinning. We need families and families are love and love pulled your number out of the lottery. Fate wanted you and your new husband, Mr Mandrake – is he the magician? – to have this honeymoon. Do you think it's possible, God, we know you're so busy. Would it be possible for you and Señor Right to stop down to our office to pick up your honeymoon? Fourteenth Street. 618 West. Ninth floor. The Honeymoon Holidays Building. Could you and Bruce toddle on down here any night after work, say seven? We could finalize arrangements for the honeymoon? Some forms to sign. (*The Piano plays a tango.*) Then you could have a lovely evening in the Village. Greenwich Village. Chianti. Pasta. Discuss your future. Discuss your honeymoon. It's all luck and love is luck and you're the luckiest girl in the world, Lisa. The past shows us the mistakes we made. The future's the place where we won't make them again. Dreams are the fuel for reality. A new family is coming into the world! Oh God! Grab the Now! The Now is all quicksilver and mercury. The Now is diamonds. Can I make an appointment for you? (*The music stops.*) Lucky you! I could squeeze you in tomorrow at seven ten. Oh, Lisa, you've made all of us so happy at *Bride's Magazine.* (*He puts on a cassette of cheering.*) See you tomorrow. (*He hangs up.*) You're the bait, baby. You lure them in here. *You* decorate the hook. *I* make the sale.

Betty   Everybody falls for it?

Raulito   Sometimes a black eye. Every now and then a death threat. But, Sweetness and Light, if I can make one sale a week, that is two trips to the Caribbean, I can make out all right. Besides what is living without a little danger?

Betty   Do they ever call *Bride's Magazine?*

Raulito   Only the smart ones and they're not exactly our clientele.

Betty   Could we be sued?

Raulito   By who?

Betty   *Bride's Magazine.*

Raulito   For what?

Betty   I don't want to go to jail. My life is beginning. I don't want to be arrested.

Raulito   Hey, hey, hey. Evidence obtained by wiretap is illegal. Can't be introduced into court. What planet you from anyway, baby?

Betty   What borough is the moon in?

Raulito   The moon is the fifty-first state. Hawaii. Alaska. The moon. Did you see the moon last night? Like a little Turkish flag waving in the sky? I saluted.

Betty   Why do you dress that way?

Raulito   That is exactly what your sister Rosalie said to me the first time we met. We would curl up on her pull-out sleep sofa, now *your* pull-out sleep sofa, and I would tell her my dream to one night turn on the TV and hear the

Late Show say, 'And tonight our guest is ME!' (*He puts on a cassette of people cheering.*) Thank you Johnny. I'm from Cuba. We lived on the other side of the island. From Havana.

The piano plays Latin-style. **Raulito** *sits beside the desk as if he were the guest on the* Tonight Show *and* **Betty** *were the host.*

Raulito   Poor. You never saw such poor. We were so poor *that.* You know those jokes? He was so fat *that.* She was so dumb *that.* Well, we were so *poor* that. When I was wearing rags, I was running around naked. This part of Cuba that we called the country, I think any normal thinking person would call it the jungle. Occasionally, a magazine would appear in our village and I'd see the pictures of evening gowns and spangles and barrettes in the hair and these high heels. I didn't know till later that was what women wore. I thought that was rich people. I thought if you were rich and lived in the city or lived in America that was what the average American family hung around in. The Revolution came. I saw Che Guevara this close. We left Cuba. We got to Florida. Where I found out that those uniforms with diamonds and lace did not belong to the typical American man. But a few years ago, I was shopping in the Salvation Army for a winter coat and I came upon this real Rita Hayworth special. A beautiful 1940s evening gown for twenty-five cents. I bought it. Why not? The dreams we have as kids, they're the dream we never get over. I put it on over my suit. I feel rich. I feel successful.

Raulito *begins to spin so the dress flares out. He advances seductively on* **Betty***, now waving his dress like a matador's cape in front of her.* **Betty** *is terrified.* **Raulito** *shows no mercy.*

Raulito   I feel I can get out of the jungle and get to America and twirl and twirl. Feeling good outside I start to feel good inside. I start Honeymoon Holidays. I want to start a family. I want to start a life. Betty, your sister went with me. Your sister would let me dance with her first. Then she would let me sleep with her after and dreams would come out of our heads like little Turkish moons. We would salute. Betty?

Betty (*getting back to work*)   It's about five thirty. I'd better call Lillibet.

Raulito   You like the name Lillibet?

Betty   It's a name. People have names. I take the Queens phone book.

Raulito   Do you know what Queen Elizabeth's secret name is? If you were in her royal family, what you would call her?

Betty   Elizabeth. They'd call her Elizabeth. They'd call her Queen Elizabeth. Elizabeth is short for Queen Elizabeth.

Raulito   They'd call her Lillibet.

Betty   I thought I was safe when I came in here, when I met you at my sister's funeral I thought, this guy's a weirdo but I'll be safe.

Raulito   Lillibet is the Queen's secret name. What Prince Philip calls her when they're alone. I read that in *People*'s magazine. Alone must mean also in the royal bed. Prince Philip calls over to her: Lillibet? He turns on the royal radio station. A little English Latin music comes on the Royal Radio. I should call you Lillibet. Tell me your story? Unfold yourself to me?

Betty   I'm Betty. Betty's short for Elizabeth. I'm a Betty. That's all I am. I have no story. I'm no guest on any talk show. No story. I am a middle-aged woman. I'm a young girl. I'm regular. Quiet. Normal. Human person. (*She is shaking violently. She puts on the cheering on the cassette and dials the telephone.*) Is Miss Lillibet Culkin there? Hi! This is *Bride's Magazine* calling. The lottery of love twirled and stopped at . . . oh? The wedding is off? The groom is dead? Head injuries? Attacked by a monkey wrench? Greenwich Village? Beaten brutally? Watch stolen? I don't care. Don't tell me your troubles. You won a honeymoon. That's all I want to tell you. That's all. (*She hangs up.*) Lillibet Culkin.

Corona, Queens. I don't want the job. I can't handle the
job. I'm not my sister. I am not Rosalie. I can't do her
job. I'm not Lillibet. I'm not Queen Elizabeth. I'm nobody.
I'm me. I can't do the job. I don't want the job.

Raulito *has picked her up. He tangos her away into the dark.*
Rosalie *appears by the piano.*

Rosalie
  Frightened of you
  All of these years
  Never secure
  In your embrace.
  Sleep through the night
  Dream that I'm dead
  Feeling your weight
  There in the bed.
  One little bag
  Never unpacked
  Hidden away
  In case
  I get the nerve
  One day to leave
  Finally that fact
  To face.
  What's getting me through my life?
  What's my excuse inside?
  What's keeping me in my life?
  The molehill of lust or the mountain of pride?
  Forgive me, my dear
  A slip of the tongue
  Forget what I said
  Erase
  I meant to say
  My life is brightened by you
  The darkness whitened by you
  Each moment heightened by you
  My life enlightened by you
  But not I'm frightened of you
  Forgive me

I'm sorry
Don't hit me
I love you

A year and a half later. Eighteen count 'em eighteen
months. My sister has moved into my life. It's like two days
before the boy's murder.

The lights upstage show **Betty** *and* **Raulito** *necking, passionately.
He has gathered his evening gown up under the trench coat he now
wears.* **Betty** *is quite snappily dressed and a lot more sure of herself
in the last months since we've seen her. The music is ominous.*
Rosalie *goes into the black.* **Raulito** *kisses* **Betty** *one time more,
and he goes into the dark. The lights come up on the apartment.*
Bert *sits on a red beanbag, winding watches. He tenses.* **Betty**
*straightens herself. She comes in the room. She begins to take off her
dress and put on a robe.*

Betty   I bought this new dress today. You like it? (*She
takes another dress out of a paper bag.*) Or do you like this one?
What do you think moving maybe to Miami? I got a
chance finally after eighteen months at Raulito's. A free
trip for two. National Airlines. There's a lot of cities we
could fly to. L.A. Round-trip ticket but we could just stay.
Stop winding all those watches. I never saw anyone for
finding so many watches. Find 'em and wind 'em. That's
your name. The watch monster. That's what I gave birth
to. Can't you say anything? Jesus. Who'd've thought you'd
grow up to be your father. To have to live through all that
again. Can't you say anything?

Bert   How's Honeymoon Holidays?

Betty   Raulito called me a professional today. He gave
me a gold star. (*She picks up the phone.*) Miss Mary Louise
Nicholson? The lottery of love twirled and twirled and
stopped at your number. It don't hurt to start a marriage
with a good honeymoon. (*She slams the phone down.*)

Bert   Did you and Daddy have a good honeymoon?

Betty   If I had a good honeymoon, you think I'd be
working at Honeymoon Holidays?

Bert You going to marry Raulito?

Betty Raulito already has a wife and about nineteen children. He gave me this butterfly pin. It was his grandmother's. (*She bends it.*) Now you bend it. I don't want anybody doing nice for me. (**Bert** *bends the pin.* **Betty** *throws the pin away.*) I don't want anybody giving me presents. I don't want to be reminded what I missed out on. We should've had a family. We could've had a family, a regular dynasty. I had a family. I should've passed one on to you. If we'd had a family, we'd go to the movies and eat at McDonald's and take summer trips to Maine to see your grandmother and see free Shakespeare in the Park and take long rides on the subway to the Bronx Zoo and the Brooklyn Botanical. If we had a family, things'd be a lot different around here.

Bert Why can't we do all those things now? They're all free.

Betty Because they're things families do together. Because they remind me how I screwed up my life. If we don't do nothing, I don't get reminded. But I don't want to turn you against your father. I want you to love your father. Your father was a god. Your father was the handsomest man I ever saw. Your father had a body you could see through his clothes. Your father had shoulders out to here and a waist you could clasp your thumb and index finger around. A brain of a fucking wizard. He could remember telephone numbers. Addresses. He could remember lottery numbers and the social security numbers of people he met a hundred years ago. Serial numbers of guys he was in the Army with. He was kind of creepy when you come to think of it.

Bert He sounds great.

Betty We bumped into an old Army buddy and your father said 'I remember you. 19769982.' The guy says 'Hey, why'd you remember my serial number?' Your father says 'Hold on. I haven't been thinking about you all these years. I just happen to have that kind of memory.'

Bert   So why's he forgot where we live?

Betty   A blind spot. He forgot you. He forgot me. For a guy with a memory. What I think is us living on Christopher Street. Ever since the Catholic Church said St Christopher doesn't exist, maybe he thinks Christopher Street doesn't exist either.

Bert   But you left him.

Betty   I didn't mind him, well, I did, him putting my head down the toilet and flushing it. But you. When he put your head down the toilet and flushed it, I said that's it. And I told him to leave.

Bert   I have dreams sometimes of water rushing by me.

Betty   That comes from your father putting your head down the toilet.

Bert   I think I'll join the Navy when I can. The submarine service.

Betty   You been seeing too many Walt Disney movies.

Joanne   (*runs in breathless*)   You know what my mother told me today? A lady in her office knew a lady who died and they couldn't find a reason why she died. She was healthy.

Betty   I don't want to hear any more black widow spiders. You get me?

Joanne   This isn't black widow spiders. This is the truth. This lady died and they traced all her steps and they found she had gone to Korvette's Department Store and on her dead body they found her wearing a beautiful Indian blouse with pieces of mirror sewn in it.

Betty   Sounds pretty. Korvette's?

Joanne   And they traced all her steps and went to Korvette's and opened the drawer where the Indian blouses came from and they reached in and the detective pulled

back his hand because it almost got bit by a cobra. Which
is what happened to the lady. These blouses had come in
from India. And cobra eggs had got woven in beneath the
mirrors while the blouses were being made and the cobra
eggs hatched from the heat of being mailed over here and
the lady reached her hand in the drawer and got bitten
and died.

Betty *serves* **Bert** *dinner,* **Bert** *eats.*

Betty   Where is this woman? How come you always have
these friends who are getting bit by black widow spiders?
Bit by cobras.

Bert   It was her mother's friend.

Betty   I don't believe her mother.

Bert   Then you don't believe me. Are you calling me a
liar?

Betty   I don't want you hanging around together. I don't
want any more stories about black widow spiders and black
widow cobras. I'm up to here with it. (**Joanne** *runs out.*)
And you be careful with her. I don't want any fourteen-
year-old fathers living in my house. I'm not ready to be a
grandmother yet.

Bert   You old hag. You old crone. I know how old you
are. You're thirty-six and you're gonna die soon and I'm
fourteen and I'm going to live forever. I hate you. You're
going to die. You know what I want for Christmas? You in
a coffin under a Christmas tree. Why did Aunt Rosalie
have to die? Why couldn't you be the one that bicycle hit.
Maybe that guy is around right now speeding down streets
looking for you.

Betty   You know why you can't hurt me? Cause I have
X-ray eyes and I can see right into your heart.

Bert   Bullshit.

Betty   Remember that old man with the pushcart in
Bangor who called out 'OLD CLOTHES'? You used to

follow him for hours. What did you do with that filthy old man? Old Clothes. I place my X-ray eyes over you and I see deep in you Old Clothes. Old Clothes. Old Clothes.

Bert Don't say that.

Betty Old clothes. Old rags. Old rats. X-ray eyes.

Bert Don't say that! Don't say that!

Betty Don't have to say it. I feel it. I'm being very quiet and saying to myself over and over. (*Wordless.*) Old clothes.

Bert *hits her. She hits him back.*

Bert Shut up! Shut up!

Betty I'm not saying anything. (*Wordless.*) Old clothes.

Bert It's what you're thinking. Can't think that. Stop! Stop!

Betty I love thinking. I can think anything I want.

Bert I've killed people.

Betty Don't make me laugh.

Bert I haven't killed them. Donny's killed them.

Betty There you are. You couldn't hurt a fly. I do not mean that as a compliment. I mean that as a truth. You could not wound a mosquito. If David and Goliath had a fight, Goliath would reach down and squeeze your head like a seedless grape.

Bert I lure them up here while you're away and Donny and I kill them. Hit them on the head with the monkey. Take their watches. Roll them out in the hall. They don't dare call the cops on us. I can so hurt a fly.

Betty (*slaps him*) Lure? Where'd you learn a word like lure?

Bert I know a lot of words.

Betty There's a whole series of murders going around.

Bert   Maybe that's me.

Betty   Decapitations.

Bert   What's that?

Betty   Down at all these rough bars down by the river, Raulito told me at work they find people with heads chopped off. The police don't bother to check them out. It's not worth the trouble. You're not part of those murders, are you? I told you to stay away from those docks, you little faggot.

Bert   What's decap – decap –

Betty   Chop their heads off!

Bert   I didn't do that! I swear! I'm just into watches. Money. The monkey wrench. I don't think any of them ever died. I swear.

A **Man** *appears at the door – a large man, carefully dressed in a white linen suit, Panama hat, and black string tie. He carries flowers.*

Betty   Yes?

Man   Betty? Betty Mandible?

Betty   I was.

Bert   Are you the police?

Man   You got married.

Betty   Oh yes. My husband here and I are very happy. Some people say he's too young. I say why not?

Man   Hello, Betty.

Bert   My mother says go away. She doesn't know you. Ma? Is this guy bothering you?

Betty   I know who you are.

Man   I was hoping you would.

Betty   In Bangor. Summer of –

Man   Nineteen years ago. I'm Durwood Peach.

Betty Durwood Peach. The Good Humor Man. Pushing that white ice-cream truck.

Durwood Name like a flavor ice cream. The special may be blueberry ripple but I'm pushing the peach.

Betty You were from North –

Durwood South.

Betty Carolina. You came up to Bangor, to visit your aunt.

Durwood Can I sit down for a minute? Excuse me for not being on my toes more. Oh, I have been driving. I drove from South Carolina straight up to Bangor, Maine, and looked up your name in the phone book. Your mother answered. She told me your swell sister had passed on. She told me you were here. You were the one I wanted. I got back in my car and drove from Maine nonstop here to Christopher Street. So this is Greenwich Village. Sure is lively. Mexican restaurant and a Chinese restaurant and an Indian restaurant all on one block. A lot of variety. Your mother didn't mention you had a little boy. Is he yours?

Bert I'm hers.

Betty Why are you here?

Durwood See. Now I should said that soon as I arrived. I never forgot you nineteen years ago and even though we never talked much and you had other boyfriends and you and me never went out, I have recently realized you are the only girl I ever loved, ever will love. My doctor gave me a note saying all this was true.

Betty Doctor?

Durwood I been in a hospital and I got out and I been going to a doctor and you appeared to me like a holy movie when the Blessed Virgin appears and tells the holy children what to do. You appeared in my analysis. Here's the note.

Betty Thank you. (*She takes the note.*)

Durwood Now my knees are shaking. I'm gonna faint.

Bert Should I call the police?

Durwood No! I'm all right. It's all the driving from South Carolina to Bangor, Maine, back to New York. Betty, I love you. I'll always love you. I've never loved anyone else. I've told my wife. She understands. She's written a note to you giving me up to you.

Betty (*reads*) 'Dear Betty. I surrender all rights to Durwood, heartbroken and bereft as that leaves me.'

Durwood My grandfather, the only surviving member of my natural family, the head of the clan, welcomes you into the family. I'm rich, Betty. I've got a farm and I lease it out to a racetrack and I make lots of money. Here's a thousand dollars in single new bills as a sign of faith. You remember me. I didn't have to introduce myself. I thought I'd have to introduce myself. That's a good sign. You remember me.

Bert You want me to get my monkey? Bang him down on his head? I can get Donny down here.

Betty I never even kissed you.

Durwood To pursue the unattainable. My doctor says that's my problem.

Betty The unattainable I'm afraid I must remain.

Durwood No, you won't. I won't lie to you. I have been sick. And to be cured, I must once in my life obtain the unobtainable or I will die. I'm staying at the Dixie Hotel on West Forty-Second Street. I'll return there now and leave this one thousand dollars to show my good faith. I'll leave these photos of my farm and all that you'll be mistress of. A mountain. A river. Caves that are closed to the public. I'll give you time to peruse my offer and would like to ask your permission to call tomorrow night after which time perhaps we could leave immediately. You cannot escape from me or the power of my mind. We will begin a family. I'll be cured. We'll be happy. All these

years. I'll be back tomorrow evening at six p.m. with my
bags packed. I'll make a reservation at the Mexican
restaurant for two.

Bert   For three.

Durwood   For two, Betty. You and me.

Betty   I don't think you need reservations at Taco
Trolley.

Durwood   Until tomorrow, Betty. Your mother's angry at
you. She said she sent you down here to bring your sister
back and you never returned. She said she had messages
for you. She said Get in touch. If I can bring you together,
you and your mother, that'll be doing good. My doctor will
be so happy. He said if you really want her, you'll find
her. I didn't have to call. You were home. One of the
largest cities in the world. You were here. Now I'm here.
I'll be back tomorrow. The special is blueberry. But I'm
pushing the peach.

Durwood *goes.* **Bert** *has been counting the money* **Durwood**
left behind.

Betty   I got to sit down.

Bert   You think it's counterfeit? You bend the face in half
on two bills and if they fit together, the two faces into one
face, that proves it's not counterfeit.

Betty   I remember him.

Bert   You must've been the prettiest girl around that
summer.

Betty   I was pretty. But not this pretty. Do you think he's
telling the truth? South Carolina? Should I go? Maybe he
does have money. Get us out of here. Who cares if he's a
nut. It's amazing how a little tomorrow can make up for a
whole lot of yesterday. It sounds like one of those uplift
songs in a musical comedy. (*She sings.*) 'It's amazing how a
little tomorrow.'

Bert (*sings*)   'Makes up for a whole lot of yesterday.'

Betty 'It's amazing how a little tomorrow.' Do you have a joint? A jay? Don't do lies to me. I found them in the Saltine box the last time.

Bert This time I hid the dope in the one place you'd never look.

Betty Stop making with the funnies ... I want to keep this moment. I feel it going away already and I'm hanging on to it. Don't go away, magic moment. I'll be right there.

Bert The one place you'd never look.

Betty I give up.

Bert The broom closet.

Betty You're right. The one place I'd never look. I like giant dustballs. It gives me a flavor of the Old West.

They sit on the day-bed and light up. The lights dim slightly on them as they smoke. **Rosalie** *and her piano appear in the light at left.* **Rosalie** *sings it like one of those rousing uplift songs in a musical comedy.*

Rosalie
   It's amazing how a little tomorrow
   Can make up for a whole lot of yesterday
   It's amazing how a little tomorrow
   Can make up for a whole lot of yesterday
   Yesterday was dreary
   Clocks kept on crawling
   Now the future's cheery
   How thrilling, how enthralling
   It's amazing how a little tomorrow
   Can recompense an awful lot of sorrow
   So get yourself a little tomorrow
   And wake up from those awful yesterdays.
   Shake up all those bore-filled yester –
   Make up those unlawful yesterdays.

She dances back to the piano, bows and goes into the darkness. **Bert** *and* **Betty** *sit on the day-bed.*

Betty   The first time I ever smoked pot, I was in a bar in Rhode Island with my girlfriend.

Bert (*bombed by the joint*)   The summer you met Durwood?

Betty   No, after. This guy asked us if we wanted to smoke reefers and my girlfriend said 'Only if you promise we'll turn into sex-crazed nymphomaniacs who won't be held responsible for any of their activities.' (*The* **Dope King** *appears upstage in the light, dressed like a beatnik.*) And the man said . . .

Dope King (*striking a match*)   Results guaranteed.

Betty   And off we went. He had a car.

Dope King (*lighting a cigarette*)   Get in.

Betty   What's that black rag?

Dope King   I'm going to have to blindfold you girls seeing as how I am the Dope King of Providence, Rhode Island.

Betty   Ooooo, I love an expert. Shut up, Betty. Just shut up.

Dope King   Look, you little twats, if you ever got caught, you couldn't reveal where I'd taken you. You couldn't betray me, but then I couldn't have you betray yourselves with the knowledge you knew where the dope headquarters of Providence, Rhode Island, was. I'm doing this for you, you little twats.

Betty   We drove, the three of us, my girlfriend, him, me. We giggled suicidally because maybe this man steering his car right then left then left then right would murder us and if he did we should remember where he took us. I had heard that directions given before death stay embroidered on your brain and the police can use that for a clue. I didn't care if we were murdered. My life was beginning. There was a hit song that summer. We drove singing it. (*She sings in a clear, pure voice.*)

  Hey Stay a While
  In the crook of my arms

All you got to do is
Look in my arms
And you'll see Home Sweet Home
I'll invest in a doormat
Hey Home Sweet Home
We'll test the mattress
Our arms are sinuous
All performances are continuous
Hey Stay a While
Feel the smile in my arms
And the smile's in my arms
All for you
Sit back/Relax
Cool brow/Tension slacks
Hey Stay a While
My arms are filled with
What the whole world lacks
Hey Stay a While

Mavis, because that was my girlfriend's name, Mavis
Brennan is squeezing my hand and I'm squeezing hers.
Where are we? I smell bread. That Portuguese bakery. I
think I know where we are.

Dope King   We're here.

Betty   He led us out of the car. We held hands like
mountain climbers. Doors open. Stairs climb.

Dope King   Okay. Open your eyes.

Betty   Three steps. One. Two. Three. Doors shut. It was
the room I had lived in the year before when I was
working in the shoe factory for the summer. I saw traces
on the wall where I had written 'Fuck You' in peanut
butter the year before one night because here I was
seventeen and my life still hadn't begun and I'm out
supporting myself. I said 'Is Miss Carter the landlady
here? Is that the shoe factory over there?' I said 'Boy, some
dope king. Living in a seventeen-dollar-a-week rooming
house with breakfast thrown in on Saturday.'

Dope King   Some breakfast.

The lights go off on the **Dope King**.

Betty (*watching where he went*)   We laughed and laughed.

Bert   That's nice. You go to a strange place and they take off your blindfold and it's a place where you lived.

Betty   That is precisely what I did not, underline the not, did *not* like. I remember Miss Carter had said, 'What's that word in peanut butter on the wall?' I said, 'Oh, you think that says Fuck? You dirty lady. That's a message in Speedwriting: If You See Kay. Kay was my girl friend,' I said. 'If you see Kay, remind us both to rd ths msj and gt a bttr jb.' Memories within memories. I'm remembering what I remembered in my memory . . .

Bert   Where's Mavis?

Betty   She died or something.

Bert   Mavis Brennan.

Betty   Don't be such a busybody.

Bert   Mavis Brennan.

Betty   What am I telling you stories about dope for? I should be telling you stories how I didn't take dope. I should be a father influence to you.

Bert   How did you die?

Betty   Who died?

Bert   Mavis Brennan.

Betty   Don't be so morbid. I didn't say she died.

Bert   You said she died.

Betty   Or something.

Bert   What's the something?

Betty   You lose touch. Touch gets lost.

Bert   Will I lose touch with you?

Betty   You're my kid. You're me. You're the fruit of my loins or the fruit of my loom. Some joke Mavis and I used to make about phrases in the Bible. Jesus came riding into town on his ass. We'd laugh. I wish sometimes you were a girl. I wish sometimes I had a friend. Mavis Brennan.

Bert   You can call me Mavis.

Betty   Mavis, I'm in love with a boy named Bert.

Bert   Do you love him a lot?

Betty   More than life itself.

Bert   Do you love life?

Betty   More than Bert himself.

Bert   Do you love me?

Betty   But Mavis, you're my best friend.

Bert   Can I rub your hair?

Betty   Oh, yes, Mavis.

Bert (*rubs her hair*)   When I rub your hair, I can feel the oil from it under my fingernails. I sit in class and the teacher says 'Get your fingers out of your nose.' He says 'You can always tell the Catholic kids from the Protestant kids.' He says 'The Catholic kids are always picking their nose and the Protestant kids are always biting their nails.' He's bald and he says 'Grass doesn't grow on busy streets.'

Betty   You tell him grass doesn't grow on rocks either. This feels so good . . . don't stop . . . Bert . . . Mavis . . .

Bert (*goes to the sink, gets a tray containing basin, pitcher, water, and shampoo*)   I'm getting the basin.

Betty   I washed my hair last night.

Bert   Let me wash it tonight? Please? Momma, we have a thousand dollars in bills of consecutive numbers. You are loved. You have decisions to make. Momma, let me clear your head. You always think better when I wash your hair.

He pours water over her hair. She leans back. Her hair is undone, and it streams out. **Bert** *soaps it.*

Betty   Make it lather up. Push all the thoughts, the bad thoughts, push them out of my head.

Bert   Push 'em out. Push 'em out.

Betty (*loving the shampoo*)   Wasn't he disgusting?

Bert   That man?

Betty (*looking at the flowers he brought*)   Durwood Peach.

Bert   If you married him, you'd be Betty Peach.

Betty   I'll give him his money back tomorrow.

Bert   Here comes the hot water!

Betty   I'll keep half the money. A consideration fee. For considering his proposal.

Bert   Keep all of it. I don't want him around.

Betty   No, I'll keep half the money in payment for a tormented night's sleep. For tossing and turning and wondering whether or not I should run away with an insane Good Humor man. Ex-Good Humor man.

Bert   Our flavor of the week: Betty Peach! Betty Peach on a stick! Here comes the shampoo. Make the bubbles come up. Work out all the bad thoughts.

Betty   I went to visit Mavis in Memorial Hospital. She was dying of everything. They had cut off her breasts and she had lots of radiation treatment and her hair had gone. And I came to visit her. She was down to about sixty pounds and she wouldn't die. And I said, 'Mavis, is there anything I can do for you?' And she said, 'Yes, there is this new book: *The Sensuous Woman*. Bring it. Read it to me.' And I went all that summer in Boston, every day for visiting hours and read her from this dirty book on how to be sensuous and how to be attractive and how to have orgasms and how to ... All summer she wouldn't die. All summer I read to her. I finished the book. Mavis said, 'Begin it again.' And I'd have to get very close to her to

read to her because it was on the ward and the other
patients did not want to hear this dirty stuff. And her gums
were black and her breath smelled like sulfur and her hair
was gone and I'm reading her how to attract a man and
she's smiling and hanging on. I never went back after one
day. I couldn't go back. Fall was coming. I hated life. I
hated Mavis. I hated. Rub the hair. Wash it out. More hot
water. More bubbles. More soap. Get it all out of my head
all the bad into a bubble and fly it away and pop it. Get it
out. (**Betty** *has torn all the petals and leaves off the flowers.*)

Bert (*very moved, tender*)   The next time my biology teacher
rubs his bald head and says 'Grass doesn't grow on busy
streets,' I'll say, 'Yeah and it doesn't grow on rocks either.'
I'll say that. I kiss your hair, Momma.

Betty   And I kiss Mavis and you and Raulito and your
father and the Dope King of Providence, Rhode Island,
and my sister Rosalie and life for bringing us a thousand
dollars through the door and I kiss life and I kiss all the
people I ever loved . . .

Bert   Me! Me! Most of all me!

Bert *pours water over her hair. The soap is washed out.*
Durwood *appears in the room. He is breathless and excited.*

Durwood   Is something wrong with me? I have you here
and say goodnight like some goon. What am I being so
polite about? I'm no goon. Good manners make you a
goon. I'm trying to learn to listen to myself. Listen to what
I want. Not what people tell me I should want. You must
think I'm a goon. Only a goon would drive thousands of
miles to find the only woman he ever loved, find her, then
leave her and go back alone to a room in the Dixie Hotel
by himself.

Betty   What did I do to make you feel all this?

Durwood   I remember riding by your house looking up
at the porch, ringing the bells extra loud so you'd come
down and buy ice cream from me. Your mother was sitting

there rocking and your father reading a paper and you and your sister crouching on the green steps holding your skirts down around your ankles talking so hard to each other.

Betty   They're all gone mostly.

Bert   You're gonna catch a cold. You got to dry the hair or the wet picks up dirt. Ma?

Durwood   You and your sister walked down the steps still talking so hard you didn't even pay any attention to me and you bought vanilla and walked back up the stairs and sat down and kept on talking.

Betty   What in God's name could we have been talking about?

Durwood   I said I want in. One day I'm going to be on that porch with that girl.

Betty   Her leaving home? Some Ava Gardner movie?

Durwood   I realize now I wanted the girl and not the porch. (*He takes out snapshots.*) You got to come back with me. This house will be yours. All this land.

Bert   Look at all the fences. Everything is outlined.

Durwood (*tearing up the photos*)   But if I had to choose between where I live and you, I'd rip up everything I own because the only landscape worth looking at is the landscape of the human body. I kiss your Blue Ridge Mountains of Virginia. I kiss your Missouri and Monongahela and Susquehanna and Shenandoah and Rio Grande. I kiss the confluence of all those rivers. I kiss your amber waves of grain. I kiss your spacious skies, your rocket's red glare, your land I love, your purple mountain'd majesty. But most of all I kiss your head. I kiss the place where we make our decisions. I kiss the place where we keep our resolves. The place where we do our dreams. I kiss the place behind the eyes where we store up secrets and knowledge to save us if we're caught in a corridor on a dark, wintry evening. And you, with your mouth, kiss my head because that's the place where I kept the pictures of you all these years. Come home with me to the hotel.

Betty   I will come with you.

Durwood (*takes her aside*)   But you can't take the kid.

Bert   What is he saying?

Durwood   I don't want you having any children except what comes out of us.

Bert   What are you talking?

Durwood   A family's like a body. A perfect body. The man's the head. The woman's the heart. The children are the limbs. I don't want any limbs from any other bodies. No transplants allowed. You hear me? Only out of us.

Bert   What are you saying?

Betty (*taking him aside, quietly*)   Let me go down there and check out the landscape. I'll send for you in a few days. I swear.

Rosalie *appears in the light at left.*

Rosalie   So they went to South Carolina. The two of them. They left the boy home.

Captain Holahan *appears in the light at right.*

Holahan   So she claims. So she claims. The fact remains the kid is dead.

Betty *holds out the money.* **Bert** *takes it.*

Curtain.

Act Two

Bert *comes downstage and sings in a clear voice:*

I used to believe
When I was young
I understood
Every note that was sung.
Voices of sparrows
Voices of blue jays
Voices of robins
Voices of eagles.

When I was young
I used to pretend
Through all of my life
I'd have a friend
We'd climb the mountains
We'd cross the deserts
We'd sail the oceans
We'd solve the mysteries.

When I was young
I used to believe
In some other life
I was an Inca
Maybe a Druid
More like Egyptian
Pyramid builder
Leader of millions.

I used to believe.
When I was young
I understood
Every note that was sung . . .

Voices of eagles . . .

The lights go out on him, come up on the interrogation room at the police station.

Holahan   We had trouble tracking you down. You left town. Everybody thought you had taken the boy with you.

Betty   I went away for a few days. He's a big kid. He's supposed to be able to take care of himself. Boy Scouts go off. Survivor camps where they go off, kids, for three months, four, in mountains. Kids go in forests for weeks and months and they come out men and parents are applauded.

Holahan   Bleecker Street ain't exactly survival camp.

Betty   He was supposed to stay with people in the building, people were supposed to look after him.

Holahan   A fourteen-year-old kid? Where's your head, lady?

Betty   Here. This whole area above the neck. I just didn't desert him. I left him with money. I left him with a thousand dollars.

Holahan   You left your kid with a thousand dollars?

Betty   My friend that I traveled with gave it to him. To me. I gave it to Bert.

Holahan   Even with inflation, a thousand's a lot of money.

Betty   What I'm saying to you is find the person stole the thousand dollars, you'll find who murdered Bert. Said it. I said murdered Bert. I promised myself everything would be all right if I never mentioned the word murdered. If I just never said the word, I'd be all right. If I never said the word, the person who – *did* it –

Holahan   The murderer –

Betty   Would be found.

Holahan   Stop running away from the fact!

Betty   I am not running away from the fact –

Holahan   Of the murder –

Betty   I just promised myself I wouldn't name the fact. Not ever. You made me say the word.

Holahan   Can I make you say another word you're avoiding?

Betty   Confess? Mister, I can say the word Confess all that I want because saying the word Confess is like saying the word desk. Chair. Necktie. Dirt. Room. You. I have nothing to confess.

Holahan   Where is this millionaire now?

Betty   It was only a thousand.

Holahan   This thousandaire. Where is he right now?

Betty   South Carolina.

Holahan   That's where you went?

Betty   Solomon Ferry. The Peach family. Durwood. His father's name. He was a junior.

The lights come down on him as **Holahan** *dials the phone.*

Rosalie *drags on a chair and she sits in it.*

Rosalie   Scene. In which Betty wishes her sister was still alive so she could tell her what happened.

Betty *sits against* **Rosalie** *'s knees.* **Rosalie** *listens with a compassion and intensity she'd never have outside of a fantasy.*

Betty   We got down to South Carolina two days after what a night at ye Olde Dixie Hotel. Durwood wasn't kidding all right. We came down this alley of trees and he says 'Close your eyes and now turn 'em on.' He had this farm with white fences. I never saw so many white fences. I'm not even talking about what went on inside the white fences. I'm a country girl. No stranger to green. The horses and cattle. I never saw such fences. And roads. White painted rocks lining the roads pointing the way where you go up to the big house. I said 'Boy, old girl, you hit pay dirt this time. Boy, old girl,' I said, 'you have been on adventures in your short lifetime, but this is the key adventure. They're going to be doing TV spinoffs and shooting sequels to this part of your life. You are going to be a Southern lady.' We stop in front of the white farmhouse and this youngish lady soon destined to be the ex-wife who wrote me the note struts out of the farmhouse followed by these two old people you just want to hug with a real nice parents' look followed by golden dogs the color gold of cough drops that rescue you in the middle of the night. Durwood gets out of the car and I let him walk around the car to let me out. And these people instead lead him in the house instead of letting him open my side of the door. The woman who would soon be Durwood's ex-wife came back out and said 'Are you the girl from Maine?' I said 'Yes, I was.' She said 'You're very kind to bring Durwood back to us. Here's money.' I got out of the car. I said 'I'm going to live here.' The old people said 'Thank you for bringing our boy back to us. Here's money. He had to get you out of his system. We let him go to you. The doctors said let him go. It was the only way.' I said 'Hey, this is going to be my house.' 'Well, one thing, Durwood isn't crazy about,' they said, 'is you. You sure are a pretty girl. He's been talking years about you. But it's time he goes back in for a rest. There's a bus leaving two oh five from Crossroads Corner going to Wheeling, West Virginia, direct and you can make connections there back to Maine.' I said 'New York. I live in New York now.' They said 'Isn't that nice.' They gave me fifty dollars and showed me the hospital where Durwood would be which was very pretty too with a little pond in the front of it and the dog rode in the car with us and licked my face and I loved those old people and asked them to take me with them. And they said 'Here's your bus,' and I got on it.

The two sisters hold each other's hands. **Captain Holahan** *puts down the phone. The lights come up.* **Rosalie** *goes into the dark.*

Holahan   We called the Peach family, honey.

Betty   Don't call me honey. Okay?

Holahan   They told us you were there.

Betty   So I'm free. Alibis.

Holahan   Honey, you don't need alibis for South
Carolina. You need alibis for Bleecker Street. That's the
required address of your alibis, honey. You could've killed
Bert before you left so you wouldn't miss out on a joy ride
to southern climes. Your boy putting cramps deep in your
life style. The Peach family of Solomon Ferry don't tell me
nothing. The main event we're conferring about took place
in New York City.

The piano plays melodramatically. The lights go out on **Betty** *and*
Holahan. **Rosalie** *appears by the piano. She speaks urgently, like
one of those action-news reporters covering a live event. She remains
onstage for the following scenes.*

Rosalie   Scenes containing information the police would
never know. Scenes containing information the mother
would never know, never could know.

Bert *and* **Donny** *appear.* **Bert** *is flashing some of* **Durwood**'s
money.

Bert   Hey, Donny my man.

Donny   Hey Mr Bert my man.

Bert   Want to see what I got? Not so close.

Donny   You want to sneak into Monosodium Glutamate?

Bert   What's your mouth talking, my man?

Donny   MSG. That's what rock musicians call Madison
Square Garden. Monosodium Glutamate. You know the
stuff they put in Chinese restaurants that makes your face
go all measles? You want to sneak in there tonight?

Bert   To a Chinese restaurant?

Donny   To Madison Square Garden. They got hockey or
a concert or a flower show.

Bert   My man, if I go to Monosodium Glutamate, I go

walking right in the front door paying my own way. (*He takes out a bill.*)

Donny   Where'd you get a ten? You pulling jobs yourself? Hey, I'm the man with the monkey. You into money now by yourself? You deal me in. I got the dibs on the monkey.

Bert   No jobs by myself.

Donny   You dealing? Coke? Pills? Is that more bills in there? They counterfeit?

Bert   No, my man. They are real as a summer's day.

Donny   Bullshit. Those are counterfeit. That's play money.

Bert   You want to see? We go into the bank.

The lights come up on a bank counter. The **Teller** *stands behind it. The music continues.*

Rosalie   They go into the bank on Sheridan Square. They wait in line.

Bert (*to the* **Teller**)   My man, is this bill negotiable? What I'm saying is there's no doubt about the accuracy of this denominational piece of merchandise.

The **Teller** *takes the proffered bill and holds it up to the light.*

Donny   They got a sign in the A & P saying beware ten-dollar bills being circulated.

The **Teller** *smiles and hands the bill back.*

Bert   It's real? There's no doubts? And if I had more with serial numbers right in line, they'd all be real too? Thank you, my man. Here's a quarter. A tip for your appraisal.

Rosalie   They walk away from the bank clerk. The bank is crowded.

Bert (*goes to a glass desk in the bank*)   Come here. I want to do something. It's a funny joke I saw about a bank. You take – anybody looking? – a deposit slip and you write on the back: Hand over all your money or I blow your brains on the wall.

Donny   Where'd you get that money?

Bert   Then you put the deposit slip back where it came from.

Donny   Come on. Tell.

Bert   Then you wait.

Raulito *enters the bank area. He takes a deposit slip, fills it out, goes to the* **Teller**, *who takes the deposit slip. The* **Teller** *looks around panicky. He pushes a button. A siren. Gun shots.* **Raulito** *looks around, his chest covered with blood. Blood comes out of his mouth.*

Raulito   I come into the bank to make deposit number seventeen in the Christmas Club. Time to make deposit number Seventeen. Christmas Club.

He falls. His trench coat opens. His evening gown trembles down. He falls against the counter. The lights go out. Music up.

Donny   Buy me something. Your money's burning holes in my pockets. Let's go.

Rosalie   They go.

The stage is bare. **Joanne** *has joined* **Bert** *and* **Donny**. *The three of them walk in circles.*

Donny (*to* **Joanne**)   Hey, Joanne, Bert's crazy. You know what he's doing? Putting razor blades in frisbees and then when we see somebody we don't like from Elizabeth Irwin High School, we toss it at them and say 'Hey, grab!'

Joanne   Papers I read a German shepherd ate a newborn baby.

Bert   Shut up, Joanne.

Donny   Bert's mother's been gone two days now. She left him a lot of money.

Joanne   The mother went out and left the baby for a moment and the dog ate the baby.

Bert   Shut up, Joanne. You're a real creep. My mother's right. You're a walking exorcism picture. All the time you're so creepy.

Joanne   Your mother likes me.

Bert   She says you give her the creeps.

Donny   Momma's boy.

Bert   I'm not!

Joanne   You are so.

Bert   I like my mother being away. I got the apartment to myself. I'm eating good. Boy, my mother's a rotten cook. I see those commercials 'Food like mother used to make'. I say Boy, that's the worst commercial God ever made.

Joanne   Momma's boy.

Bert   Shut up. There's the restaurant where the bicycle got my aunt.

Donny   What kind of bicycle?

Bert   Ten-speed Raleigh. Yellow.

Joanne   You got the money. You could buy a ten-speed Raleigh yellow. If you weren't so chintzy.

Bert   No way. Money's got to last me.

Donny   She was a nice lady.

Bert   That's how we came down to New York from Maine. We had her funeral, then we stayed and stayed. Wasn't for that ten-speed Raleigh whizzing around the corner, we'd still be in Maine.

Joanne   Momma's boy.

Donny   Where's your father? My mother says how come we never see Bert's father?

Bert   He's away on secret duty.

Joanne   Oh sure.

Bert   He's on the payroll of foreign governments. He calls me all the time and asks me not to tell where he is because if it got out.

Joanne   Oh sure.

Donny   The CIA?

Bert   More secret than the CIA.

Joanne   Nothing is more secret than the CIA.

Bert   If it's such a good secret then how come you know about the CIA. The place my father works for is so secret it don't have no name or initials or nothing.

Joanne   Or existence. (*She calls in the distance.*) Hey, Margie? Want to sneak in to what's playing at the Greenwich? The Waverly? I don't care. (*She goes.*)

Bert   What a creep.

Donny   German shepherds are gonna eat her some day.

Bert   Suppose one day your money runs out and you don't know anybody, what do you do?

Donny   You work.

Bert   Fourteen you can't work. They put you in orphanages? You go to the police, they arrest you? What do you do?

Donny   You got all this money.

Bert   Suppose it runs out.

Donny   Thousand dollars don't run out.

Bert   Sure it can.

Donny   You sure you got it.

Bert   You want to see it?

They run. Music plays. Threatening. Blackness. Then one spotlight shining down at center stage. They're in **Bert**'s *apartment.*

Bert   Hello?

Donny   You think there's anybody here?

Bert   Ma?

Donny   Is she here?

Bert *runs in and out of the light.*

Bert   I hid the money behind the curtains. I hid the money in the toilet. I hid the money in the freezer. I hid the money under the bed. I hid the money in the oven. I hid the money under the carpet. I hid the money in the shower. I hid the money in our shoes. I hid the money in pockets of clothes we don't wear. I hid the money. (*His arms are filled with the bills.*) How long can it last me? Suppose somebody comes in the window? Suppose they steal the money? Who am I gonna call? It's not me. It's a friend. I'm talking about a friend. What if my friend gets locked out? How will he get back in? Is there an earthquake? Why is the room shaking? I can't stop shaking? Hold down the floor! I don't know where she is! She went away and left me! She went out the door! She left me! She went away! I'm turning to water! My stomach's coming up! The floor is moving! (*He hugs* **Donny**.)

Donny (*pauses*)   Hey. Don't you hug me. Hey. You don't touch me. You hear me? You get your mitts off me. You hear.

Bert   I'm going away. Hang on to me.

Donny   You keep your hands to yourself. You keep your hands. It was your idea bringing those guys up here and hitting them. You the one that brought them up. You brought up too many. You got too many watches, Bert. You stay away from me.

Bert   Suppose she never comes back?

Donny (*takes out his monkey wrench*)   I know what this is.
You brought me up here to get my watches, didn't you.
You earned all that money. You brought me up here.
You're doing recruiting for those old guys down at the
docks who want kids.

Bert   Suppose she don't ever come back.

Bert *clutches* **Donny** *around his knees.* **Donny** *lifts his monkey
wrench over* **Bert***'s head. They freeze.* **Rosalie** *appears.*

Rosalie   And all the dead people, the people who have
died, me, Raulito, Durwood, the Dope King of Providence,
Mavis Brennan, the man on the ten-speed bike, all the
dead people in our lives join together and lead Donny to
the wrench and put his hands around the wrench and lead
the wrench to Bert's head and we hold Bert's head so
Donny can bring the wrench down onto Bert's head with
greater ease. Bert falls. Donny takes the thousand dollars.
And at this time precisely, Betty was being put on a
Greyhound bus at Crossroads Corner, South Carolina, and
being sent back to New York. Betty turns around in the
window and sees the parents of Durwood and Durwood's
wife waving goodbye.

Joanne *runs into the apartment area. She knocks on the door.*

Joanne   Bert? Donny?

Donny   Go away.

Joanne   You in there?

Donny   Get out of here, Joanne.

Joanne   I'm coming in.

Donny   You stay outside there.

Joanne   I just got a summer job.

Donny   Don't come in.

Joanne   Checkout girl at the A & P.

Joanne *is trying to push the door in.* **Donny** *is trying to hold it* *shut.* **Joanne** *pushes the door in.* **Donny** *falls back.*

Joanne   You got to be very strong to be a checkout girl at the A & P.

Donny   You tell and I'll.

Joanne (*after walking around and around* **Bert**)   That's what a dead person looks like?

Donny   He made me do it.

Joanne   All the time you read about dead people and hear about dead people but this is my first. Not embalmed or anything.

Donny   He tried to touch me.

Joanne   Just regular dead.

Donny   He put his hands on me.

Joanne   I'm glad it's Bert. I'd hate my first dead person to be a stranger.

Donny   I'm not ever going to not believe in dreams again. I dreamed the other night and the night before that and once about six months ago that a yellow checker cab stopped and a man got out and dragged me in and when the cab stopped we were in a quiet warehouse so you could look down and see the river and waiting in a line was all these men with drool coming out of their mouths and my feet were in cement and the old man touched me only he wasn't old anymore and that dream came true just now. Bert was the old man. My feet were in cement. I am not going to end up my life in any dream. I stopped that dream. Anybody tells you dreams don't tell the future you send them to me.

Joanne *holds* **Donny**.

Joanne   We'll say somebody killed him.

Donny   Who killed him?

Joanne   One of those guys you bring up here with the watches.

Donny   I don't want any part of it. Cops up here. They'll find fingerprints.

Joanne   Okay. They've had all those murders down at the docks. We'll put Bert in a bag and bring him down the river and leave him there. By the warehouse.

Donny   But those murders. The school-crossing lady told me those bodies – they had no heads. The maniac takes the heads off.

Joanne   You got a saw?

Donny   There's one out there.

Joanne   You start cutting. Put papers down.

Donny   Is this a crime!

Joanne   He's already dead. You're making a mess.

Donny   My uncle saw a dirty movie and he told me Bert's mother was in it.

They take **Bert** *by the feet and drag him into the dark.*

Joanne   Bert wasn't from here. Bert never belonged here.

Rosalie *steps forward.* **Betty** *appears in the light, at a phone. She dials.*

Rosalie   Betty is now in Washington, DC. She roams around Washington, DC, looking at monuments. She buys a dress to calm herself. She calls Bert at a pay phone.

The phone rings.

Joanne   Don't get it.

Donny   It might be for me.

Joanne   Don't get it. I'll wait for you outside.

The lights go out on **Donny** *and* **Joanne** *and* **Betty**.

Rosalie   Betty hangs up. She walks to the Capitol

building to look for the Declaration of Independence she saw printed on parchment paper like the original. She will bring it home to Bert for a present.

The lights come up center stage to signify the street. **Donny** *and* **Joanne** *drag on the bag.*

Donny   I'm finished. I put him in a duffel bag.

Joanne   I got a shopping cart.

Donny   We can't steal that. The A & P arrests you.

Joanne   I'm going to be working there this summer. Employees are allowed to use them.

They load **Bert**'s *body in the bag into the cart. They begin pushing.*

Donny   You can smell the river tonight.

Margie *comes up.*

Margie   Hi. Joanne, could I talk to you?

Joanne   Go away, Margie.

Margie   I got to talk to you.

Joanne   Later, Margie.

Margie   What's in there?

Donny   Margie, I believe Joanne was talking to you.

Margie   I want to see what you're pushing.

Joanne   My grandmother's dog died and we're going to bury it in the river.

Margie   Can I talk with you? I don't want to go home yet. My mother's watching television. My father's kicking ass in the living room. (*The three of them walk.*) I went to the Waverly. My girlfriend held open the exit door. They had this movie there. A French picture. Reading the bottom lines in English while they're all above talking French. This picture was all about children. And a little French baby in the picture falls out of the nine-story window and lands

nine stories on the ground and all the grownups scared
shitless and the baby – God, I screamed – lands on a bush
and jumps up and says Baby fall boom boom. The
audience cheered. And later on this French grownup says
That's childhood. They're protected forever. In a magic
circle. Bad things happen to grownups but children are
magic. I think that's what it said. I had to read fast and I
was crying. I don't ever want to grow up. I'm afraid of
getting out of school. I hate what's happening to my body.
It's like it's a sin. I keep going to confession and confessing
that things are happening to my body and the priest says
But that's growing up and I say I don't want to grow up. I
mean, I want to grow up so I can leave home and get a
job and make some money and get a record player and get
married, but I want my body to stop doing what it's doing.
What kind of dog was it?

Donny   I don't like it down here.

Joanne   Look at the yellow cabs. People pulling up.
Going into those warehouses. People climbing into those
trucks.

Donny   It's like my dream.

The cart tips over. **Bert***'s head rolls out.* **Margie** *screams.*
Donny *puts it back in the bag.* **Joanne** *takes* **Margie***'s hands.*
She and **Donny** *put* **Margie***'s hands in the bag.*

Joanne   You're part of this forever and ever. You're part
of it.

Margie   I'm out taking a walk.

Donny   Here's money. Don't tell.

Joanne   Shut up, Donny.

Margie   Where'd you get that money?

Joanne   Don't give it to her.

Donny   She'll tell.

Joanne   She won't.

Margie I got to go home!

Joanne You are a part of this.

Margie I never saw nothing. My brain is dead. You hear me? I swear? My eyes are blind. I was never out. My ears don't hear. My brain is dead. I'm just out taking a walk. My brain don't register nothing. My eyes don't see. Forever. I'm never seeing nothing. Please. I'll see you. Later. School. I'll see you tomorrow. That's all.

Donny *and* **Joanne** *push the cart into the darkness. There is a splash. Darkness.* **Rosalie** *steps forward. The piano plays 'Hey, Stay a While', very bouncily, cheerily.* **Rosalie** *does the stripper's walk while talking to us in the audience.*

Rosalie So Betty returned to New York, called Raulito to make sure her job was still safe with Honeymoon Holidays and to make a wonderful joke about her southern adventure of the past few days and she smiled because she would make it sound funny like a wonderful guest on the Johnny Carson show. Some Cuban relative answered the phone and told her Raulito was dead, shot while trying to hold up the Chase Manhattan Bank. Betty laughed till she realized a truth was being told. She ran home and found police waiting there and when they told her Bert was dead, her son was dead, for a moment got Bert and Raulito mixed up in her head. They both couldn't be dead. She had this picture that her apartment had become a branch of Chase Manhattan and that's what Raulito was holding up. They took her down to the morgue and she asked why her son was on two tables. One large and one small. She identified his body. She identified his head. The room was identical to the one she had identified her sister in two years ago and somehow that comforted her, that she had been here before. She did not know, Betty, nor would she ever know that two drawers over from her son's was Raulito's body. Betty was taken into custody. Betty was questioned for a long time. Betty was released. Months went by. A summer. Joanne and Donny were very nice to her for a while but kids get new friends and kids forget and Betty hardly ever saw Bert's friends anymore. She draws a circle on a map and sees an island thirty miles off the coast of Massachusetts is the furthest she can get away from New York, from the mainland, with the sixty-odd dollars she has in her account. She gives up the apartment. She takes the bus to Massachusetts. She steps onto the ferry. She looks at the houses of great families on the shore. She talks with a man of quintuplets born many years ago. Talk of family and children. The sea is autumn calm. Seagulls fly above.

The music stops. The stage is filled with light. We are on the deck of the boat as at the beginning. **Holahan** *and* **Betty** *appear at the ship's railing.* **Rosalie** *goes into the black.*

Holahan   You recognized me?

Betty   Captain Marvin Holahan. Sixth Precinct Homicide.

Holahan (*pulls off his disguise*)   What did you write in that note?

Betty *throws sheets of small papers into the wind. They blow away. She pours bottles overboard.*

Betty   A confession. A full confession. I wrote down everything that happened. And it's all gone. There it goes. There's your case.

Holahan   I got bounced. From the force. About six days after our meeting. I took a lot out on you. I was on probation at the time of that interrogation. I had a lot of secret pressures on me. I thought if I nailed you, they'd overlook this minor nothing drug bribe extortion rap they pinned on me which if the truth be known everybody on the force is involved with in one way or another. But they were looking for a patsy. I loved the way you stood up to me. I wanted you to be the killer. If I stayed on the force I would've found your boy's killer.

Betty   No matter. I got on the bus this morning and I started writing on little pieces of paper everything I ever knew. Everything that ever happened to me. Sentences.

Places. People's names. Secrets. Things I wanted to be. I thought maybe out of all that I'd find the magic clue who killed my kid. I'd say I see.

Holahan I tried to do investigations on my own to find the killer for a present to you. But you can't investigate outside the force. You need that power. You need . . . that secret power the force offers.

Betty It bothered me at first not knowing who killed Bert. But then I thought of all the things we don't know. All the secrets in the world got put in a bottle and thrown in the sea and maybe someday I'll be walking along a beach and the bottle containing the message for me will wash up. If I don't know the answer, it's out there and one day maybe an incredible coincidence will occur and I'll know all I need to know. Or the murderer will come forward. Or I'll even forget once I had a secret. I'll remember I had a boy like I'll remember I once had a mother and once had a father and I'll try to keep piling the weight on to the present, so I'll stay alive and won't slide back. If I don't know, somebody knows. My life is a triumph of all the things I don't know. I don't have to know everything. I read Agatha Christies and throw them away when the detective says 'And the murderer is . . .' The mystery's always greater than the solution. I was terrified to have a kid. I said before I got pregnant, I'll have a kid and the eyes will end up on one side of the face and all the fingers on one hand and all the toes on one foot and both ears on one side of the head. And Bert was born and he was perfect. And this is the only thing I know. There's got to be some order in there. I'm moving to this new place and it has big houses with classical columns and maybe I'll find a job in one of them in a house owned by an old man who has an art collection and I'll read up on classical painters and maybe he'll ask me to marry him or maybe I'll kill him and get him to sign the collection over to me or maybe I'll love him and marry him. Or maybe I'll discover a secret inside me that will make the whole world better. I'm not discounting nothing.

Maybe I'll be transplanted into somebody great who knows the secret, my secret, or maybe I'll never know and a tornado or a water spout will whisk me up and I'll turn into rain and end up in that sea.

Holahan   All I know is I know more about you than anyone I know. All those months doing dossiers on you. All disconnected. All disjointed. Still I know more about you. We both have to begin again. Maybe together? I could reveal myself to you slowly. That was not me who interrogated you. That was my job talking. That was unseen pressures talking to you. That was saving my skin talking to you. I feel for you. All what you've been through. I feel for you. I read stories people falling in love who threw acid in each other's faces and they get out of prison and they still love each other. I read stories people try to kill each other and end up loving each other. Give me a chance? I got severance pay? I got enough to get us through a winter?

Betty *looks at him. She turns.* **Rosalie** *appears at left. The piano plays 'Voices of Eagles'.*

Rosalie   Last scene. In which Betty remembers the conversation she and I had so many years ago, the intensity of it burned into the Good Humor man's head. Betty has tried to remember since that day what Rosalie, what I had told her. She remembers. She and I sat on a summer afternoon on the green porch steps. Our mother over there. Our father over there. We pulled our skirts over our legs.

Betty *and* **Rosalie** *sit side by side as young girls.*

Rosalie   Stop shaking. Don't let them see. (*To their parents.*) It's nothing, Dad.

Betty   It's like my stomach's going to come up all the time.

Rosalie   You're all right.

Betty   How am I going to get through my life?

Rosalie   Would you let me explain? Our spirits – it's so simple – float around in space and it all makes sense when you realize the planet Earth has these fishing hooks on it. What we call gravity is fishing hooks and all the nice things in the world are baited on those hooks and our spirits, floating up there all loose and aimless, spy those baited hooks and we bite. And we are reeled down onto this planet and we spend the rest of our stay on this planet trying to free our mouths of that hook, fighting, fighting.

Betty   But what do you do?

Rosalie   You travel alone because other people are only there to remind you how much that hook hurts that we all bit down on. Wait for that one day we can bite free and get back out there in space where we belong, sail back over water, over skies, into space, the hook finally out of our mouths and we wander back out there in space spawning to other planets never to return hurrah to earth and we'll look back and can't even see these lives here anymore. Only the taste of blood to remind us we ever existed. The earth is small. We're gone. We're dead. We're safe.

Betty   But Momma says –

Rosalie   Oh, Momma says. Momma says. When are you gonna think for yourself?

Betty   How do you . . . How can I think for myself?

Rosalie *has no answer. Bells ring.*

Betty   Vanilla? You want vanilla? We hear you, Durwood!

Rosalie *runs off.* **Betty** *looks at* **Holahan**. *A long pause. She moves towards him.*

Curtain.

> The greatest poverty is not to live
> In a physical world, to feel that one's desire
> Is too difficult to tell from despair.
>
> Wallace Stevens, *Esthétique du Mal*

Bosoms and Neglect

For Adele

Bosoms and Neglect was first presented by Bernard Gersten and John Wulp in association with Marc Howard, at the Goodman Theater, Chicago, on 1 March 1979 and subsequently at the Longacre Theater, New York, on 3 May 1979. It was directed by Mel Shapiro with the following cast:

Henny	Kate Reid
Scooper	Paul Rudd
Deirdre	Marian Mercer

Scenery by John Wulp
Costumes by Willa Kim
Lighting by Jennifer Tipton

In a production of *Bosoms and Neglect*, directed by Larry Arrick, with a cast including Richard Kavanaugh, April Shawhan and Anne Meara as Henny, presented at the Perry Street Theater through the auspices of the New York Theater Workshop, 26 March–20 April 1986, a number of additional lines and scenes were written into the play.

In December 1998, the Signature Theater, New York, presented this play in a production directed by Nicholas Martin, with David Aaron Baker, Katie Finneran and Mary Louise Wilson as Henny. I again made more changes. The text reproduced here incorporates all those changes.

Bosoms and Neglect was first produced in the UK by Theatro Technis, London, on 7 February 1992, with Eve Pearce, Campbell Graham and Deborah Weston, directed by Daniel Banks.

Prologue   Henny's apartment
Act One   Deirdre's apartment
Act Two   Henny's hospital room

Act One

Darkness. Two pools of light. In one, **Scooper**, *forty, fit, trim, is in agony curled on a couch in a fetal position.* **Deirdre**, *thirties, beautiful, intense, in another pool of light, sits at a distance.*

Deirdre Try.

Scooper No . . .

Deirdre Try. Tell me. You're in a safe place.

Scooper I . . . found a doctor who'd make house calls.

Deirdre's *light fades. In the darkness* **Henny** *raucously sings an old song like 'When the Red Red Robin Comes Bob Bob Bobbin' Along'. We are in* **Scooper**'s *story. He stands in a shaft of light, carrying a small jar.*

Scooper (*calls brightly*) I found a doctor who'll make house calls. Talk about *Mission Impossible.* I'm sorry I'm late. He'll be here in about fifteen minutes.

Henny (*in dark*) Oh God. Oh God. Oh God.

Henny *comes into his light, her fingers in her ears, still singing. She is old. She is blind. Her spirit is strong.*

Henny I don't have to go.

Scooper This house-call doctor wants you to fill up a jar so he can take it to the lab. I have to bring it up to the pharmacy on Eighty-Second Street. Can you fill this up?

Henny I don't have to go.

Scooper *Now* you don't have to go.

Deirdre Cystitis?

Scooper (*to* **Henny**) Cystitis?

Henny I don't have any cystitis.

Scooper Don't go screaming and crying and shaking so

hard. He can't get a look at you if you're screaming and crying and shaking so hard. I told him it burns when you pee. I told him it's probably cystitis. Don't close your ears and hum.

Henny   My bladder fell out.

Scooper   This magic doctor says 'What does this mean, her bladder fell out.' I said 'That's what she says, her bladder fell out.'

Henny   My bladder fell out.

Scooper (*to* **Deirdre**)   It burnt when she peed.

Henny   It burns when I pee.

Scooper (*hands her the bottle*)   He has a Spanish accent so when he comes don't go running out because he's a foreigner. He's a real Latin Lover type is what he sounds like. Take the bottle! And don't go falling in love with him when you hear his Latin accent.

Henny (*feeling the bottle*)   You'd have to be a contortionist in a circus to fit on this. What's wrong with you?

Scooper   What's wrong with *me* who finds a doctor who makes house calls? You got a juice bottle?

Henny   My bladder fell out. I can feel it. Give me your hand. Touch it. Oh God. You can feel it.

Scooper   I'm not the doctor. Don't go using me as the doctor. I'm not going to touch you there. (*To* **Deirdre**.) I went out of the room.

Scooper *goes into dark.*

Henny   This doctor's going to lock me up when he sees me. When he sees this bladder.

Scooper   The doctor's not the enemy.

Henny   How do you know? You never saw him before. He's going to run out of here screaming when he sees me.

Scooper (*comes back into the light, holding a quart-sized juice* *jar*) Doctors don't run out on patients. Crazy patients do the running out so the doctors can't treat them, fix them. Fill this jar.

Henny It's . . . it's not just my bladder.

Scooper (*something catches his eye*) Why does an eighty-three-year-old woman have a giant box of Super Kotex? You're not having reverse change of life? Medical marvels. What is this Kotex doing here?

Henny I thought it would go away.

Scooper What would go away?

Henny I prayed to Saint Jude and said Saint Jude Patron Saint of Lost Causes, Patron Saint of the Impossible, Patron Saint of the Damned, take this away from me.

Scooper Take what away from you?

Henny It bleeds and bleeds and I put Kotex over it and stand in front of the window all night in the dark looking up waving a statue of Saint Jude over it so it'll dry by the morning. But it never dries. It never stops bleeding. I sent out for more Kotex. It never stops bleeding. You're hurting my arm!

Scooper What never stops bleeding?

Henny I never would've told you about this other incident, except my insides are falling out and I can't pee and I told you and I could cut my tongue out because it don't hurt that much when I pee. I could live with it. It's not so bad.

Scooper This other incident?

Henny It doesn't hurt. If I could see, I could see it was nothing. But I can't see so I make it up in my mind that it's more than it is, you see.

Scooper Where is this incident?

Henny It's not hide-and-seek, for Christ's sake. I haven't got it hidden in the back of the stove. It's here. It's me. The incident is me.

Scooper   How long?

Henny   Not long.

Scooper   Deal straight. How long?

Henny   It started in a way I could notice the day you and Valerie and Ted came out here.

Scooper   That was two years ago.

Henny   It started that day.

Scooper   What started that day?

Henny   The skin broke that day.

Scooper   Skin where?

Henny   It's not important.

Scooper   What skin broke?

Henny   I can deal with this. My Kotex and Saint Jude and I are very happy. I don't have to pee. If I can just work it so I don't have to pee, I'm all right.

Scooper (*to* **Deirdre**)   The doorbell rang. (*To* **Henny**.)   He's here. The doctor is here.

Henny   Send him away.

Scooper   We'll hold you down and strip you and find this incident.

Henny   It feels better. Go away.

Scooper   What skin broke?

Henny (*impatiently*)   Oh God. Here. (*She opens her blouse. He steps back.*) It doesn't look so bad. Does it? Real false alarm. Girl who cried wolf. One day something will be wrong with me and you won't bother to help me because I dragged you out here once before for a little nothing. You're too young to have problems. I don't want to burden you with my problems. You want to send out to that new Italian deli for shrimp salad? They use real shrimp. None of those little plastic pinkies. I buy it to last two days and it's gone before I'm even ready for dinner.

Scooper Oh dear God. Oh Christ. Jesus H fucking Christ.

Henny There is no reason for such language. Saint Jude does not like it. Want me to go to the door and tell the doctor to go away? False alarm time? I'll give him five dollars. See my system? The five-dollar bills have one safety pin in them. The tens I have the girl put two safety pins in. The ones are on their own. (*The door chime sounds.*) Tell him April Fool. Say Saint Jude helped a supposed lost cause make a miraculous recovery.

Scooper Doctor, you'd better get in here.

Henny No!

Henny *goes into darkness. Light comes up on:*

Deirdre*'s apartment in the East Sixties. Lots of books. A sofa. Light streams in. A section of the room is used as an office, with Jiffy mailing envelopes, wrapping paper, twine, a stamp machine, and a scale.*

Deirdre *holds a drink and leans forward listening to* **Scooper**. *He sits on the couch. A packed suitcase is by the door. It is* **Scooper***'s.*

Scooper Imagine a peach that had an enormous bite taken out of it.

Deirdre Oh Christ.

Scooper I'm not finished. Then. Then.

Deirdre Calm.

Scooper Was left in the back of a disconnected refrigerator for the winter months and you come back in the spring and open the ice-box door and find the peach rotted where the bite was taken out. This poison gauze.

This penicillin rot-mold. You could put your fist into the hole in her breast. The cancer was that deep.

Deirdre　Wait.

Scooper　She stood there, her blouse off. It's not so bad, she keeps saying. It is not so bad.

Deirdre　It's impossible. What you're describing.

Scooper　I saw it.

Deirdre　Cancer works slowly.

Scooper　I am telling you – I can't believe you are not believing me. I pour this out and your response is . . .

Deirdre　I'm not saying you're hallucinating. I'm saying cancer works inside, silently. Not like some horror show in a Drive-In.

Scooper　She had so neglected herself that the disease was sick of not being noticed. The disease finally burst through her skin. The ulceration was like this screaming flesh, this breast – screaming how loud do you have to go to get noticed?

Deirdre　Oh Christ.

Scooper　The good part about being that old the metabolism moves so slowly that the cancer takes just that much longer.

Deirdre　And she had no medical aid?

Scooper　Sure. For two years, she's been laying Kotex over the wound, waving this tan plastic statue of Saint Jude, Patron of Lost Causes, over this small, expanding cavity in her chest, standing all night in the dark privacy of her open window so the midnight air would dry it out.

Deirdre　You never noticed?

Scooper　I never saw her.

Deirdre　In two years?

Scooper   She only likes talking on the phone. I can't see her. She can't see me. Gives her equal footing.

Deirdre   But her bladder –

Scooper   It was her uterus.

Deirdre   Oh dear God.

Scooper   It fell out.

Deirdre   Oh no.

Scooper   Eighty-three-year-old muscles give out.

Deirdre   But still –

Scooper   The doctor who made the house call said this woman is finished. This woman will not make it through the day. 'It's not so bad. Girl who cried wolf. False alarm.' I paid off the doctor. Got Doctor James on the phone. Got her up to Columbia-Presbyterian.

Deirdre   The best.

Scooper   Doctor James waiting right there. He had a bed waiting, the best surgeon all lined up to see her.

Deirdre   That was yesterday?

Scooper   That was yesterday.

Deirdre   And today she's on the table?

Scooper   Right now.

Deirdre   It makes *me* feel so well taken care of, like a great fringe benefit, if anything happened to me.

Scooper   Thanks to Doctor James.

Deirdre   A toast to you.

Scooper   To me?

Deirdre   To him.

She pours wine. White, chilled. Cool. They toast.

Scooper   After two years of lying and hiding.

Deirdre   You?

Scooper   Her. (*They sip.*)

Deirdre   Poor tragic lady. Outliving her friends. Standing all night at a window. Not trusting any human being enough to reach out.

Scooper   Don't forget the statue she's waving over her breast. Significant detail. Saint Jude. Patron of Lost Causes.

Deirdre   I suddenly have this image of being blind. Oh God. Never to be able to browse. I could never learn braille. The skin on my fingers might be too tough to let the words come through.

Scooper   She elected to go blind.

Deirdre   You don't cast votes to be blind.

Scooper   Twenty years ago she did. She marched right up to the polling booth with her glaucoma and cataracts. Her hysteria rendered her untreatable. She looked at my father and me with these eyes turning to milk, the sight curdling out of them. 'You're lying to me, it's something worse. Tell me the truth. No, don't tell me the truth. Lie to me.' She begged us to lie to her. We said we *were* telling the truth. She said that's the biggest lie. And she invented some exotic disease for herself. And she proceeded to go bonkers and embark on a series of suicide attempts as if the *Guinness Book of Records* suddenly had an opening.

Deirdre   And she's still nuts?

Scooper   As soon as she went blind, her mind snapped back like the price of gold. She was still alive. Nothing worse had gone wrong with her. She believed the disaster. She was only blind. That she could live with. You become saner much quicker than you go mad. So we had ten years of suicide attempts. And now the last ten she's been feeling her way around like a lost company of *The Miracle Worker*.

Deirdre   Your father?

Scooper   He stroked out along the way. One day he just

shortcircuited while she was eating a light bulb . . . or a knife. Stop looking at me that way.

Deirdre   Do you find it so difficult taking care of another human being?

Scooper   She did it herself.

Deirdre   I see why you go to Doctor James.

Scooper   Sight is a collaborative act, requiring subject and object working together in trust and tranquillity. You have to tell the doctor what you're seeing and if you're screaming and have flames shooting out of your ears – (*He downs his drink. He looks around at all her books.*) Are you in publishing?

Deirdre   I buy and sell. From estates. First editions.

Scooper   You could have two lions in front of your door.

Deirdre   How old is she?

Scooper   Eighty-three.

Deirdre   Then why don't you let her die?

Scooper   Because I don't want that solution of self-destruction in me. She is not allowed to take that *out*. Hysteria is not an *out*. Fantasy and panic are not *outs*. I don't want the solution of suicide in my genes. I want courage in my genes. I want strength in my genes. I want seeing problems *through* in my genes. That old lady is going to stay alive and die of old age and plain old-fashioned wearing out. She is not going to be killed by an overactivity of the most valuable thing we have, our imagination. Look, you've got your own problems.

Deirdre   No! No! Really! I'm an ear. I love to be an ear.

Scooper   Still. He died right here? (*He touches her hand.*) It must have been a shock.

Deirdre   The air conditioner was off. I thought I'd suffocate and I couldn't open any windows, all sealed shut to keep the air conditioning *in*, and I turned on the lights and they flickered and went out and my Walkman said it was three a.m. and a hundred degrees. I had this flashlight and picked up anything to read, just for the reading, just till it got light ... *Tess of the D'Urbervilles.*

Scooper   Thomas Hardy!

Deirdre   And Raymond leaps up. His paws cover the text. I say 'Down, Raymond!' And Raymond gasped with the lack of air and falls over. Right here. Tongue hanging out. I didn't know what to do. Please let it be light! Finally it got to be time and I put on this dress and ran out.

Scooper   And you come back and he's gone?

Deirdre   Wait. The air conditioner's on.

Scooper   Who'd break in and kidnap a dead dog?

Deirdre   I see! My husband! Of course.

Scooper   Your husband?

Deirdre   Came back. Saw what happened. Took Raymond up to the animal hospital for disposal. Or the ASPCA. I'm glad that's solved. And the air conditioner turned on. Oh dear, the idea of a thief who breaks in and takes only dead pets. That's even too strange for a city of strange tales. Raymond will be back soon and all questions will be solved.

Scooper   Raymond? Will be back?

Deirdre   My husband. (*She resumes packing books in boxes.*) I really have to get back to work. Charles Dickens off to Honolulu. (*She packs books busily.*)

Scooper   Your husband and your dog have the same name?

Deirdre   That should tell you all you need to know about my marriage.

Scooper   I'm sorry.

Deirdre   It's all over. Nothing. Really. Hand me John Updike.

Scooper (*bringing her the book*)   He must be a great help.

Deirdre   John Updike?

Scooper   Doctor James.

Deirdre   I read somewhere once the reason people have to go to doctors is the impossibility of the human being to say goodbye.

Scooper (*picks up some books*)   Beautiful bindings. Uncut.

Deirdre   I specialize in uncut.

Scooper   The weight. The smell. The feel. (*She takes the books away from him.*)

Deirdre   I was touched when you introduced yourself.

Scooper   You didn't say 'Who is this asshole coming up to me in a Fifth Avenue bookstore?'

Deirdre   You're hardly a stranger.

Scooper   I stumbled out in the street this morning. Have a wonderful vacation, Doctor James. Don't dare ask him where he's going. Ooops, didn't mean to ask. Should I kiss him? Filial peck on the cheek? Yearly affection. Will he think it's a pass? Decide against. Out in the street. Jesus. Only Nine Fucking Forty Fucking Five a.m. How am I going to get through this day?

Deirdre   Already eighty-eight degrees.

Scooper   I run to a bookstore.

Deirdre   Not one of the big chains?

Scooper   No! Rizzoli's. Fifty-Seventh off Fifth. Wait for it to open. Cool. See what new books have come in since yesterday.

Deirdre   But it was like two degrees Celsius.

Scooper   Spy. Sex. Show Biz. Something to turn the page.

Deirdre   I cannot figure out Celsius.

Scooper   And what do I see when I get to the corner? You. Looking in the bookstore window. Waiting for it to open. Your dress swaying slightly. How did your legs find the only breeze?

Deirdre   I mean, who *is* Celsius?

Scooper   You looked so healthy.

Deirdre   I *am* healthy.

Scooper   I didn't think you'd.

Deirdre   Of course I.

Scooper   But you moved away.

Deirdre   I didn't think you'd. After months of silence.

Scooper   I'd never seen you move. Only sit. The waiting room. Turning pages. Reading copies of *Vogue*.

Deirdre   Long gone out of vogue.

Scooper   I looked at you staring in the bookshop window and I said this woman and I share the deepest experience of a lifetime and we have never spoken a word. I have even come from a couch that was still warm from you.

Deirdre   You followed me.

Scooper   Into Rizzoli's.

Deirdre   The foreign bookstore.

Scooper   Is that woman as paralyzed as I am about Doctor James going away for a month?

Deirdre   Thumbing through glossy foreign magazines, looking around to see if you were following me. I pick up *Oggi, Paris Match, L'Express*.

Scooper   I thought you'd be glad to hear an American voice.

Deirdre   Just because someone speaks the same language

doesn't mean you can trust them.

Scooper   You recognized me.

Deirdre   I recognized you.

Scooper   'Would you like to have a drink?'

Deirdre   'My dog's died and it's eighty-eight degrees and it's just ten a.m. and I don't know what to do.'

Scooper   'I could help you.'

Deirdre   'I live around the corner.'

Scooper   'Around the corner.' My God, across the street from Doctor James. I didn't think real people lived on this street. All the Mercedes lined up to haul our pains away. I thought you had to be a shrink to live here.

Deirdre   A friend of mine calls this street the Mental Block.

Scooper   A close friend?

Deirdre (*avoiding the question*)   Actually I read it.

Scooper   Who's with him now?

Deirdre   The mother who drinks.

Scooper   Oh Jesus. She once came out of the office and asked me for drink money right in the waiting room.

Deirdre   She did the same to me!

Scooper   I felt so guilty refusing her.

Deirdre   I had to have my session switched.

Scooper   Look! There she is!

Deirdre   Get down!

Deirdre *reaches for a pair of binoculars she keeps by the window. She looks through them.*

Scooper   She's walking so straight.

Deirdre (*watching her go*)   Sober.

Scooper   Healed.

Deirdre   A cab pulls up. Out gets the pianist. He runs in, late for his appointment.

Scooper   He didn't play for years. That poor genius. Too crazy to play.

Deirdre   I have his new CD!

Scooper   I went to his concert.

Deirdre   I was there!

Deirdre *puts on a CD of the first movement of the Scriabin Piano Sonata No. 3 in F♯ Minor.* **Scooper** *starts to speak.* **Deirdre** *shushes him.* **Scooper** *and* **Deirdre** *listen intently.*

Scooper   I thought: Doctor James healed this man so he can play again.

Deirdre   I felt the same thing.

Scooper   It's like we're all related.

Deirdre   Brothers and sisters sent in for a private loving audience with our father.

Scooper (*calling*)   We love you, Doctor James!!!!

Deirdre   This is no spy turret!

She turns off the music abruptly. **Scooper** *comes away from the window and pours another drink.*

Scooper   You must know so much about him.

Deirdre   I know he's got a wife.

Scooper   Oh, I knew that.

Deirdre   Poor Doctor James.

Scooper   Poor?

Deirdre   That tragic marriage.

Scooper   Did he tell you he had a tragic marriage?

Deirdre   How could he understand my pain if he didn't

have his own? I hear it. There in his voice. That
tormented way his fingers rub that birthmark on his hand.
Talk about Rorschach tests. I never thought I had any
imagination at all until I saw Doctor James's wine-colored
birthmark ... like a magic token transforming me into
whatever I want to be. Clouds. Scudding by in the
birthmark.

Scooper   What birthmark?

Deirdre   On his hand.

Scooper   Which hand?

Deirdre   I lie like this. Look over like this. Yes, the left
hand.

Scooper   I never noticed any birthmark.

Deirdre   Did you notice FDR was in a wheelchair?

Scooper   Are you calling Doctor James a cripple?

Deirdre   It's the most obvious thing about him.

Scooper   You see a spot from luncheon. And you
romanticize the coagulation into a birthmark.

Deirdre   I have seen that birthmark every day for the
past – *number* of years and it is impossible to spill that
much gravy in the selfsame spot for the past – *number* of
years. Let's not make this one of those events like the song
in *Gigi* – 'I Remember It Well' – based on Colette, where
we talk about the same thing and have completely different
perceptions of it. You have your Doctor James.

Scooper   I have *my* Doctor James.

Deirdre   I have my birthmarks. You keep of him
whatever you want.

Scooper   All I ever see of Doctor James are his wing-tip
shoes. I love the guy, but I hate his wing-tip shoes. They're
like shoes that belong to some CIA agent.

Deirdre   How can you see his wing-tips?

Scooper   He crosses his legs. I quick turn up off the couch and look down and see the tips of his shoes.

Deirdre   Hating the wings at the tips of his shoes. So fascinating. Hating the fact that Doctor James can fly.

Scooper   Do you hear us romanticizing our doctor? We will have to tell him next September. He will laugh.

Deirdre   You think?

Scooper   You have to take risks.

Deirdre   I can never forgive them for taking the month of August off.

Scooper   They only do it so we won't run off to other doctors while they're away.

Deirdre   As if we'd go to anyone else.

Scooper   Sometimes I'll look at a friend in trouble and say Boy, if I trusted you more. Boy, do I have a doctor for you. Boy, could he tie those loose ends up in a minute.

Deirdre   But you don't.

Scooper   He's my secret weapon.

Deirdre   That's not being selfish.

Scooper   That's being protective.

Deirdre   I think you'd better go.

Scooper   Have I said –

Deirdre   I don't think it's healthy talking about our doctor this way.

Scooper   I think he'd be thrilled. I can't wait to tell him.

Deirdre   You wouldn't dare tell him!

Scooper   To bring Doctor James a new character in my life that he knows so well? You have to tell him about me. You'll bring him me. I'll bring him you. To play his version of you against my version of you. To play your me against his me. It'll be like *The Alexandria Quartet*. The air carbonated with all these realities and people! Poor Lawrence Durrell. He's become so neglected.

Deirdre   Am I a major character or a minor character?

Scooper   Friends are always major characters.

Deirdre   Friendships are major responsibilities.

Scooper   I'm a wonderful friend.

Deirdre   Are you a five a.m. friend?

Scooper   A five a.m. friend?

Deirdre   A friend you can call and say stay on the phone till it gets light.

Scooper   I read a book.

Deirdre   Sometimes a book doesn't help.

Scooper   You need a voice. I am a five a.m. friend.

They look at each other.

Deirdre   Thank you for telling me about your mother, your father.

Scooper   *Life with Father*. Clarence Day.

Deirdre   I have that. I love books about families. They read to me like science fiction.

Scooper   You don't have any family?

Deirdre   They were killed when I was very young.

Scooper   Oh dear.

Deirdre   Car crash home from skiing.

Scooper   Stowe?

Deirdre   Lake Placid.

Scooper   Never been to Lake Placid.

Deirdre   I went there once.

Scooper   I go to Stowe.

Deirdre   I have this golden photo of my parents. (*She picks up a picture in a frame.*)You can see the wit in their eyes. I've learned more about life staring at this picture taken shortly before their deaths trying to riddle out their smiles. Trying to find some injunction in their wrinkled noses. At one point in my life the picture seemed spiritual. I was going to school at a convent. I became a nun for a while.

Scooper   You were a nun?

Deirdre   I mistook gratitude for a vocation.

Scooper   I can't imagine you as a nun.

Deirdre   Believe me.

Scooper   I'd love to see that picture.

Deirdre   I show it to no one. (*She puts it away in a drawer.*) Doctor James says I read so much to make up their voices reading to me. I hear what I imagine their voices to be telling me about their lives. I read only the finest works. Their voices are very golden in my ear.

Scooper   You must be some patient for Doctor James.

Deirdre   When you said you'd come from the couch warm with me, you were saying you're in analysis. You don't sit up. I mean, you're not in therapy.

Scooper   I'm in analysis.

Deirdre   I couldn't talk to you if you were just in therapy.

Scooper   You can talk to me.

Deirdre   It's so snobbish but I wouldn't have respect for you if you were in therapy – I wish you'd get away from the window. I don't want him looking up and –

Scooper   Remember that fat girl – did you ever get a look at her? She must've weighed in at a good four hundred pounds. I used to follow her at one time and I thought the couch would cave in –

Deirdre *Ivanhoe* is an amazing book. It speaks with such an urgent clarity to today. Who'd think Sir Walter Scott would achieve –

Scooper Oh my God, that wasn't you . . . was it?

Deirdre Good God, I don't even know who you're talking about. Is that your idea of why people go to Doctor James? He's hardly a fat farm.

Scooper It's just this girl –

Deirdre Why did you go to Doctor James? Weight?

Scooper One little problem that needed tying up.

Deirdre One little problem? No such animal.

Scooper I don't want to tell you anything that'll change your impression of me –

Deirdre Luckily I have no impression of you at all. (*She uncorks a wine bottle.*)

Scooper I think you're right. (*He starts to go.*)

Deirdre You were saying why you went –

Scooper He might be angry if he knew we were –

Deirdre Try lying down on the couch –

Scooper I don't want to tell you –

Deirdre It might make it easier.

Scooper He's not lucky enough to get orphans and nuns and husbands and dogs with the same name from me.

Deirdre You're afraid you're not complicated enough? How silly! It's not a competition. How often do we get to share this magic part of our lives?

Scooper It is almost religious with him.

Deirdre Pater Noster. You and I. Brothers. Sisters.

Scooper   I'm an only child.

Deirdre   Family. That's what we are. We share family secrets.

Scooper   I started going to Doctor James because – ahhh. Sherlock Holmes. Beautiful edition . . . (*She takes the book from him.*) I started going to him because I was so happy.

Deirdre   So happy?

Scooper   I could live with my mother's suicide attempts and my father's strokes. That was like wartime. That was easy. But for one period I stumbled inadvertently into some kind of happiness. Everything was strangely productive and rewarding and simple. I beamed out in this seraphic five a.m. joy why is everything so wonderful? And the Lispenards – *my* five a.m. friends – got me Doctor James's number to find out in a few quick sessions how this wanderer had stumbled into Shangri-La and how he could stay there.

Deirdre   And that was –

Scooper   Six years ago.

Deirdre   Are you still happy?

Scooper   Well, one thing led to another. And also Val.

Deirdre   Valium?

Scooper   Valerie.

Deirdre   Valerie?

Scooper   My old lady.

Deirdre   You don't mean your mother.

Scooper   My lady. My girl. My mistress. My blood. My brain. My heart. My wonder.

Deirdre   How nice of her to stand by you today.

Scooper   No, she's up in New Hampshire putting her

kids in camp. Three of them. God, I'll be a father.

Deirdre   They're not by you.

Scooper   That's a whole other saga. She had Bradley and Kim and Sophie by Caesarean so she is still tight like a young girl and you come into her so firm and then suddenly it's like coming into St Peter's in Rome, the way you round a small corner and the entire Basilica is wide open in front of you. We have a good time in bed. She'll moan. I'll say 'Darling, is that passion?' She says 'No, for Christ's sake, I got this Joseph Conrad stuck in my ribs.' We both have to have books in our pockets at all times. In our beds. On our walls. (*He takes a paperback from his right jacket pocket.*) Right now I'm traveling with Rilke. *Duino Elegies.* 'All this was a trust and I was not up to it.' Best poems written this century. (*He takes a paperback from the left jacket pocket.*) P. G. Wodehouse. *Luck of the Bodkins.*

Deirdre   Hardly neglected.

Scooper   All the time I have to have a book. Words on the eyeball ... it must create an erotic pressure. The physical rubbing of the words against the eyeball, kneading, prodding, massaging, grazing like this sensuous cow on the green pastures of your eye. And the thought, the illumination, the comprehension! Yes, that's the orgasm. You'd love her.

Deirdre   I must meet her.

Scooper   I even think of Doctor James as a literary experience. Before Doctor James, my life was pages spilled all over the floor. Grim. Violent. Aimless. He's edited my life into a novel I am so proud to be a part of. Jane Austen. That kind of clarity and effervescence. And intelligence.

Deirdre   Nothing's worth it if it's not a great artistic event.

Scooper   She wouldn't continue with me unless I kept up the therapy. I started doing the therapy as a bouquet for her. Then the therapy turned into analysis and here we are.

Deirdre   She sounds very positive.

Scooper   She is so healthy. She's been going to the shrink since she was about two. She has grown up on the couch. Then our affair sent her back into therapy.

Deirdre   Not Doctor James.

Scooper   No! She goes to group.

Deirdre   Group. Eccch.

Scooper   And her husband is in another.

Deirdre   She's married.

Scooper   The Loch Ness Monster lives.

Deirdre   Oh dear. Of course. The three children. St Peter's Basilica.

Scooper   She was so unhappy over our affair and guilty that her husband began to feel guilty because he didn't know about our affair and started blaming himself for her grief, so he went into therapy and he was in one group and asked her to join him in his group but she was already in another group and she wanted me to join the group her husband was in and then she'd join too, and I said I did not think that was a good idea.

Deirdre   I'm with you all the way there.

Scooper   I said I'll go to Doctor James for you, but no group analysis.

Deirdre   Only teaches you another kind of social chitchat.

Scooper   Unless it helps.

Deirdre   Of course. And what do your five a.m. friends say to all this?

Scooper   The Lispenards? It *is* the Lispenards. Valerie is one half of the Lispenards.

Deirdre   And the other half is –

Scooper   Ted. My college friend. My business partner. I suddenly see something so clearly. I get in a panic and I can't think straight. You have cleared my head. My God. I see. That vicious rotten human being. Literally rotten.

Deirdre   Valerie?

Cacophonous music. Red and purple lights. **Henny** *appears clutching a statue of St Jude. She walks blindly through the room.* **Scooper** *follows her.*

Scooper   My mother. She did it on purpose. She knew I was leaving. That's why she waited till yesterday. This operation. This cancer caper. All designed to keep me from going. I don't know how she knew but she knew. Mystic connection.

Henny *is gone. Lights to normal.*

Deirdre   Don't assign her magic powers.

Scooper   You don't think she died.

Deirdre   On the table?

Scooper   Eighty-three. Wouldn't be unheard of. Oh Christ.

Deirdre   Believe it or not, mastectomy is simple surgery.

Scooper *takes out a cellular phone and dials.*

Deirdre   The breast doesn't involve any major body function like breathing or digesting.

Scooper (*speaks into the phone*)   I'm trying to get information on the outcome of an operation? Could you connect me with – (*To* **Deirdre**.) They put me on hold.

Deirdre   She'll be all right.

Scooper   That breast nursed me. Fed me. My first connection. All the time I spend pursuing wombs, hidden

under infinities of skirts, entry to that warm darkness, and
to see what I'm searching for, hanging there. Light shining
on what no light should ever shine. This fucking old lady
thinks it's her bladder. If I'm conceived out of a bladder,
what does that make me? Get me off hold! Operator!
Operator! (*He snaps the wine glass in his hand.*) Godammit!!!

Deirdre *runs out of the room.*

Scooper   I want the recovery room! Okay. Back on hold.
If that's the way you want it.

Deirdre *returns with a basin of water and bandages. She takes his
bleeding hand and washes the cut.*

Deirdre   'All happy families are alike': I don't know
about you but I find Tolstoy very comforting.

Scooper   Are you a nurse?

Deirdre (*avoiding the question*)   I hope you're not a concert
pianist. Don't have to give a concert tonight.

Scooper   I'm an analyst.

Deirdre   But Doctor James –

Scooper   A computer analyst. Don't laugh.

Deirdre   I just had this mental image of all these angst-
ridden computers jumping up on your couch. Help me!
Help me!

Scooper   This customer calls me up, falling apart like the
Flight Deck at Bellevue and he tells me his secretary wiped
out a systems file and now his computer screen only
displays the Blue Screen of Death, rows of zeros and
ones, undecipherable hexadecimal code. 'Calm down,' I
say, 'we'll restore the system using the Emergency Repair
Disk. Do a hard reset, run the repair option, restore the
original system files, run the Scandisk Utility and the
operating system will come back up,' and that's how I
speak all day.

Deirdre   What does Hanna Arendt say? 'Without

passport and language we are nothing.'

Scooper   Well, exactly. I love the way the light streams in your apartment.

Deirdre   I said once before I died I'd finally live in a place filled with light.

Scooper   Heat banging its fists against the window trying to get in. (*Into the phone.*) Operator! I'm here! Don't go away! (*But she has.*) Should I dial again?

Deirdre   Hang on there.

Scooper   Okay. Oh God. (*He buries his face in his hands.*)

Pause.

Deirdre   You know who's tragically neglected? The Japanese. Kawabata.

Scooper   Is he the one with the private army who disemboweled himself?

Deirdre   That's Mishima.

Scooper   Is Kawabata the one who has the Japanese married couple traveling to all the puppet shows in Japan? A dying art to mirror a dying marriage?

Deirdre   No, that's Tanazaki.

Scooper   Is Kawabata the one who writes about the whorehouse where an old man rents drugged young girls and holds them in his arms all night, never fucking them. Just holding them.

Deirdre   That's Kawabata.

Scooper   So *that's* Kawabata. So neglected.

Deirdre   He won the Nobel Prize.

Scooper (*disdainful*)   Pearl Buck won the Nobel Prize. (*Impressed.*) Now Isaac Bashevis Singer!

Deirdre   I cut something out of an old *TV Guide.* 'Dick

Cavett Show. Dick's guest tonight will be the singer, Isaac Bashevis.'

Scooper   You have to show that to me.

Deirdre   I showed it to Saul Bellow and he was sending it out for Christmas cards.

Scooper   You know Saul Bellow?????

Deirdre   Well . . .

Scooper   You know someone who won the Nobel Prize?????

Deirdre   Oh, he's not my only Nobel Prize winner. I cradled Joseph Brodsky in my arms right over there. Derek Walcott passed out there. I have authors in and out of here.

Scooper (*into the phone*)   Yes? I'm calling to see if my mother has come down from surgery yet? I know you're busy but – her name is – has she even gone into surgery? I'm not trying to sell this info to the Chinese, believe me. You advise me not to stay at the hospital while the operation's on but then you won't – she's blind, she'll wake up and not know where – there was a brownout?

Deirdre   Happened here this morning. Lights just dim.

Scooper   Nobody's gone into surgery yet? When are they going into surgery? I have a plane to catch! (*He slams the phone down.*) She hasn't even gone in yet.

Deirdre   Leaving?

Scooper   Five o'clock.

Deirdre   Tonight?

Scooper   Haiti.

Deirdre   This time of year?

Scooper   She's trying to stop me.

Deirdre   The sidewalks are buckling and you're going to the jungle?

Scooper   It's so blindingly clear.

Deirdre   Don't people usually go to Haiti in the winter?

Cacophony. Colors. **Henny** *crosses the room blindly, waving her statue of St Jude.*

Scooper   She's been saving that breast to whip out just at an instant like this.

Deirdre   The heat in August. Frying pan. Fire.

Scooper   Hiding that whammy there in her bra.

Deirdre   But I suppose it's a different kind of heat.

Scooper   To stop me with guilt. Stop me with caring.

Deirdre   But people *always* say a different kind of heat.

Scooper   The caring is over.

Henny *is gone. Lights back to normal.*

Deirdre   Still hot is hot.

Scooper   My heart is sealed up.

Deirdre   On the other hand –

Scooper   I have to keep reminding myself she is a crazy old lady crippled by fear. Two years at a window waving plastic statues of fictional saints over a bleeding breast. God, Haiti. Tropic. Lush.

Deirdre   Isn't there a revolution in Haiti?

Scooper   Everything's in revolution. She's not stopping me. Olaffson's Hotel. Great white Victorian bric-a-brac gingerbread hotel there in the jungle. Victorian. Voodoo. Volcanoes.

Deirdre   If you need any Valium.

Scooper   I'll have Valerie.

Deirdre   You're taking Valerie?

Scooper   Our first trip together. Finally. The decision.

Deirdre   What does her husband say to all this?

Scooper   We haven't told him yet. We've left a letter for
him at his group tonight. We felt that was the kindest thing
to do. He goes right from work to group. He couldn't read
a letter like the one we've left him alone. He's so
dependent on his group. Poor weak . . . don't get me
started on Ted.

Deirdre   Should be an interesting session.

Scooper   In a way I'd like to be there. What was
Hemingway's phrase? Grace under pressure? I don't think
Ted Lispenard will personify grace under pressure.

Deirdre   And you'll be in Haiti.

Scooper   Four weeks.

Deirdre   The time Doctor James is away.

Scooper   Her sister will take the kids. When we get back
we'll start looking for a place in Maine. Get out of this
neurotic city. Find a beat-up ramshackle house by the sea.
Remodel it. Books. Music. Comfort. Valerie says she wants
a house like us. Simple on the outside. But inside. Inside!
We have this dream of buying up every book in Maine.

Deirdre   That shouldn't be hard.

Scooper   Open the world's greatest bookstore. Get out of
computers and machinery. Publish newsletters written by
people telling what books they love. A bookstore open
twenty-four hours a day. 800-numbers! Web-sites!

Deirdre   Like L. L. Bean.

Scooper   Yes! People will flock to us from all over the
world and we'll grow and grow until one day the entire
town is one bookstore.

Deirdre   The elephant graveyard.

Scooper   A Vatican of books. 'If we don't have it, they
didn't write it.'

Deirdre   You'll finish your treatment?

Scooper   Finishing my treatment is not the most important thing in the world. I'm almost finished with Doctor James anyway. Except for this one dream I have that even the great dream-decipherer himself can't figure out.

Deirdre   Please? I might be able to help –

Scooper   I am this little boy. All dressed up.

Deirdre   New clothes. Masquerade.

Scooper   A strange city.

Deirdre   Outsider. Go on.

Scooper   Facing a strange man.

Deirdre   And you're a small child. And it's not your father. Hmmm.

Scooper   And my mother who is all dolled up –

Deirdre   A new beginning?

Scooper   Picks me up and begins hitting this man with me.

Deirdre   Using you as a weapon?

Scooper   And she's screaming You neglected me! You neglected me!

Deirdre   And then you wake up?

Scooper   It's so alive in my mind.

Deirdre   I could figure that out.

Scooper   I really wish you wouldn't.

Deirdre   Strange city. Outsider. A dream of betrayal.

Scooper   I didn't say betrayal. I said neglect.

Deirdre   Neglect is always betrayal.

Scooper   Is that a quote?

Deirdre   That's a belief.

Scooper   If he can't figure it out – talk about Pride and Prejudice – I don't think you can. Stay out of it, okay?

Deirdre   I'll butt out of your head. Fine.

Scooper   But I know the key to everything is in that dream.

Deirdre   Oh, I see! If you solve the dream, you'll have to leave him.

Scooper   I want to leave him!

Deirdre   I didn't say you didn't.

Scooper   He's getting a postcard from me with a volcano on it and the message reads Doctor, see this volcano? This is me . . . Suppose she's dead. Suppose she died?
(*He picks up the phone and dials.*) Columbia-Presbyterian – is this? What number have I?

He puts the phone down in agony, then gets his face into a big smile. He lifts the phone again.

Ted. Hi! What are you doing home? No, my fingers were just dialing. And I dialed. Summer cold? Oh no. They're the worst. Go back to sleep. You shouldn't answer the phone if you're sick. Are you going to group tonight? No, you mustn't miss that. Take care. Oh. Valerie called? What time did she leave for New Hampshire? Great. Listen, thank you for the flowers. She was barely in the hospital when the flowers arrived. Really sweet. I don't know yet. But the best doctors. Could you do me a favor? Valerie wanted a report on how my mother is. I'm not at home. Could you tell her to call my cellular? Yes . . . Thank you. I'll tell her . . . Very sweet . . . Yes . . . Okay . . . Yes . . . Bye. Yes . . . Bye. (*He hangs up. He is furious.*) Asshole. You don't send flowers to a blind person. You treat her senses. You send candy. That's Ted in a nutshell. Oh, fuck. This atmosphere of lying. Every day for the past five years, living life with this Pavlovian smile trapped on my face. Inside I'm dying. A Madame Tussaud's perfect wax smile.

Deirdre *turns away from him. She looks back at him with disdain.*

Deirdre   Betraying your five a.m. friends.

Scooper   It didn't seem like betraying. The love sweetened everything.

Deirdre   You mean it poisoned everything. Like the silence of your mother's sickness.

Scooper (*reaching for a book*)   Joseph Conrad. *Chance*! This is one of the books stuck in Valerie's ribs.

Deirdre (*disillusioned*)   One of the great neglected masterpieces.

Scooper   I love this damned book.

Deirdre   So did I.

Scooper   'Life demands a man and a woman.' (*He searches through the book.*)

Deirdre   Page 432. 'Pairing off is the fate of mankind.'

Scooper (*reading*)   'If two beings thrown together, mutually attract . . . voluntarily stop short of the – the *embrace* –'

Deirdre (*quoting*)   'they are committing a sin against life. The call of which is simple.'

Both   'Perhaps sacred.'

A pause. They look at each other.

Scooper   It's taken Valerie and me five years to get to this day. I don't want to get mixed up with another married lady.

Deirdre   I'm not married.

Scooper   Raymond.

Deirdre   There is no Raymond. I only told you that – a girl has to be – a woman has to be – I call myself a woman when I'm working, but when I'm alone in this apartment, I'm a girl. A girl has to be careful. I don't know you. A patient. I don't know what you're seeing him for. You might be a psychopath. I wanted you to think someone was coming home.

Scooper   You wear a wedding ring.

Deirdre   A friend advised me to. It avoids hassles.

Scooper   A close friend?

Deirdre   What time is your plane?

Scooper   Five o'clock.

Deirdre   Busy day. Very active. Very healthy. Haiti. *Comedians.*

Scooper   I don't know who's playing down there.

Deirdre   Graham Greene. Novel. Haiti. In this pile.

Scooper   I've never read that.

Deirdre   I'd like to give it to you.

Scooper   Sign it?

Deirdre (*digging angrily in the stacks*)   Where the fuck is it? Here. In the Evelyn Waugh pile. That's neglected. When one author ends up in another author's pile.

Scooper   They're all English. Easy mistake.

Deirdre   Your hand is all right?

Scooper   All fine.

Deirdre (*writing in the book*)   'Be careful in the jungle.'

Scooper   You sound like my mother.

Deirdre   Why did you pick me up today?

Scooper   I told you. The breeze around your legs –

Deirdre   We shared the same waiting room for so many months in silence. I spend so many sessions asking Doctor James, Why isn't that man looking at me? I even got it into my head that Doctor James had hired you to drive me mad, to ignore me, to come for your session even before my session.

Scooper   I came to prepare. To calm myself. A quiet place to read.

Deirdre   You'd loom outside that door. I'd be inside on the couch. You'd be out there, doing God knows what. Listening at the door. Laughing at me.

Scooper   Never. I was reading.

Deirdre   I begged Doctor James to change appointments. Please! I don't want to be annihilated by that man.

Scooper   And he only said Why does the presence of that man annoy you?

Deirdre   You *were* listening.

Scooper   How could I hear with his air conditioner on?

Deirdre   You became my father. My lovers. My teachers. My uncles. My bosses. Every man who's ever gone out of his way to ignore me. I found myself dressing for you. Would he notice this? I'll show him. I would stand up naked in this window and wait for you to come out of your appointment. I'd do hypnotism things. Now he'll look up. Now he'll see me.

Scooper   I was deep in my own problems.

Deirdre   So you missed my breakdown.

Scooper   When was it?

Deirdre   Last October.

Scooper   Last October. That was a rough time for me last October.

Deirdre   I had one of the world's greatest uninstitutionalized breakdowns with weeping and moaning and Doctor James pulling magic tricks out of the air to keep me out of a hospital and you sit there turning the pages.

Scooper   I was reading Herman Melville. *Pierre*. His last novel. His most misunderstood –

Deirdre   You ignore me for eleven months and today you are suddenly obsessed with unculminated desire to pick me up.

Scooper   *Pierre* is Melville's only novel that takes place on land ... You're an attractive woman.

Deirdre   I have been for the last eleven months. It's still the same flesh.

Scooper   Edith Wharton says beauty is genius of the skin.

Deirdre   Did Doctor James say 'Take her? She's lonely. She's mad. She's out roaming the streets right now. My going-away present from doctor to patient. I can't mess around with her because of the Hippocratic Oath, but you give her a good boff for me.' Is that what the mind butcher said to you? Is that how you spend your sessions? Talking about me? How many other patients has old stud Doctor James fixed you up with? The mother who drinks? Is she another one of your old discards? You are wasting your one hundred and forty bucks an hour. The two of you. Two Freudian mind fuckers. He tells you all my secrets? The two of you having a bloody good laugh on my account? I thought you and I *shared* Doctor James. Brothers and sisters? Going in to visit our father? Brothers and sisters? Hah!

Scooper   A hundred and forty dollars an hour?

Deirdre   I suddenly understand incest.

Scooper   A hundred and forty dollars an hour?????

Deirdre   You have successfully ruined Doctor James for this analysand. I can never go back to him again.

Scooper   He charges me a hundred and fifty dollars an hour.

Deirdre   A hundred and fifty dollars an hour?

Scooper   He charges you a hundred and forty dollars an hour?

Deirdre   A hundred and forty.

Scooper   Why does he charge me a hundred and fifty?

Deirdre   He charges you a hundred and fifty?

Scooper   A hundred and fifty and a hundred and forty? It doesn't seem fair.

Deirdre   He charges me a hundred and forty because I am his favorite patient.

Scooper   Don't say that.

Deirdre   Sometimes he doesn't even charge me. Sometimes he says you are so interesting, I should be giving you money just for the privilege of listening to you pour out your heart.

Scooper   He doesn't say that.

Deirdre   No, he doesn't.

Scooper   But he does charge you a hundred and forty.

Deirdre   A hundred and forty.

Scooper   How many days a week?

Deirdre   Five.

Scooper   How many years?

Deirdre   Eight.

Scooper   You must be very sick.

Deirdre   How long for you?

Scooper   Six.

Deirdre   How many days a week?

Scooper   The three I see you.

Deirdre   Oh, therapy. You're only in therapy.

Scooper   I'm in analysis.

Deirdre   Three days a week? Gerber's Baby Food
analysis. On the other hand, we have me! Five days a
week! Depths of my psyche! Sonar waves into my soul!
Psychic barium cocktails.

Scooper   Wait. You go early in the morning.

Deirdre   Gallop straight from my dreams to the couch.

Scooper   Oh, I know what you're in.

Deirdre   Doctor can't wait to start off his day with a
high.

Scooper   You're in supportive analysis.

Deirdre   Deep classical.

Scooper   You're one of those sad neurotics who have to
go first thing in the morning just to get enough courage –

Deirdre (*holding her ears*)   What Beethoven is to the sonata,
I am to the couch!

Scooper   – just to get through the day.

Deirdre   I am *not* in supportive.

Scooper   You're one of those cripples who can only take
life in twenty-four-hour doses. Then off to Daddy.

Deirdre   I am very strong.

Scooper   When did he say you were strong?

Deirdre   You're the one who listens at the door. You tell
me.

Scooper   He hardly says anything ever to me.

Deirdre   To me he gives wonders.

Scooper   All I know is I possess enough strength to get
through a simple day.

Deirdre   To me he tells secrets of living.

Scooper   I only need him three days a week.

Deirdre He reads me from the Secret Freud Handbook.

Scooper I don't use him for a crutch.

Deirdre He wants me to be free.

Scooper I don't think Doctor James likes the kind of patient who uses him for a crutch.

Deirdre He says Deirdre, I learn from you!

Scooper He has you first just to get the worst out of the way.

Deirdre It boils down to this.

Scooper He's not helping you if he's charging you charity fees.

Deirdre I am in analysis. You are in therapy. You are going to him for one specific problem. Your girlfriend. Your mother. I am going to him for my whole life. All the fantasies I wasted on you. I had you trapped in this Dostoevskian turmoil. A fellow tormentee. Someone who is my match. Someone who understands. What do I get picked up by? Cuticle despair. Is that why the little baby's going to Doctor James? His little cuticle hurts?

Scooper You're being very hostile.

Deirdre You have discovered the mouth of the River Hostility. You are drowning in the Great Lakes of Hostility.

Scooper Don't say that.

Deirdre Oh, little baby can dish it out. But little baby can't take it. You want to know why I'm spending the best years of my life on Doctor James's couch? And it looks like my sunset years. You want to know the magic event that will clarify everything for you? Little magic key revelations? I hurt someone. Hurt them very badly.

Scooper You don't mean breaking hearts.

Deirdre We both share a relationship of a long nature with a married person.

Scooper   Of which sex.

Deirdre   A married person. This married person sat in a
hotel room and told me this person was going back to their
mate. Finally. Over. I had trouble hearing because the
ashtray on the table between us started talking to me. The
ashtray was empty because both of us had stopped
smoking. We had met at a Smokenders clinic and it made
us think we had a great deal in common and we had both
not smoked for a long time now and I felt proud of that.
But now words like Over and Returning became our
vocabularies' main themes and this ashtray says to me Just
because you don't smoke anymore doesn't mean you have
to neglect me. And the ashtray starts singing in this lovely
clear voice the old Jerome Kern standard 'Why Was I
Born?' And this person whose lungs I have helped clear
packs a suitcase and calls room service and orders a pack
of cigarettes. Camels. Lucky Strikes. Anything without a
filter. And I knew it was over. And we sat there a long
time. Room service brings the smokes. A pot of
decaffeinated coffee. And the ashtray suddenly stops singing
and says I'll tell you why you were born. To free yourself.
Do it. Use me! I picked up the ashtray and could see the
person all distorted in its glass base. I brought it down on
the side of this person's head.

Scooper   Did you kill this person?

Deirdre   The person turned to light the cigarette. The
match flew out of my friend's hand and landed on blue
pajamas which I thought were silk but were this incendiary
Orlon and the suitcase burst into flame and I threw the de-
caf coffee on the bed and put out the fire and called room
service to take care of this person with the gash on the
person's head and in a secret way found Doctor James and
have been going to him every day since that day.

Scooper   This person. Was it a man or a woman?

Deirdre   It was a man, goddamit. (*She picks up an ashtray.*)
A man! You're like every other man I ever met in my life.
You come on like this great oral aggressive, but at heart

you're this anal retentive . . .

Scooper I think . . . really wish you would put that down. I'm not like your friend. I stopped smoking and have not started up. Put it down. (*She puts the ashtray down quietly.*) I saw you in the waiting room. I couldn't look at you because of the desperation smeared all over your face. I said Is that what I look like?

Deirdre Then you must have felt some sympathy for me. If you saw my agony.

Scooper There's no sympathy in a doctor's waiting room. Only me next! Me next! I picked you up today because I was sad Doctor James was leaving, crazy because I am finally leaving with the woman I love after a trillion years of waiting. I'm losing a close friend, Ted, my old college roommate. And my mother's body bursts open and I'm furious at her for not trusting me enough to tell me two years ago and I see you, by the books, and I just wanted to connect to you.

Deirdre E. M. Forster says that. Connect. Only connect.

Scooper Fuck E. M. Forster. I just wanted to sit down and share.

Deirdre And what did you find out?

Scooper That I'm being overcharged.

Deirdre I'm sorry I said you were only in therapy.

Scooper It's the meanest thing anybody ever said to me.

Deirdre Well, if that's the meanest thing –

Scooper I'd better go. Up to the hospital. Find out what I can before I'm off. (*He picks up his suitcase and stands at the door.*) We'll meet again.

Deirdre You'll be all healthy, living with the world's most perfect woman. I don't think we'll meet.

Scooper Thank you for the Greene. (*He starts to go.*)

Deirdre My father lives in New Jersey.

Scooper (*pausing*) Recuperating from his death in the Lake Placid car crash?

Deirdre He lives in a nursing home. Which is why I asked you before if your mother was in a nursing home. If I can help in any way. We both share a guilt about the way we neglected a parent.

Scooper I haven't neglected anybody . . .

Deirdre It's a very good nursing home. It's a lot but the Medicare helps out. My father was in the Mafia. You don't have to be Italian to be in the Mafia. He was in charge of all the pinball machines in the state of New Jersey. Atlantic City. Up through the Jersey shore. I didn't mind that. But when I was twenty, I found out that he had gone over to drugs and was pushing drugs. Fairly large quantities in the same areas where he previously had had the pinballs . . . I found that out inadvertently. He kept things from me. Loved that I read and was smart. But when I found out about the drugs. Heroin. Did I tell you it was heroin? I blew the whistle on him. I called the FBI. They arrested him. It was on the front pages of lots of papers. Daughter Turns In Father. Do you remember me? Sometimes for a while after that, people would recognize my face. I wrote a book about it.

Scooper (*in awe*) You wrote one of *these*?

Deirdre Long before the day of the big paperback sale. Still I got an advance you'd call tidy. *Turn-In: The Story of a Daughter*.

Scooper I don't know it.

Deirdre Talk about neglected. It never took off the way they hoped. Out of print. No copies. The FBI gave me a new identity. After I named names and after I named Papa, our family no longer existed. I no longer had the right to use my family name.

Scooper Deirdre is not your name?

Deirdre   No, that's all I kept. Deirdre I kept. But this hair . . . this face . . . this body, all new.

Scooper   All new?

Deirdre   The FBI set me up here. Helped me get started.

Scooper   This is a government bookstore?

Deirdre   No. Then they left me on my own. All I had was my books.

Scooper   Do you miss your old life? My God, losing everything. You're quite beautiful now. They did . . . whoever, a wonderful job.

Deirdre   Do I miss my old life? No, strangely, what I miss . . . the moment I can't lose is the moment I turned my father in. The moment I called.

Scooper   You can't do that too often.

Deirdre   I know, and now that he's not available, I do the next best thing.

Scooper   Which is?

Deirdre   I call up the spouses of authors who mean the world to me.

Scooper   And say what?

Deirdre   Look up Norman Mailer. I know how to sow the seeds.

Scooper   You don't have a computer! I could set you up!

Deirdre   The Rolodex is my last concession to the future.

Scooper   That is so admirable!

Scooper *looks through the Rolodex.*

Scooper   My God, the names here: Saul Bellow. William Styron.

Deirdre   Dial Norman Mailer.

Scooper   Brooklyn. 718 area code. (*He dials the phone.*) It's ringing.

Deirdre(*takes the phone*)   Mrs Mailer? Mrs Norman Mailer? Yes. Could you please give Norman – I mean Mr Mailer – a message? Tell him it's Deirdre calling. Tell him his *book* is ready. Tell him his special order is ready. The special order. The one he was dying for. (*She hangs up.*)

Scooper   But you could get him in trouble.

Deirdre   Why do you think he's been married so many times?

Scooper   You are incredible. Do another one.

Deirdre   Spin the Rolodex!

Scooper (*spins*)   Doctorow, E. L.

Deirdre   Dial!

Scooper (*dials*)   It's a machine.

Deirdre (*takes the phone*)   Edgar. It's Deirdre waiting for you again and again and again, Edgar, we can repeat the past. Yes. Yes. Yes. (*She hangs up.*)

Scooper   I want to try one!

Scooper *finds a name and dials.*

Scooper   May I speak to Joan Didion? Is this her husband? Yes, Mr Dunne, I'd like to leave a message. Tell her it's ... Tell her it's Herman Melville and I want to hear Joan cry out 'Omoo' once more. I want to hear her cry out 'Typee.' Do you have that? 'Omoo! Typee!' (*He hangs up.*) Holy Christ, this is fantastic! I want to call Susan Sontag!

Deirdre (*takes phone from him*)   My father was in the Big House for a long time.

Scooper   Is he still in the Big House?

Deirdre   He's out now. He developed this very bad arthritis in prison. And his stomach is gone from taking so many aspirins for his arthritis. I'm hoping one day before he dies we can clear the books. He will lean over and take my hand and say I understand why you did what you did. So I go out there every weekend, sit there, read. Out loud. Wait for the scene. That moment that will clarify all. I've gone through James Joyce and Wallace Stevens.

Scooper   Does a Mafia chief understand it?

Deirdre   I don't know. I only hope he'll hear the voice underneath. English has the largest vocabulary of any language and perhaps one day I'll come up with the right combination and my father will forgive me for putting him away for ten years in the slammer.

Scooper   You put a lot of faith in the language.

Deirdre   Yes. Yes, I do. (*They embrace.*)

Scooper   What you've been through. I'd like to show you how much I care for you.

Deirdre (*undoes his tie*)   Care for Doctor James. Care for our work.

Scooper   What are you reading to your father now?

Deirdre (*unbuttons his collar button*)   The South Americans.

Scooper (*pulls the tie off his shirt*)   Don't get me started on the South Americans.

Deirdre   Jorge Amado. (*She undoes her skirt.*)

Scooper (*undresses as fast as he can*)   *The Two Loves of Doña Flor.*

Deirdre *opens a cabinet and rolls out a bed.*

Deirdre   *Gabriella Clove and Cinnamon.*

Scooper (*undoes his tie*)   *A Hundred Years of Solitude.*

Deirdre (*steps out of the other shoe*)   Marquez is hardly neglected.

Scooper (*takes off a shoe*)   A cult book.

Deirdre (*unbuttons her blouse*)   But not neglected. Overpraised.

Scooper (*unbuttons his shirt*)   But perfect.

Deirdre (*drawing the shades*)   Of its kind. (*The room is dark except for one lamp over the bed.*) But like all cult books ultimately overpraised.

Scooper   Think of me as an eclipse.

Deirdre   An eclipse?

Scooper   Let me move into your orbit. Let me blot out the vision of your father. Oh God – you poor girl – what you've been through – I'd like to show you how much I care for you – (*They are on the bed.*)

Deirdre   Care for Doctor James, care for our work –

Scooper   Care for our meeting –

Deirdre   Have you ever been to South America?

Scooper   No. No. But emotionally I identify with the South Americans.

Deirdre   I'd like to put another woman's body between you and the image of that half-rotten peach. That poisoned gauze. Restore the womb to its proper dark place. Do you read Valéry?

Scooper   Do I read to Valerie?

Deirdre   Paul Valéry.

Scooper   I don't read French.

Deirdre   I don't either.

Scooper   Your first edition of Byron.

Deirdre   Shall we read it?

Scooper   It's uncut. (*She takes a paper knife.*) It'll reduce the value. I'll cut just one page. (*He takes the paper knife from her. He takes one of the Byron volumes. He slices the page, opens the book carefully and reads:*) 'But some are dead and some are gone

And some are scattered and alone And some are rebels on the hills . . .' (*He gives her the book and the knife.*)

She slices open a page and reads.

Deirdre Ahhh. He says, 'Had Orpheus fiddled at the present hour He'd see lions waltzing in the tower.'

Scooper The pressure.

Deirdre The sound.

Scooper The pages resist.

Deirdre Gentle. (*She cuts another page.*)

Scooper Feels good. (*He cuts another page.*)

Deirdre Firm. (*She cuts another page.*)

Scooper Slice. (*He cuts another page.*)

Deirdre The odor.

Scooper The feel.

Deirdre The paper.

Scooper The binding.

Deirdre The print.

Scooper The ink.

Deirdre So neglected.

Scooper So neglected.

They each cut a page. They drop the books. They embrace hungrily. She turns off the light. Dark. Quiet. Breathing. Laughter. Joy. The phone rings. It rings.

Deirdre No.

Scooper (*picks up the phone*) Hospital! Hospital! Yes? Valerie! (**Deirdre** *turns on the light.* **Scooper** *is naked.*) How was New Hampshire? (*He signals* **Deirdre** *to turn off that light. Darkness again.*) I'm just at a friend's house. The operation – I don't know – there was a brownout. Chicken

pox? What are you talking about. She has cancer. Bradley
has chicken pox? (*He turns on the light. He now has his shorts
and one stocking on.* **Deirdre** *lies on the couch, the sheet over her,
her arms over her eyes.*) They turned you back from the camp?
Sophie might have chicken pox? Kim might have it?
They're all home with you? You drove all the way up to
New Hampshire with them and now they're all back with
you? Can't your sister – (*He turns the light off. Blackness.*) It's
very difficult to talk right now. Why didn't you give him
shots? You have no right to say that – what are you
saying? Our affair took up so much time that you have
neglected your kids? Stop crying. (*He turns the light back on.
He is pacing back and forth. He now has his shirt on.*) Chicken
pox is not dangerous. You are not a terrible woman.
(**Deirdre** *turns on another light. She goes off.*) I don't care if
you've never had chicken pox. *I've* never had chicken pox.
We can still get on the plane. We'll start a world-wide
epidemic of chicken pox. I don't care. I want us to be off.
Don't cry, Val! Val! Valerie! Hi, Ted. Listen, Ted, we
might as well cut the shit – Valerie is not unpacking from
New Hampshire. Those bags are for me. She is packing for
me. Ted, you might as well know. Valerie and I are going
to Haiti tonight. When you get to your group, you'll find a
letter from us. Ted, Valerie and I – Val, get off the
extension. Let me tell him! Valerie, I'll be right over there
to pick you up. Ted, we have been screwing right under
your nose for the past five years. Valerie, put that phone
down. Valerie, it's the only time we can go. With the
doctor away. I've met a wonderful person who'll help us
with our books. Valerie? I'll be right over. Ted. Put Valerie
on. Hello? (*He hangs up.* **Deirdre** *returns in a bathrobe. Pause.*)
Her kid's got chicken pox.

Deirdre (*so pleased*)   Oh. I'm sorry.

Scooper   Psychosomatic chicken pox.

Deirdre   What a month we can have! New York in
August! You can get into any restaurant. Movies are empty
and cool! Movies! We'll see every movie in town and get

icicles on us from watching! Should we see only films
adapted from books and sit in the theater with flashlights
and read along with the movie? Day trips to the beach!
Museums! (*She opens the curtains. Afternoon light floods the room.*)
The pianist comes out. Is he weeping? No, the pianist is
dancing! He is healed! (*She puts on a Bach partita.*) When you
said you were reading Rilke, I couldn't believe it. I fell in
love with you at that moment. I can mark my love.

Scooper   I just picked up Rilke. I'm not familiar with
Rilke.

Deirdre   Rilke couldn't write for ten years. But he trusted
his angels would return to him. And they did. That book
in your pocket, *The Duino Elegies*. That's the only reason
we're going to Doctor James. To keep ourselves open so
we can recognize our angels when they finally show up.
We have been given a gift!

Scooper   She didn't leave him.

Deirdre   One day you will write that lady such a thank-
you note!

Scooper   She promised she'd leave him.

Deirdre   And people make promises and people break
promises –

Scooper   You know what I blame it all on?

Deirdre   Don't blame it on anybody. To be our ages and
unattached.

Scooper   I never read a book that had a thing to do with
my life. (*He stacks books in a pile as tall as he is.*)

Deirdre   Don't you hear me?

Scooper   We're the subsidiary characters in everybody's
lives. That's the joke, the joke of our lives. We spend all
our time babbling to Herr Doktor across the street about
ourselves and we don't figure in anyone's life. I bring my
life to Doctor James and we turn my life into a lullaby
until I am as fictional to myself as any one of these books

are to me. (*He punches the pile of books and begins ripping them.*)
I wish I were blind! And illiterate! I wish I could rip all the
sight out of my head. (*He rips a pile of books. He hurls a book
at the CD. The music stops.*) Were you a nun? Were you an
orphan! Is your father in the Mafia! Are you even in
books!

Deirdre (*throws herself on her books*)   Don't rip my books!
Stop it!

Scooper *pushes her out of the way. She falls against a tall
bookcase which tips over and spills out its volumes. He destroys lots of
books.*

Deirdre   My ankle!

Scooper   I want to get all this fiction out of my eyes!

Deirdre *picks up the paper knife. She stabs him. He is in such a
fury he doesn't even feel it.*

Scooper   Throw them all out the window!

Scooper *runs to the window with his arms full of books. His shirt
is covered with blood.* **Deirdre** *is hysterical.* **Scooper** *stops.*

Scooper   There's Doctor James. Coming out of his office.

Deirdre (*hopping to the window*)   Who's driving the blue
Mercedes?

Scooper   A woman.

Deirdre   Three children.

Scooper   They put the luggage in the trunk.

Deirdre   He kisses them all.

Scooper   He gets in the driver's seat.

Deirdre   They drive away.

Scooper   Come back.

Deirdre   Come back!

Scooper   Doctor James, come back!

Deirdre   Doctor James, come back!

They press against the glass.

Scooper   I see the car.

Deirdre   Turning onto Park.

Scooper   Doctor James.

Deirdre   He's gone.

Scooper   Doctor James.

Deirdre   He's gone.

They punch each other. They stab each other. They are weeping and hitting and attacking each other. They stop. They gasp for breath.

Scooper   Put down that paper knife. I'm bleeding.

Deirdre   Oh dear Christ. I stabbed you. I tried to kill you.

Scooper   I ruined your apartment. I tried to kill you!

Deirdre   What's the last eight years been for? Are you dying? Are you bleeding?

Scooper   Is it all for naught? The last six years? All for naught?

Deirdre   The last eight years? All for zero? Have to get out to my father. To read to him.

Scooper   It can't be. Back to go. The mother.

Deirdre   Back to zero. The father.

Henny *appears in the room, clutching the statue of St Jude.*
Scooper *looks up in terror.*

Blackout.

Act Two

A hospital room. **Henny** *sits up in the bed. It's two days after the operation. Her I.V. has been disconnected. In spite of her bandaging, it's the first time she's felt comfortable in years.* **Scooper** *is a patient in the hospital. He has a bathrobe on over pajamas. His side is bandaged. His arm is bandaged. He sits in a wheelchair.*

Scooper Ma. I'm having a lot of trouble relating to people.

Henny Every time I call you, you're reading a book. And they're these books no one ever heard of.

Scooper I'm having trouble with women.

Henny Don't you ever read anything by a writer who's alive?

Scooper And you are the key woman in my life. The first woman.

Henny Writers write books and then they go on promotion tours on the radio and TV and a person like myself who can't read can at least hear about the person who did the writing.

Scooper I would like to examine in this time we have –

Henny But you don't read them unless they sold two copies and been dead nine hundred years and nobody ever made a movie out of it or heard of it.

Scooper This relationship in a way, a manner, that might shed light on future relationships with –

Henny My friend, Roberta Schildhauer, has always got her nose in a book. She wore out her library card. They had to laminate it, and she never heard of any of the stuff you read.

Scooper *holds his side by his spleen. He makes a sudden retching noise, but then is quiet.*

Henny   Is that you?

Scooper   I got a crick in my side. (*He gets out of the wheelchair.*)

Henny   Why did the nurse come and say 'Get back in bed.'

Scooper   There's other people in the room. She was talking to them.

Henny   It sounded like she was talking to you.

Scooper   Get back to bed? She was being sexy.

Henny   What does the nurse look like?

Scooper   She's the shortest nurse you ever saw with this great white cap on her head. It looks like this seagull has made this rest stop on her head on his way out to the horizon.

Henny   What do you have on?

Scooper   Blue striped seersucker suit. Blue shirt. Blue tie with red apples on it for the Big Apple.

Henny   You must look nice. No wonder she's being sexy. I'll get special attention if the nurses know I got a sexy son.

Scooper   Henny, you've been lying to me, to yourself for the past two years. You're going home in ten or twelve days. I want to make sure you won't ever lie –

Henny   I wasn't lying –

Scooper   You were sick for two years and couldn't trust me. I called you most every day and saw you at Christmas and on your birthday and in all that time you acted like you were sneaking a thermos of martinis onto the beach for Daddy to drink.

Henny   I was going to tell you –

Scooper   Tell me what?

Henny (*sharply*)   Tell you I was frightened. What do you think?

Scooper   And you couldn't.

Henny   I couldn't give you my problems.

Scooper   You didn't trust me?

Henny   I was going to call the priest one day and have him come to the house and confess about the sore down there.

Scooper   Sores are not sins. Something in you said I do not trust this man who is my son.

Henny   Did you put the double lock on my apartment? I don't want those people next door raiding my apartment. Oh, the old witch is finally gone. Let's get the furniture. Let's get the dishes. Wheel out the piano.

Scooper   Nobody wants anything in that apartment.

Henny   You do. I'm leaving things for you. I'm collecting sheets for you. I send the girl to open bank accounts and get electric blankets and electric kettles so when you finally get married you'll be all set. You're the only boy on the block with a hope chest.

Scooper   I'm not a boy, Henny. I'm forty years old.

Henny   Forty? Old? You know what old is? When you look back and say Christ, to be seventy-nine again. Nostalgia for eighty. Even eighty-one. That wasn't so bad. To be that young. To be handsome.

Scooper   You haven't seen me in years. You don't even know what I look like.

Henny   You look like Robert Redford.

Scooper   You don't know what Robert Redford looks like.

Henny   He looks like you.

Scooper   Henny –

Henny   The lucky part is I don't know what I look like either.

Scooper   The lucky part is this operation –

Henny (*holds her ears*)   Don't talk about the operation!

Scooper   It was a success.

Henny   What was a success?

Scooper   They got it. You're okay.

Henny   Between my legs?

Scooper   They put a pessary.

Henny   They put a pet between my legs?

Scooper   A silver disc to hold the uterus.

Henny   My bladder!

Scooper   You don't know. You make everything up for yourself.

Henny (*reaches out her hands*)   I can drink water? It won't burn? I want water.

Scooper *gives her the pitcher. She takes it and drinks right out of the pitcher. She falls back.*

Scooper   The irony is you're probably in the best health you've ever been in in your life. They said for all the neglect, you had the body of a fifty-two-year-old woman.

Henny   Well, if they find a fifty-two-year-old soul stuck in a six-thousand-year-old body, we can do a complete switch.

Scooper   The good thing about being old –

Henny   Twenty-five-thousand words or less please.

Scooper   The cancer moves slow.

Henny   Stop harping that word!

Scooper   They got it. It's out of you. Hallelujah, Saint Jude. Maybe Kotex and Saint Jude are the secret of life.

The disease in Fort Bosom is captured. I don't want you leaving this hospital galloping pronto back to the old evasions. Doing anything to avoid hitting center. Not lying. Just evading. I'm talking to myself as well as you. If you're in trouble, you have to tell me.

Henny   How hot is it in this room? I'm burning up.

Scooper   The thermometer here on the window. Eighty-nine degrees.

Henny   A miracle. An age I haven't been. Pick a number. Any number. I've been it. Who cares how hot it is. I'm in hell and isn't hell supposed to be hot?

Scooper   You got yourself in hell all by yourself.

Henny   And I'll get myself out all by myself.

Scooper   Did you show your breast to me –

Henny   Bosom!

Scooper   To stop me from going? I have to know this.

Henny   Where are you going?

Scooper   I was only going away for a few weeks.

Henny   You going on a trip?

Scooper   You had it hidden for two years. Why did you have to pick that time –

Henny   You can't leave.

Scooper   I canceled the trip. Did you know?

Henny   I'm sorry such a minor thing as this *bosom* incident has fouled up your summer plans.

Scooper   Cut the dramatics.

Henny   I'm eighty-three. I won't be around much longer to screw up your summer vacations. If you write a piece on 'My Summer Vacation', don't forget to send me a copy. I'm learning braille with my ass. I'll sit on it and learn all I need to know.

Scooper   Did you show me your breast to stop me from going?

Henny   I hate that word. 'Breast beating.' Why do you have to use that word, Breast? Sounds like something a chicken has. I always loved my bosoms. Your father loved my bosoms. Bosom buddies. Bosoms are fun. Bosoms are round. I may not have had good legs, or had the straightest teeth, but did my bosoms get attention at the beach. I couldn't wait for summer. I'm a topless dancer now. Half a topless dancer.

Scooper   Did you know I was going away?

Henny   Where are you going? I don't keep track of your life. Who'd tell me?

Scooper   Val. Did she let anything slip?

Henny   I never talk to Valerie.

Scooper   She let something slip about a trip?

Henny   She and Ted sent flowers.

Scooper   That we were going away.

Henny   I wish they sent candy instead. I could eat that bouquet. The food I'll tell you is not so hot here. But don't have them come visit me. They're good friends to you, but I don't want anybody up here seeing me.

Scooper   Believe me, they won't be coming.

Henny   I wish Jack were here. Where is my Jack?

Scooper   So you could kill him again?

Henny   Your father died because he drank and he was drunk all the time and then he drank even more and then he died.

Scooper   So why do you wish such a drunk here by your side?

Henny   To have a man with me.

Scooper   You have me.

Henny   Like I was saying. Where are those nurses? What
do you think Medicare's paying for? I want a cool white
towel. Is it daytime? Night-time? I'm burning up. My head
is so . . . Scooper? Are you still in the room? (*A pause.*)

Scooper   I'm here.

Henny   I was going to tell you but I thought how can I
tell him with so many worries so deep on his mind? Don't
you think I know you're lonely? You got nobody in your
life. Things aren't working out. I don't need optometrists to
see all that. And now this. Nurses. Me coming home.
Who's going to pay for it?

Scooper   The Medicare takes it. Relax. When Jack died
and you had that suicide –

Henny   It wasn't suicide. I reached for the wrong pills. I
couldn't see. I thought they were breath fresheners. Life
Savers.

Scooper   Nobody takes eighty-six Life Savers. Nobody's
breath is that bad. Jack dying in one hospital. You
suiciding in another. Me racing back and forth to see
who'd die first. A five-day race. He went. You survived.
When it was all over, the Medicare, for some reason I
never followed up on, sent me a rebate of forty-four
dollars. I made forty-four bucks off the two of you being in
the hospital. Who knows what'll happen this time? Jackpot.

Henny   How did I get in here so quickly? I thought
hospitals had waiting lists. I thought you had to wait weeks
to get appointments and beds. Three days ago you come
see me and that very day I'm taken here and two days ago
I'm operated on. How did we get in so quickly?

Scooper   It was an emergency.

Henny   Pearl Harbor is an emergency. An old lady with
female problems is no emergency. You didn't have to panic
and carry me out.

Scooper You were in pain. Why would you do that to yourself all these years? Put yourself in solitary confinement.

Henny Is there anyone else in the room?

Scooper A lady over there. Asleep. Tubes coming out of her. Another lady was here. I guess being operated.

Henny Are they ack-blay?

Scooper Both of them.

Henny Couldn't you get me a room with ite-whay people in it?

Scooper You're lucky to have this room.

Henny Did you stick me on the charity ward?

Scooper It's no charity ward.

Henny Let the nurses know I'm somebody. Tell them I am not run-of-the-mill. Tell them I used to be somebody.

Scooper Who did you used to be?

Henny Make up somebody. You're the one who reads the books.

Scooper Why don't you ever tell me the truth?

Henny Why don't you ever ask me the truth?

Scooper Why did you try to kill yourself ten years ago?

Henny Why aren't you married?

Scooper Why did you get married so late?

Henny Who is this Doctor James who got me in here?

Scooper A doctor.

Henny What kind of a doctor?

Scooper I don't know. He's. They have to be everything.

Henny Who does he look like?

Scooper He looks like – believe it or not – he looks like Jack.

Henny   My Jack? Your father?

Scooper   Same slicked-back hair.

Henny   Your father. So embarrassed about his curls. I said why God wasted curls on you. He said it was a present from heaven: beautiful brains. Doctor James looks like Jack? I can't wait for him to come in again.

Scooper   He won't. He's away.

Henny   Jack could've had anybody. He had me. Biggest shock of my life when he said, Henny, give a guy a break. Marry me. He could've had any girl.

Scooper   What did Dad mean when he said 'That's what I get for marrying a forty-two-year-old virgin.' Why would you scream 'I can't help it if I'm a good girl.' Why would you scream over and over 'I can't help it if I'm not a whore like your other women. I can't help it if I kept it for the man I married.'

Henny   I didn't realize I had given birth to a little cassette recorder.

Scooper   What kept you two together?

Henny   I would've called you Xerox, bought stock in you and sold you.

Scooper   What was your life like before you married Jack? Before you had me? I'm almost the age you and Jack were when you met. What was your life like?

Henny   Life like? Life like? Our life was life-like. You like this Doctor James a lot. I can hear a blush in your voice.

Scooper   Did you ever have nightmares? You were thirty-eight, thirty-nine, forty. Alone. Unmarried. Not walking the streets like Jack's other girls.

Henny   Your father and I went to dances.

Scooper   Why did two forty-year-old people get married

for the first time?

Henny   To hold up their pants? To get to the other side of the road? I'll bite. Why did two forty-year-old people get married for the first time? We had money to spend on ourselves. We were lonely. Is that a sin? To be lonely. My father had died. I was alone.

Scooper   How lonely were you?

Henny   I met your father in a bar.

Scooper   Did it make you wake up in the middle of the night?

Henny   We'd do this funny dance. I'd pull my bloomers down like a harem girl. We'd do this Egyptian dance.

Scooper   My father. Was he lonely?

Henny   Why would he be lonely?

Scooper   You never asked him?

Henny   I'm supposed to wake him up in the middle of the night and say to my husband I'm lucky to get 'Are you lonely?' He'd thwack me in the head. A man is never lonely. A man on his deathbed can pick up the phone and get a date. A woman's different. I had buck teeth. They should've straightened my teeth while I was under the knife. They should've left my bosoms alone and broken my legs and reset them straight. I had grey hair when I was twenty-seven. Too honest to dye it. I made myself attractive telling jokes and acting the life of the party. Slaving in the kitchen. I was always afraid your father would leave. I was glad when he died. The worries were over. He couldn't leave me.

Scooper   Then why did you try to kill yourself?

Henny   What are you? J. Edgar Hoover? Is this the Warren Commission?

Scooper   I'm trying to be honest.

Henny   You just can't start being honest. You don't walk up to a fella and say Hey, today I'm honest.

Scooper There must be something you want to know about me.

Henny I'm proud I never pried.

Scooper You never knew how much money your own husband made.

Henny I waited for him to tell me.

Scooper You didn't know how old he was.

Henny Not my business to ask.

Scooper Your own husband?

Henny There was food on the table. You never went hungry.

Scooper He didn't know how old you were.

Henny I was older. He would've left me.

Scooper Two years older! Two years!

Henny Do they know here? How old I am?

Scooper Your birthday's on your wrist on a little plastic tag.

Henny Take it off. Change the date!

Scooper To what?

Henny Anything! Make it even older so they'll say I look swell for a ninety-five-year-old woman.

Scooper You're going to die and I'm not going to know anything about you.

Henny You know enough about me.

Scooper How you felt?

Henny (*angry*) Felt? Felt? You make hats out of felt.

Scooper I'm dying I'm so crazy. If I can straighten things out with you, maybe I can do it with all women –

Henny   Don't you think I know you're unhappy? Don't you think I know that you know that I'm unhappy? You think I tried to kill myself for fun?

Scooper   That's the first time I ever heard you admit you tried to kill yourself. Did it hurt? There. That's a start. That's a start.

Henny   I told the truth. Did the Red Sea part? I'm this old woman who does not want to live in the past and I have this son who is like living in a time capsule. They call it the past because it's over with, done, passed. Bury him with his copy of *Gone With the Wind*.

Scooper   You're going to be dead and I'm not going to know you.

Henny   You put me in hospitals.

Scooper   Now? You blame me for this?

Henny   You put me in hospitals before.

Scooper   You were crazy. You needed help.

Henny   Causing blackouts all the electricity they put in me.

Scooper   You needed care.

Henny   Whole coastlines blacked out because of me.

Scooper   No one could help you.

Henny   Major cities. Industry crippled. Airlines. Television. Looting results because of the electricity they put in me to straighten out my head.

Scooper   You wouldn't trust anyone.

Henny   Lot of good it did.

Scooper   You wouldn't listen to anyone. You wouldn't ask anyone anything.

Henny   Okay. Who's this Doctor James that got me in here? I never heard you mention him before. I could hear

the blush in your voice. As a kid you were a blusher.
You're older. I bet your skin doesn't blush, but my ear is
attuned to voices. I can hear the blush in your voice.

Scooper   Who do you think he is?

Henny   What?

Scooper   I'm curious to know who you think he is.

Henny   Twenty Questions? Don't *you* know? I think he's
your –

Scooper   Speak up. Come on.

Henny   I don't want the nurses to hear.

Scooper   To hear what?

Henny   I think he's your boyfriend. Am I right?

Scooper (*laughing*)   Why do you think he's my boyfriend?

Henny   My friend, Roberta Schildhauer, saw you at East
Sixty-Eighth Street where she was doing practical nursing
across the street for a very wealthy lady and saw you going
in and out of the building across the street. She asked the
doorman who you went to visit.

Scooper   You don't need to see! You have a little blind
person's Mafia.

Henny   She told the doorman you were her daughter's
ex-husband and owed alimony. The doorman said you
went to see Doctor Virgil James. Roberta asked me who
Doctor Virgil James was. I lied to her. I said Oh, an old
college chum. They're scribbling away alumni notes.

Scooper   Doctor James is a psychiatrist.

Henny   I know about those shrinkolas. They're all so
cuckoo themselves I'm not surprised that's who you got
mixed up with. Just don't let him give you drugs. There's
nothing those mind shrinkers like better than getting you
deep on the drugs. A man was on the Diane Sawyer show
talking how those mind shrinkers had screwed him up.

Scooper   He's my doctor.

Henny   This man says in his book they're all junkies themselves.

Scooper   My doctor.

Henny   Why don't you read nice books like that? Books I hear about on the radio that I could talk to you about. *You* needing a psychiatrist? You'd have to be an ingrate! Everything you got. A nice business.

Scooper   I'm selling the business. My share to Ted. All over. Finished. Can't work together anymore.

Henny   Your best friends. Teddy and Valerie. They love you.

Scooper   Friends no more.

Henny   They told me that. They called at Christmas. It's like a home for you.

Scooper   Like a home. I want my own home.

Henny   Never be lonely with friends like that.

Scooper   I have been fucking Valerie for the past five years.

Henny   They sent me flowers.

Scooper   She was going to leave Ted but at the last moment she developed this paralysis of the threshold (*Pause.*)

Henny   You and Valerie?

Scooper   That's carved on secret trees all over town.

Henny   What about you and Doctor James?

Scooper   I'm his patient. (*She puts her hands over her face.*) You'd rather I were homosexual than had to go to a doctor?

Henny   There's nothing sick in being homosexual.

Scooper   But going to a psychiatrist?

Henny   That's sick. (**Scooper** *howls.*) I love to hear you laugh. When you laugh, the world's back in place. Laughter!! That's the best medicine! Laughter! Doctors know that'll put them out of business! Laugh, Scooper. (*Quiet.*) Scooper, are you here? (*A pause.*) Scooper?

Scooper   You've been in bug houses. I've had to put you there myself. I've seen you put in the back of trucks and taken away. You're up there in the Loony Hall of Fame. You have gold stars on your strait jackets. I've seen them.

Henny   And a lot of good it did me. Psychiatrists. My son.

Scooper   Six years ago, your son found himself walking barefoot down Fifth Avenue in the dead of winter carrying a red plastic machine gun. Your son followed a young girl for five blocks because he knew she would be kidnapped and he had to protect her from the aliens who would kill her. Very Stephen King. Just in the nick of time, your son pulled this girl into a sidestreet to let her know she was protected from those who would do harm to her hair and her skin and her fingernails. She screamed not knowing that your son was her savior. A passer-by heard her scream and grabbed your son. Your son pulled the cigarette out of his lips and put it in the Good Samaritan's face. Your son ran down Fifth Avenue to the Gotham Book Mart that sells old books. Your son ran into the bookshop to find a different character for himself. Charles Dickens. Something with an eccentricity he could live with. The police got your son there. Took him to Bellevue. Thanks to Ted and Valerie, your son got transferred to the Psychiatric Institute here in this hospital. Your son's doctor was Doctor James, and he has been my doctor ever since.

Henny   Did she press charges?

Scooper   No. But a few days later I got a book in the

hospital. *The Letters of Mozart.* She had written inside 'I am the girl you attacked. I want you to know I forgive you. Maybe a little contact with Mozart might heal you.'

Henny   I hope you sent her a thank-you note.

Scooper   She didn't sign it. I had nowhere to send the letter. I loved those letters of Mozart.

Henny (*groans*)   He loves the letters of Mozart.

Scooper   I said for years I look for the perfect girl. One day I snap. It all goes. I become a mugger. What do I do? I mug Miss Right. Nowhere to find her. I spent my time going after women to love them, to chase them, to hassle them, to talk to them, to touch them, to see them, to smell them, to feel them, to wound them, to heal them, to taste them . . .

Henny   Are you one of those transvestites?

Scooper   No, Ma.

Henny   I hear about them on the radio. There's nothing wrong in being a transvestite.

Scooper   I'm trying to clear my life out. I don't want to be crazy like you.

Henny   When you were eight years old, you put on my dress. And my make-up.

Scooper   Maybe I was trying to find out who you were.

Henny   We made a joke. When you were being born we didn't know if we wanted a boy or a girl so we got a little bit of both.

Scooper   I have this fantasy that one day you and I will have a scene that will clear everything out between us and I can lay you to rest while you're still alive.

Henny   Did you have one with your father?

Scooper   Yes.

Henny   Oh no! You couldn't've. He was too busy fighting to share anything. Too busy ripping the tops off beer bottles. Bourbon bottles.

Scooper   He had his stroke. I got a cab because that could come quicker than an ambulance.

Henny   I don't want to hear this.

Scooper   He couldn't speak. Left leg couldn't move. Left arm. No voice. We drove up to this hospital. Over the Triborough Bridge. I held him in my arms. 'All right, Jack,' I said. 'All right, Dad. Everything is going to be great! Remember when I was a kid, Dad, and we'd ride over a bridge and you'd say "You count all the boats on that side of the bridge, I count 'em on this side, whoever has the most is King for a Day!" Dad, I'll count boats for you. Six. Eight. Nine! You win! You're King for a Day! I love you, Dad.' I told him that. I held him. I felt the right side of his body answer me.

Henny   Then I'll twitch and you can hold me and we'll call it quits.

Scooper   Ma, feel these pajamas. Feel this robe. I'm not in a seersucker suit. I'm a patient here. I got stabbed, Ma. In the spleen.

Henny   In the subway! I tell you to ride taxis! I tell you it's dangerous out there –

Scooper   No muggers, Ma. I tried to hurt somebody again. The words all short-circuited. I didn't mean . . . she didn't mean to.

Henny   Valerie? Ted stabbed you?

Scooper   Deirdre.

Henny   Deirdre?

Scooper   You don't know her.

Henny   That's what I tell Roberta Schildhauer. You got a million of them.

Scooper   Why didn't you trust me? Why didn't you tell me? For two years why didn't you tell me you were standing in front of windows waving statues of impossible saints over you?

Henny   Where's the spleen?

Scooper   I stay away from you because you are all chaos. Your body bursting open. I need my life structured, enclosed. I pick up a book. The page's rectangular shape, obvious but important, *constant* from book to book, dependable, the passion, wisdom, excitement captured in the center of the page tamed by the white margin. I lie on the rectangular couch of Doctor James and yes I become the words on the page. I can face my dreams.

Henny   Your father and I had that song we'd dance to. 'I had a dream, dear, you had one too.'

Scooper   Ma, I have dreams that you picked me up and used me like a weapon against a strange man.

Henny   Where's the spleen?

Scooper   I feel you holding my feet and my face so close to this strange man and my head is hitting his. My friendships with men are all fucked up. My friendships with women are all fucked up. The doctors says you can't live alone anymore.

Henny   Doctor James?

Scooper   He's away. The surgeon said it.

Henny   No homes.

Scooper   I can't take care of you.

Henny   Never asked you to.

Scooper   Why do you want to stay alive?

Henny   Did I hear the question right? Why? Why!!!!

Scooper   After devoting fifteen solid, very unsolid years to trying to bump yourself off –

Henny   They were accidents! Household tragedies!

Scooper   Now when it's all over are you trying to hang on?

Henny   It's not all over. You said they got it.

Scooper   They got it so it won't kill you immediately. They didn't go into the lymph glands. You couldn't have stood up to that. They got rid of the discomfort.

Henny   How much . . .

Scooper   What are you saying?

Henny   Time.

Scooper   He said –

Henny   Who said?

Scooper   The doctor said.

Henny   I don't want any Doctor James said.

Scooper   The surgeon said.

Henny   Get to it.

Scooper   In spite of everything, you were in remarkable health. He said the cancer –

Henny   I hate that word.

Scooper   Could take ten years till it got you.

Henny   Ten years?

Scooper   Ten years.

Henny   Ten years! You gotta be joking: ten more years of this?

Scooper   Ten more years of this.

Henny   I must be an awful burden to you.

Scooper   You're an awful burden to me. I want to get to a new town, a new country, change the name, you over, start all over again.

Henny   Ten years.

Scooper (*very quietly*)   Ma. In the drawer of the table to the right of your bed are your pills. Your sleeping pills. I put all your belongings into a plastic bag and put them in that drawer. Ma. You can't live in dignity. You have a chance right now to die in it.

Henny   You want me to take the pills?

Scooper   I want you to take the pills.

Henny   Are there enough?

Scooper   A lot.

Henny   We'll do it?

Scooper   We'll do it.

Henny   You won't feel badly?

Scooper   I won't feel badly.

Henny   Give me the pills.

Scooper *takes the pills out of her bedside table, looking around to make sure no one sees him. He gives her the vial.*

Scooper   Ma?

Henny   Are these the pills?

Scooper   I loved you.

Henny   Is this our scene?

Scooper   We'll give each other a hold.

Henny   Don't do that. It hurts.

Scooper   Your hand.

Henny   Where's your hand? (*They connect hands.*)

Scooper   Thank you.

Henny   Thank you?

Scooper   For life. Caring for me.

Henny   Oh, that.

Scooper   We'll forgive each other.

Henny   You won't get into trouble over this?

Scooper   With your history?

Henny   I don't want you getting into any trouble for this.

Scooper   Open your hands. (*He pours the pills in.*)

Henny   Give me water. (*He pours her water. She drinks.*) I'll need lots of water. It feels like a lot there. It's so exciting to drink water again. (*She shakes the vial.*) You're sure you won't get in trouble for this?

Scooper   I'll stay by your side. You'll fall asleep.

Henny   To drink water and not have it burn.

Scooper   I'm by your side.

Henny   Water shouldn't burn.

Scooper   Still. Quiet.

Henny   550-2219. That's the butcher. He delivers. If you ever want anything delivered.

Scooper   550-2219.

Henny   I keep a hundred numbers right up here in my head.

Scooper   I loved you.

Henny   I loved your father.

Scooper   Thank you. That's important to know.

Henny   I love you.

Scooper   Goodbye.

Henny   You sure you'll light a lot of candles for me?

Scooper   They'll see the glow in Helena, Montana.

Henny   When I was a little girl, I dreamed of being a

great actress and I would change my name to Helena Montana.

Scooper   Your own name is all right.

Henny   Goodbye.

Scooper   Goodbye.

Henny (*flings the pills across the room*)   You rotten little shit, do you think they're going to let me bring killer pills in here? These are for my gas. You'd have done it? You'd have let me die?

Scooper   Take these pills! (*He picks them off the floor.*)

Henny   Nurse! Nurse!

Scooper   Quiet. (*He turns to the door. He speaks to the nurse.*) She's all right. Was dreaming. (*A pause. He waits for the nurse to leave. He sits by her bed.*) I want you dead.

Henny   God help me if I get gas in this hospital. (*She tosses the empty vial away.*)

Scooper   What keeps you alive?

Henny   You. I want to know what happens to you.

Scooper   I want to kill you.

Henny   That interests me.

Scooper   I want you to die.

Henny   That, my God, amazes me.

Scooper   Nothing's working out for me.

Henny (*thrilled*)   I know.

Scooper   What am I going to do? I put all this time into Valerie.

Henny   That's what I want to know about.

Scooper (*sits in his wheelchair*)   What am I telling you? You can't help me.

Henny   I'm not trying to.

Scooper   Ma, I'm not a book you sit there passively and keep turning the pages.

Henny   Oh yes, you are. You're my book. The day the nurse put you in my arms, I looked down at you. This complete stranger had come out of me. That I could produce this stranger. Would you take my breast? Would you drink? Would you live? Would you die? Would you be run over? Would you get polio or crib death or meningitis or be kidnapped? Would you learn? Who would you look like? You've always come up trumps, Scooper. Just when I'm about to give up on you and I say I knew what that boy is all about, out of the blue, I realize you're trying to kill me. That's so exciting. And to find out about you and Valerie! You could knock me over. Will she leave? Will she stay with Ted? How will Ted take it? Can you even keep Valerie? You want me to be open? Here I am. Open. (*Silence.*) But you're not ready to be. Poor Scooper.

Scooper   I'm not Scooper. My name is James.

Henny   Now see that. I wondered how long you want to keep being called Scooper.

Scooper   You named me!

Henny   I beg to differ. You were always scooping sand and putting it in your bucket. I said 'You're like a little ostrich scooping sand for his head.' You said 'Scooper!' 'Scooper!' You made us call you Scooper. If we wouldn't call you Scooper, you wouldn't come. It's awful having a kid with a silly name like Scooper. It could've been worse. You could've wanted to be called Ostrich. People would look at me as if actually calling another human being Scooper was my idea. Not my idea! His idea. Scooper. No wonder nobody can take you seriously. Or trust you. This is so interesting. I was wondering when you'd get around to changing your name back to what we named you. James! After my father. A wonderful man. James. The first. You're James the Second.

Deirdre *appears in the door. She has a robe over her hospital gown and hobbles in on crutches, her ankle in a splint.*

Deirdre I called my father.

Henny Who's there?

Deirdre I said a man tried to kill me.

Henny Who is that?

Deirdre I said it fast so he wouldn't hang up on me. He didn't speak but he didn't hang up. I poured it all out. I told him I was in the hospital and I wouldn't be out to see him for a few days and finally he spoke to me. He said 'Give me his name. I will tell certain men to see him.'

Henny Get out of my room. My son and I are –

Deirdre 'You don't touch a hair on the head of my Deirdre of the Sorrows.' He said that.

Henny Is this for you, Scooper?

Scooper Yes, Ma.

Deirdre I said 'Poppa, that's a play by John Millington Synge.' He said 'I named you after that play. Didn't I ever tell you?' He's going to kill you.

Henny Girl trouble?

Scooper Yes, Ma.

Henny Scooper! *(She leans forward, concentrating intently.)*

Deirdre He's going to send people out, find you and kill you for hurting the daughter of the professor. We talked! My father and I *talked.*

Henny Say something, Scooper!

Scooper I think you're going to extremes. I'm very happy you and your father –

Deirdre *(hits the wheels of his chair with her crutches)* Don't even mention him.

Scooper   You don't have to operate out of his code.

Deirdre   My father and I connected.

Scooper   You don't have to kill me to make up for all the years he didn't pay any attention to you.

Deirdre   I don't want his name in your mouth!

Scooper   You of all people should understand panic and losing control.

Deirdre   You did something worse. Worse than hitting me.

Scooper   You stabbed me.

Henny   Stabbed! Scooper, this is wonderful!

Deirdre   Worse than making me stab you. Worse than screwing up Doctor James for me.

Scooper   In a way we had a wonderful afternoon. I had hoped we'd –

Deirdre   We'd what? You had your chance. You had me. You touched me. You dropped me.

Scooper   And you're going to have me killed?

Deirdre   You made me afraid. I want to find Doctor James. I want him to see you for what you are.

Henny   Doctor James again! The Mystery Man!

Scooper   In a month you can tell him all.

Deirdre   Oh, I'll tell him. He'll throw you out in the gutter if you ever show up there again.

Scooper   Tell him whatever you want. It's one way to finish with Doctor James.

Deirdre (*hits the wheels of his chair with her crutches*)   Don't you say one word against him.

Scooper   I don't know where he is.

Deirdre   How am I going to get through this goddam month?

Scooper   I could put an emergency call into the AMA.

Deirdre   Who said April was the cruelest month?

Scooper   T. S. Eliot.

Deirdre   August. August. August.

Henny   I know where he is. (*A pause.*)

Deirdre   Who is this woman?

Henny   Hi! I'm him. But I don't want to butt in.

Scooper   What do you mean? You know where he is.

Henny   When you went to check me in, we stood out on the sidewalk. Talk about heat. Sidewalks buckling beneath me. This strange hand holding on to me. I don't know where I am.

Scooper   What did he say?

Henny   Don't get on the bed! You're worse than a cat! (**Scooper** *backs off.*) Is there such a place as Haiti?

Deirdre   Doctor James is in Haiti?

Scooper   Are you making this up?

Henny   No! We were making conversation. I said New York's like a jungle. He said I'm going to the jungle. A big white hotel. Talk about creepy.

Scooper   Haiti! I could go there.

Deirdre   Haiti? I could go there.

Scooper   Talk to him.

Deirdre   Explain to him.

Scooper   He'd want to see me.

Deirdre   He'd weep to see me.

Scooper   I have the tickets.

Deirdre   I'll call my travel agent.

Scooper   I have the reservations at the same hotel. (*He takes his wallet out. He fishes out the airline tickets.*)

Deirdre   Fly down. See him. Fly right back. I could swing that.

Scooper   Take one ticket.

Deirdre   I don't want anything from you.

Scooper   Don't let it go to waste.

Deirdre (*takes the ticket*)   I'll pay you later.

Scooper   Fine.

Deirdre   I don't want any free rides.

Scooper   And none of us will ever get them.

Deirdre   He'll help us. He'll help *you*.

Scooper   He'll help you.

Deirdre   And I'm doomed to travel with you? It's like some plot.

Scooper   Shoes like a CIA agent. Not one crease in them. Silently sliding through our lives . . . my God! You don't think –

Deirdre   It *is* a plot? You never mentioned to him you were going to Haiti?

Scooper   Haiti never came up.

Deirdre   And yet he knows. He's planned to drive us crazy all along. And bring us down there. He's arranged all this. Maybe he did it unconsciously. Even a shrink can have a subconscious. Doctor James is sitting under a palm tree. We're face to face. Finally. 'So our little odyssey has brought us to the jungle . . .'

Scooper   What is he trying to do to us?

Deirdre   That devil –

Scooper   That evil –

Deirdre   Diabolical.

Scooper   No. Good.

Deirdre   Wonderful.

Scooper   See him!

Deirdre   Face him! Knock on the door of his hotel room. She'll answer the door. 'Oh, hello, Mrs James, may I see the doctor? It's Deirdre.'

Scooper   'Hi Doctor. It's Scooper.'

Deirdre   Scooper?

Henny   Scooper. His name is Scooper. Not my idea.

Deirdre   I can't go into the jungle with anyone named Scooper.

Henny   It's a nickname for James.

Deirdre   Your name is James? (*Pause.*)

Scooper   I never made the connection!!!! Doctor James. Me James.

Deirdre (*in awe*)   You've done it. You have devoured Doctor James. He is in you. The transference is complete. His wisdom has unlocked your wisdom. James. James!!!! How lucky you are. (*She turns to go.*) Goodbye. (*Pause.*)

Scooper   Jane Bowles is neglected.

Deirdre (*stopping – but not turning*)   Carson McCullers.

Scooper   Joyce Carol Oates.

Deirdre (*turning*)   How can you say she's neglected? She writes a book a week.

Scooper   I never read them.

Deirdre   A neglected author is not one you choose to neglect. (*She turns to go.*)

Scooper   Joseph Conrad.

Deirdre   *Chance*?

Scooper   'Sacred call of life.' Page 432.

Deirdre   Page 432. 'The greatest sin to resist the embrace.'

Scooper   Are we that couple?

Deirdre   I can't. I can't keep starting . . .

Scooper   Your father – was he really in the Mafia?

Deirdre   He's a librarian.

Scooper   What's your truth?

Deirdre   Like everyone else's. Sordid, banal – of interest only to myself.

Scooper   Tell me one truth.

Deirdre   New York really is empty in August. (*Pause.*)

Scooper *stands.* **Deirdre** *motions him not to disturb* **Henny**, *who has fallen asleep.* **Scooper** *gestures to go outside. He pushes his wheelchair to the bed.* **Scooper** *and* **Deirdre** *go out.* **Henny** *wakes.*

Henny   James? James? Is she gone? Take my hand, James? (*Pause.*) Okay. Play the Quiet Man. Hearing the name James over and over, I keep thinking of my father. He was a wonderful man. After he died, I was lost. His dying broke me in about a million pieces but after a while I pasted myself together into some kind of new tea cup and toddled off to Boston for a new drink of water. I loved Boston. They laughed at my New York accent. It made me stand out. I met a man. Don Walker. He was Amish. I said 'You must be nuts to love me.' He said 'No, because I have all my buttons.' I said 'Which makes you ex-Amish, seeing as how you are not allowed to have buttons.' And he said, 'Well, you're no great shakes,' and I said 'Neither are you or you'd still be a Shaker.' Believe me, it was funny at the time. We loved each other. I felt my father in heaven was paying attention to me and had sent Don to me as a heavenly present. But Don's Quaker mother who unfortunately was still on this earth would not have her precious ex-Amish son hitched up with a shanty Irish

Catholic girl from Manhattan. Even though we were *very* lace curtain. Maybe rayon curtain. But not shanty. Not trash. But only a Quaker girl was good enough for her son. He buckled under. Stopped calling me. Neglected to keep dates. I got the message. I moved my broken tea cup of heart back to New York. Moved into 214 Riverside Drive. Met your father in the lobby. One disappointed person? Meet another disappointed person. Years went by. We got married. To show we could. We stayed together. We had you. And one day I dressed you up and got on the morning train to Boston. I waited outside my old office on Summer Street until Don Walker came out for lunch. I acted like I was just passing by. I wanted it to seem like I had just bumped into him, act casual, show him how great my life was, show off my beautiful child that was not his. And I saw him and I loved him so much. And after we said hellos and fancy meeting yous and acted surprised, I picked you up to show him what he missed and instead I hit him with you. Because he wasn't your father. Because he hadn't trusted me. Because I hadn't meant enough to him. I kept hitting him with you, pushing your face into his, till I realized your nose was bleeding. He was so shocked. I kept saying 'You neglected me.' I kept screaming like some shanty Irish Banshee: 'I loved you.' Finally he ran off. I wiped off your face. We got back on the next train to New York. Your father was home. He didn't ask why we were late, what we had done. He read his paper. Had his drinks. Slept. I put you to bed. I took off all my clothes and stood in front of the mirror. This body was not good enough. It couldn't get me what I wanted . . . maybe if . . . maybe . . . I got dressed. Sat by your bed. Stared and stared at you. This was my prayer. A better life for you. You woke up. You looked at me. I want that for you. I want that for you . . . James?

She reaches out for her son.

Curtain.

Six Degrees of Separation

Six Degrees of Separation was premièred at the Mitzi E. Newhouse Theater, Lincoln Center, New York, on 19 May 1990.

It was first performed in the UK at the Royal Court Theatre, London, on 11 June 1992, with the following cast:

Ouisa	Stockard Channing
Flan	Paul Shelley
Geoffrey	Gary Waldhorn
Paul	Adrian Lester
Doorman	John Grillo
Hustler	Mark Bowden
Kitty	Deborah Norton
Larkin	Barry Stanton
Detective	Gary Waldhorn
Tess	Caroline Catz
Woody	David Groves
Ben	Andrew Muir
Dr Fine	John Grillo
Doug	Glenn Hugill
Policeman	Ian Dunn
Trent	John Padden
Rick	Ian Dunn
Elizabeth	Zara Turner

Directed by Phyllida Lloyd
Designed by Mark Thompson
Lighting by Rick Fisher
Sound by Bryan Bowen

This production subsequently transferred to the Comedy Theatre, London.

A painting revolves slowly high over the stage. The painting is by Kandinsky. He has painted on either side of the canvas in two different styles. One side is geometric and somber. The other side is wild and vivid. The painting stops its revolve and opts for the geometric side.

A couple runs on stage, in night dress, very agitated. **Flanders Kittredge** *is forty-four.* **Louisa Kittredge** *is forty-three. They are very attractive. They speak to us.*

Ouisa Tell them!

Flan I am shaking.

Ouisa You have to do *something*!

Flan It's awful.

Ouisa Is anything gone?

Flan How can I look? I'm shaking.

Ouisa *(to us)* Did he take anything?

Flan Would you concentrate on yourself?

Ouisa I want to know if anything's gone?

Flan *(to us)* We came in the room.

Ouisa I went in first. You didn't see what I saw.

Flan Calm down.

Ouisa We could have been killed.

Flan The silver Victorian inkwell.

Ouisa How can you think of *things*? We could have been murdered.

An actor appears for a moment holding up an ornate Victorian inkwell capped by a silver beaver.

Flan There's the inkwell. Silver beaver. Why?

Ouisa Slashed – our throats slashed.

Another actor appears for a moment holding up a framed portrait of a dog, say, a pug.

Flan And there's the watercolor. Our dog.

Ouisa Go to bed at night happy and then murdered. Would we have woken up?

Flan Now I lay me down to sleep – the most terrifying words – just think of it –

Ouisa I pray the Lord my soul to keep –

Flan The nightmare part – if I should die before I wake –

Ouisa If I should die – I pray the Lord my soul to take –

Flan *and* **Ouisa** Oh.

Ouisa It's awful.

Flan We're alive.

Flan *stops, frightened suddenly, listening.*

Hello?

He holds her.

Hello!

Ouisa (*whispers*) You don't call out Hello unless –

Flan I think we'd tell if someone else were here.

Ouisa We didn't all night. Oh, it was awful awful awful awful.

They pull off their robes and are smartly dressed for dinner.

Flan (*to us*) We were having a wonderful evening last night.

Ouisa (*to us*) A friend we hadn't seen for many years came by for dinner.

Flan (*portentously*) A friend from South Africa –

Ouisa Don't say it so portentously.

Flan (*bright*)   A friend from South Africa.

Ouisa   Don't be ga-ga.

Flan (*to us*)   I'm an art dealer. Private sales. Purchases.

Ouisa (*to us*)   We knew our friend from South Africa –

Flan   – through our children when they all lived in New York.

Ouisa   They had gone back to South Africa.

Flan   He was here in New York briefly on business and asked us to ask him for dinner.

Ouisa   He's King Midas rich. Literally. Gold mines.

Flan   Seventy thousand workers in just one gold mine.

Ouisa   But he is always short of cash because his government won't let its people –

Flan   it's *white* people –

Ouisa   – its white people take out any money. So it's like taking in a War Baby.

Flan   When he called it was like a bolt from the blue as I had a deal coming up and was short by

Ouisa   two million.

Flan   The figure is superfluous.

Ouisa   I hate when you use the word 'superfluous'. I mean, he needed two million and we hadn't seen Geoffrey in a long time and while Geoffrey might not have the price of a dinner he easily might have two million dollars.

Flan   The currents last night were very churny.

Ouisa   We weren't sucking up. We like Geoffrey.

Flan   It's that awful thing of having truly rich folk for friends.

Ouisa   Face it. The money does get in the –

Flan   Only if you let it. The fact of the money shouldn't get in –

Ouisa   Having a rich friend is like drowning and your friend makes life boats. But the friend gets very touchy if you say one word: life boat. Well, that's two words. We were afraid our South African friend might say 'You only love me for my life boats?' But we *like* Geoffrey.

Flan   It wasn't a life-threatening evening.

Ouisa   Rich people can do something for you even if you're not sure what it is you want them to do.

Flan   Hardly a life boat evening –

Ouisa   (*sing-song*) Portentous.

Flan   But when he called and asked us to take him for dinner, he made a sudden pattern in life's little tea leaves because who wants to go to banks? Geoffrey called and our tempests settled into showers and life was manageable. What more can you want?

Geoffrey *is there, an elegant, impeccably British South African, slightly older than* **Ouisa** *and* **Flan**. **Flan** *passes drinks.*

Geoffrey   Listen. (*They do.*) It always amazes me when New York is so quiet.

Ouisa   With the kids away, we get used to a lower noise quotient.

Flan   Geoffrey, you have to move out of South Africa. You'll be killed. Why do you stay in South Africa?

Geoffrey   One has to stay there to educate the black workers and we'll know we've been successful when they kill us.

Flan   Planning the revolution that will destroy you.

Ouisa   Putting your life on the line.

Geoffrey   You don't think of it like that. I wish you'd come visit.

Ouisa   But we'd visit you and sit in your gorgeous house planning trips into the townships demanding to see the poorest of the poor. 'Are you sure they're the worst off? I mean, we've come all this way. We don't want to see people just mildly victimized by apartheid. We demand shock.' It doesn't seem right sitting on the East Side talking about revolution.

Flan   Only small murky cafés for Pepe le Moko here.

Ouisa   No. La Pasionaria. I will come to South Africa and build barricades and lean against them, singing.

Flan   And the people would follow.

Ouisa   'Follow Follow Follow.' What's that song?

Flan   The way Gorbachev cheered on the striking coal miners in the Ukraine – yes, you must strike – it is your role in history to dismantle this system. Russia and Poland – you can't believe the developments in the world – The Fantasticks, 'Follow Follow Follow'.

Ouisa   China.

Flan *and* **Ouisa** (*despair*)   Oh.

Geoffrey   Oy vay China. As my grandmother would say. (*They all laugh.*) Our role in history. And we offer ourselves up to it.

Flan   That is your role in history. Not our role.

Ouisa   A role in history. To say that so easily.

Flan (*to* **Geoffrey**)   Do you want another drink before we go out?

Ouisa   The phrase – striking coal miners – I see all these very striking coal miners modelling the fall fashions –

Geoffrey   Where should we?

Flan   There's good Szechuan. And Hunan.

Ouisa   The sign painter screwed up the sign. Instead of The Hunan Wok, he painted The Human Wok.

Geoffrey   God! The restaurants! New York has become the Florence of the sixteenth century. Genius on every corner.

Ouisa   I don't think genius has kissed the Human Wok.

Geoffrey   The new Italian looked cheery.

Flan *and* **Ouisa**   Good.

Flan   We made reservations.

Ouisa   They wrap ravioli up like salt water taffy.

Flan   Six on a plate for a few hundred dollars.

Geoffrey   You have to come to South Africa so I can pay you back. I'll take you on my plane into the Okavango Swamps –

Ouisa   Did you hear – to take back to Johannesburg. Out in East Hampton

Flan   last weekend

Ouisa   a guy goes into one of the better food stores –

Flan   Dean and DeLuca –

Ouisa   one of the Dean and DeLuca look alikes. Gets a pack of cigarettes and an ice-cream bar. Goes up front. Sees there's a line at the register. Slaps down two twenty dollar bills and goes out.

Flan   We sent it to the *Times*.

Ouisa   They have a joke page of things around New York.

Flan   They send you a bottle of champagne.

They all laugh brightly.

Ouisa (*to us*)   We weren't auditioning but I kept thinking Two million dollars two million dollars.

Flan (*to us*)   It's like when people say 'Don't think about elephants' and all you can think about is elephants

elephants.

Ouisa (*to us*)   Two million dollars two million dollars.

They laugh brightly. The doorbell rings.

Ouisa (*to Flan*)   Whatever you do, don't think about elephants.

Ouisa *goes.*

Geoffrey   Elephants?

Flan   Louisa is a Dada manifesto.

Geoffrey   Tell me about the Cézanne?

Flan   Mid-period. Landscape of a dark green forest. In the far distance you see the sunlight. One of his first uses of a pale color being forced to carry the weight of the picture. The experiment that would pay off in the apples. A burst of color asked to carry so much. The Japanese don't like anything about it except it's a Cézanne –

*A young black man – **Paul** – enters, supported by the **Doorman**. **Paul** is in his early twenties, very handsome, very preppy. He has been beaten badly. Blood seeps through his white Brooks Brothers shirt. **Ouisa** follows at a loss. The **Doorman** helps **Paul** to the sofa and stands at the door warily.*

Paul   I'm so sorry to bother you, but I've been hurt and I've lost everything and I didn't know where to go. Your children – I'm a friend of –

Ouisa (*to us*)   And he mentioned our daughter's name.

Flan (*to us*)   And the school where they went.

Ouisa (*to Flan*)   Harvard. You can say Harvard.

Flan (*to us*)   We don't want to get into libel.

Paul   I was mugged. Out there. In Central Park. By the statue of that Alaskan husky. I was standing there trying to figure out why there is a statue of a dog who saved lives in the Yukon in Central Park and I was standing there trying to puzzle it out when –

Ouisa   Are you okay?

Paul   They took my money and my briefcase. I said my thesis is in there –

Flan   His shirt's bleeding.

Ouisa   His shirt is not bleeding. *He's* bleeding.

Paul (*a wave of nausea*)   I get this way around blood.

Flan   Not on the rug.

Paul   I don't mind the money. But in this age of mechanical reproduction they managed to get the only copy of my thesis.

Flan   Eddie, get the doctor –

Paul   No! I'll survive.

Flan   You'll be fine.

Flan *helps* **Paul** *out of the room. The* **Doorman** *goes.*

Ouisa (*to us*)   We bathed him. We did First Aid.

Geoffrey (*leaving*)   It's been wonderful seeing you –

Ouisa (*very cheery*)   No no no! Stay! – (*To us.*) Two million dollars two million dollars –

Geoffrey   My time is so short – before I leave America, I really should see –

Flan (*calling from the hall*)   Where are the bandages!?

Ouisa   The Red Cross advises: Press edges of the wound firmly together, wash area with water –

Geoffrey   May I use your phone?

Ouisa   You darling old poop – just sit back – this'll only take a mo – (*Calling.*) Flan, go into Woody's room and get him a clean shirt. Geoffrey, have you seen the new book on Cézanne? (*To us.*) I ran down the hall to get the book on Cézanne, got the gauze from my bathroom, gave the Cézanne to Flan who wanted the gauze, gave the gauze to

Geoffrey who wanted Cézanne. Two million dollars two million dollars –

Flan *comes back in the room.*

Flan   He's going to be fine.

Ouisa *(to us)*   And peace was restored.

Paul *enters, slightly recovered, wearing a clean pink shirt. He winces as he pulls on his blazer.*

Paul   Your children said you were kind. All the kids were sitting around the dorm one night dishing the shit out of their parents. But your kids were silent and said, No, not our parents. Not Flan and Ouisa. Not the Kittredges. The Kittredges are kind. So after the muggers left, I looked up and saw these Fifth Avenue apartments. Mrs Onassis lives there. I know the Babcocks live over there. The Auchinclosses live there. But you lived here. I came here.

Ouisa   Can you believe what the kids said?

Flan *(to us)*   We mentioned our kids' names.

Ouisa   We can mention our kids' names. Our children are not going to sue us for using their names.

Paul   But your kids – I love them. Talbot and Woody mean the world to me.

Flan   He lets you call him Woody? Nobody's called him Woody in years.

Paul   They described this apartment in detail. The Kandinsky! – that's a double. One painted on either side.

Flan   We flip it around for variety.

Paul   It's wonderful.

Flan *(to us)*   Wassily Kandinsky. Born 1866 Moscow. Blue Rider Exhibition 1914. He said 'It is clear that the choice of object that is one of the elements in the harmony of form must be decided only by a corresponding vibration in the human soul.' Died 1944 France.

Paul It's the way they said it would be.

Ouisa (*to us*) Geoffrey had been silent up to now.

Geoffrey Did you bitch your parents?

Paul As a matter of fact. No. Your kids and I . . . we both liked our parents . . . loved our – look, am I getting in the way? I burst in here, hysterical. Blood. I didn't mean to –

Flan *and* **Ouisa** No!

Ouisa Tell us about our children.

Flan (*to us*) Three. Two at Harvard. Another girl at Groton.

Ouisa How is Harvard?

Paul Well, fine. It's just there. Everyone's in a constant state of luxurious despair and constant discovery and paralysis.

Ouisa (*to us*) We asked him where home was.

Flan (*to us*) Out West, he said.

Paul Although I've lived all over. My folks are divorced. He's remarried. He's doing a movie.

Ouisa He's in the movies?

Paul He's directing this one but he does act.

Flan What's he directing?

Paul *Cats*.

Ouisa Someone is directing a film of *Cats*?

Flan Don't be snooty.

Paul You've seen it? T.S. Eliot –

Flan Well, yes. Years ago.

Ouisa A benefit for some disease or school –

Flan Surely they can't make the movie of *Cats*.

Ouisa   Of course they can.

Paul   They're going to try. My father'll be here auditioning –

Ouisa   Cats?

Paul   He's going to use people.

Ouisa   What a courageous stand!

Paul   They thought of lots of ways to go. Animation.

Flan   Animation would be nice.

Paul   But he found a better way. As a matter of fact, he turned it down at first. He went to tell the producers – as a courtesy – all the reasons why you couldn't make a movie of *Cats* and in going through all the reasons why you couldn't make a movie of *Cats*, he suddenly saw how you could make a movie of *Cats* –

Ouisa   Eureka in the bathtub. How wonderful.

Flan   May we ask who –

Ouisa (*to us*)   And it was here we pulled up – ever so slightly – pulled up closer –

Flan (*to us*)   And he told us.

Ouisa (*to us*)   He named the greatest black star in movies. Sidney –

Flan   Don't say it. We're trying to keep this abstract. Plus libel laws.

Ouisa   Sidney Poitier! There. I don't care. We have to have truth. (*To us.*) He started out as a lawyer and is terrified of libel. I'm not.

Paul *steps forward cheerily.*

Paul (*to us*)   Sidney Poitier, the future Jackie Robinson of films, was born the twenty-fourth of February 1927 in Miami during a visit his parents made in Florida – legally? – to sell tomatoes they had grown on their farm in the

Bahamas. He grew up on Cat Island, 'so poor they didn't even own dirt' he has said. Neglected by his family, my father would sit on the shore, and, as he told me many times, 'conjure up the kind of worlds that were on the other side and what I'd do in them.' He arrived in New York City from the Bahamas in the winter of 1943 at age fifteen and a half and lived in the pay toilet of the bus station across from the old Madison Square Garden at Fiftieth and Eighth Avenue. He moved to the roof of the Brill Building, commonly known as Tin Pan Alley, and washed dishes at the Turf Restaurant for $4.11 a night. He taught himself to read by reading the newspaper. In the black newspaper, the theater page was opposite the want ad page. Among his forty-two films are *No Way Out*, 1950; *Cry the Beloved Country*, 1952; *Blackboard Jungle*, 1955; *The Defiant Ones*, 1958; *Raisin in the Sun*, 1961; *Lilies of the Field*, 1963; *In the Heat of the Night*, 1967; *To Sir With Love*, 1967; *Shoot to Kill*, 1988; and, of course, *Guess Who's Coming to Dinner*. He won the Oscar for *Lilies of the Field* and was twice named top male box-office star in the country. My father made no films from 1977 to 1987 but worked as director and author. Dad said to me once, 'I still don't fully understand how all that came about in the sequence it came about.'

Paul *returns to the sofa.*

Dad's not in till tomorrow at the Sherry. I came down from Cambridge. Thought I'd stay at some flea-bag for adventure. Orwell. Down and Out. I really don't know New York. I know Rome and Paris and Los Angeles a lot better.

Ouisa   We're going out to dinner. You'll come.

Paul   Out to dinner?

Flan   Out to dinner.

Paul   But why go out to dinner?

Ouisa   Because we have reservations and oh my God what time is it? Have we lost the reservations and we don't

have a damn thing in the house and it's sixteenth-century
Florence and there's genius on every block.

Geoffrey   Don't mock.

She kisses **Geoffrey** *lightly.*

Paul   You must have something in the fridge.

Flan   A frozen steak from the Ice Age.

Paul   Why spend a hundred dollars on a bowl of rice?
Let me into the kitchen. Cooking calms me. What I'd like
to do is calm down, pay back your kids –

Ouisa (*to us*)   He mentioned our kids' names –

Flan (*to us*)   Two. Two at Harvard. A daughter at Groton.

Paul   who've been wonderful to me.

Ouisa   They've never mentioned you.

Flan   What are they supposed to say? We've become
friends with the son of Sidney Poitier, barrier-breaker of
the fifties and sixties?

Geoffrey   Your father means a great deal in South
Africa.

Ouisa (*to us*)   Even Geoffrey was touched.

Paul   I'm glad of that. Dad and I went to Russia once to
a film festival and he was truly amazed how much his
presence meant –

Ouisa   Oh no! Tell us stories of movie stars tying up
their children and being cruel.

Paul   I wish.

Geoffrey   You wish?

Paul   If I wanted to write a book about him, I really
couldn't. No one would want to read it. He's decent. I
admire him.

Ouisa   He's married to an actress who was in one of –

she's white? Am I right?

Paul   That is not my mother. That is his second wife. He met Joanna making *The Lost Man*. He left my mother, who had stuck by him in the lean years. I had just been born. *The Lost Man* is the only film of my father's I can't bring myself to see.

Ouisa   Oh, I'm sorry. We didn't mean to –

Paul (*bright*)   No! We're all good friends now. His kids from that marriage. Us – the old kids. I'd love to get in that kitchen.

Flan (*to* **Ouisa**)   What should we do?

Ouisa (*to us*)   It's Geoffrey's only night in New York.

Geoffrey   I vote stay in.

Ouisa, **Flan** *and* **Paul**   Good!

Paul goes off to the kitchen.

Ouisa (*to us*)   We moved into the kitchen.

Flan (*to us*)   We watched him cook.

Ouisa (*to us*)   We watched him cook and chop.

Flan (*to us*)   He sort of did wizardry –

Ouisa (*to us*)   An old jar of sun-dried tomatoes –

Flan (*to us*)   Leftovers – tuna fish – olives – onions –

Paul returns with three dishes heaped with food.

Paul   Here's dinner. All ready.

Ouisa   Shall we move into the dining room?

Paul   No, let's stay here. It's nice in here.

Ouisa, **Flan** *and* **Geoffrey** *take plates skeptically.*

Ouisa   Have you declared your major yet?

Paul   You're like all parents. What's your major?

Flan   Geoffrey, Harvard has all those great titles the students give courses.

Ouisa   The Holocaust and Ethics –

Flan   Krauts and Doubts.

They eat. Surprise. It's delicious.

Geoffrey   This is the best pasta I've ever –

Paul   My father insisted we learn to cook.

Flan   Isn't he from Jamaica? There's a taste of –

Geoffrey   The islands.

Paul   Yes. Before he made it, he ran four restaurants in Harlem. You have good buds!

Geoffrey   See? Good buds, I've never been complimented on my buds –

Paul (to **Geoffrey**)   You're from –

Geoffrey   Johannesberg.

Pause.

Paul   My dad took me to a movie shot in South Africa. The camera moved from this vile rioting in the streets to a villa where people picked at lunch on a terrace, the only riot the flowers and the birds – gorgeous plumage and petals. And I didn't understand. And Dad said to me, 'You meet these young blacks who are having a terrible time. They've had a totally inadequate education and yet in '76 – the year of the Soweto riots – they took on a tremendous political responsibility. It just makes you wonder at the maturity that is in them. It makes you realize that the "crummy childhood" theory, that everything can be blamed in a Freudian fashion on the fact that you've had a bad upbringing, just doesn't hold water.' Is everything okay?

Flan, **Ouisa** and **Geoffrey** *are mesmerized, and then resume eating.*

Flan, **Ouisa** and **Geoffrey** (*while eating*)   Mmmmmm . . . yes.

Geoffrey What about being black in America?

Paul My problem is I've never felt American. I grew up in Switzerland. Boarding school. Villa Rosey.

Ouisa There is a boarding school in Switzerland that takes you at age eighteen months.

Paul That's not me. I've never felt people liked me for my connections. Movie star kid problems. None of those. May I?

Flan Oh, please.

Paul *pours a brandy.*

Paul But I never knew I was black in that racist way till I was sixteen and came back here. Very protected. White servants. After the divorce we moved to Switzerland, my mother, brother and I. I don't feel American. I don't even feel black. I suppose that's very lucky for me even though Freud says there's no such thing as luck. Just what you make.

Ouisa Does Freud say that? I think we're lucky having this dinner. Isn't this the finest time? A toast to you.

Geoffrey To *Cats*!

Flan Blunt question. What's he like?

Ouisa Let's not be star fuckers.

Flan I'm not a star fucker.

Paul My father, being an actor, has no real identity. You say to him, Pop, what's new? And he says, 'I got an interesting script today. I was asked to play a lumberjack up in the Yukon. Now, I've been trained as a preacher, but my church fell apart. My wife says we have to get money to get through this winter. And I sign up as part of this team where all my beliefs are challenged. But I hold firm. In spite of prejudice. Because I want to get back to you. Out of this forest, back to the church . . .' And my

father is in tears and I say, Pop, this is not a real event,
this is some script that was sent to you. And my father says
'I'm trying it out to see how it fits on me.' But he has no
life – he has no memory – only the scripts producers send
him in the mail through his agents. That's his past.

Ouisa (*to us*)   I just loved the kid so much. I wanted to
reach out to him.

Flan (*to us*)   And then we asked him what his thesis was
on.

Geoffrey   The one that was stolen. Please?

Paul   Well . . .

A substitute teacher out on Long Island was dropped from
his job for fighting with a student. A few weeks later, the
teacher returned to the classroom, shot the student
unsuccessfully, held the class hostage and then shot himself.
Successfully. This fact caught my eye: last sentence. *Times*.
A neighbor described him as a nice boy. Always reading
Catcher in the Rye.

The nitwit – Chapman – who shot John Lennon said he
did it because he wanted to draw the attention of the
world to *The Catcher in the Rye* and the reading of that book
would be his defense.

And young Hinckley, the whiz kid who shot Reagan and
his press secretary, said if you want my defense all you
have to do is read *Catcher in the Rye*. It seemed to be time
to read it again.

Flan   I haven't read it in years.

Ouisa *shushes* **Flan**.

Paul   I borrowed a copy from a young friend of mine
because I wanted to see what she had underlined and I
read this book to find out why this touching, beautiful,
sensitive story published in July 1951 had turned into this
manifesto of hate.

I started reading. It's exactly as I remembered. Everybody's a phoney. Page two: 'My brother's in Hollywood being a prostitute.' Page three: 'What a phoney slob his father was.' Page nine: 'People never notice anything.'

Then on page twenty-two my hair stood up. Remember Holden Caulfield – the definitive sensitive youth – wearing his red hunter's cap. 'A deer-hunter hat? Like hell it is. I sort of closed one eye like I was taking aim at it. This is a people-shooting hat. I shoot people in this hat.'

Hmmm, I said. This book is preparing people for bigger moments in their lives than I ever dreamed of. Then on page eighty-nine: 'I'd rather push a guy out the window or chop his head off with an ax than sock him in the jaw. I hate fist fights ... what scares me most is the other guy's face ...'

I finished the book. It's a touching story, comic because the boy wants to do so much and can't do anything. Hates all phoniness and only lies to others. Wants everyone to like him, is only hateful, and is completely self-involved. In other words, a pretty accurate picture of a male adolescent.

And what alarms me about the book – not the book so much as the aura about it – is this: The book is primarily about paralysis. The boy can't function. And at the end, before he can run away and start a new life, it starts to rain and he folds.

Now there's nothing wrong in writing about emotional and intellectual paralysis. It may indeed, thanks to Chekhov and Samuel Beckett, be the great modern theme.

The extraordinary last lines of *Waiting For Godot* – 'Let's go.' 'Yes, let's go.' Stage directions: They do not move.

But the aura around this book of Salinger's – which perhaps should be read by everyone *but* young men – is this: It mirrors like a fun-house mirror and amplifies like a distorted speaker one of the great tragedies of our times – the death of the imagination.

Because what else is paralysis?

The imagination has been so debased that imagination –
being imaginative – rather than being the linch-pin of our
existence now stands as a synonym for something outside
ourselves like science fiction or some new use for tangerine
slices on raw pork chops – what an imaginative summer
recipe – and *Star Wars*! So imaginative! And *Star Trek* – so
imaginative! And *Lord of the Rings* – all those dwarves – so
imaginative – The imagination has moved out of the realm
of being our link, our most personal link, with our inner
lives and the world outside that world – this world we
share. What is schizophrenia but a horrifying state where
what's in here doesn't match up with what's out there?

Why has imagination become a synonym for style?

I believe that the imagination is the passport we create to
take us into the real world.

I believe the imagination is another phrase for what is most
uniquely *us*.

Jung says the greatest sin is to be unconscious.

Our boy Holden says 'What scares me most is the other
guy's face – it wouldn't be so bad if you could both be
blindfolded – most of the time the faces we face are not
the other guys' but our own faces. And it's the worst kind
of yellowness to be so scared of yourself you put blindfolds
on rather than deal with yourself . . .'

To face ourselves.

That's the hard thing.

The imagination.

That's God's gift to make the act of self-examination
bearable.

Pause.

Ouisa   Well, indeed.

Pause.

Flan I hope your muggers read every word.

Ouisa Darling.

Geoffrey I'm going to buy a copy of *Catcher in the Rye* at the airport and read it.

Ouisa Cover to cover.

Paul I'll test you. I should be going.

Flan Where will you stay?

Ouisa Not some flea-bag.

Paul I get into the Sherry tomorrow morning. It's not so far off. I can walk around. I don't think they'll mug me twice in one evening.

Ouisa You'll stay here tonight.

Paul No! I have to be there at seven.

Ouisa We'll get you up.

Paul I have to be at the hotel at seven sharp or Dad will have a fit.

Ouisa Up at six-fifteen, which is any moment now, and we have that wedding in Roxbury –

Flan There's an alarm in that room.

Paul If it's any problem –

Flan It's only a problem if you leave.

Paul Six-fifteen? I'll tiptoe out.

Flan And we want to be in *Cats*.

Ouisa Flan!

Paul It's done.

Geoffrey I'll fly back. With my wife.

Ouisa Pushy. Both of you.

Paul He's not. Dad said I could be in charge of the

extras. You'd just be extras. That's all I can promise.

Flan In cat suits?

Paul No. You can be humans.

Flan That's very important. It has to be in our contracts. We are humans.

Geoffrey We haven't got any business done tonight.

Flan Forget it. It was only an evening at home.

Ouisa Whatever you do, don't think about elephants.

Paul Did I intrude?

Flan *and* **Ouisa** No!

Paul I'm sorry – oh Christ –

Geoffrey (*to* **Flan**) There's all ways of doing business. Flanders, walk me to the elevator.

Ouisa Love to Diana. (*To us.*) We embraced. And Flan and Geoffrey left –

Flan *and* **Geoffrey** *go.*

Pause. **Paul** *and* **Ouisa** *look at each other. Is it uncomfortable? Then:*

Paul Let me clean up –

Ouisa No! Leave it for –

Paul Nobody comes in on Sunday.

Ouisa Yvonne will be in on Tuesday.

Paul You'll have every bug in Christendom –

They both reach for the dishes.

Ouisa Let me –

Paul *takes the dishes.*

Paul No. You watch. It gives me a thrill to be looked at.

Pause. **Paul** *goes off.*

Ouisa (*to us, amazed*)   He washed up.

Flan *returns, amazed.*

Flan   He's in.

Ouisa   He's in?

Flan   He's in for two million.

Ouisa   Two million!

Flan   He says the Cézanne is a great investment. We should get it for six million and sell it to the Tokyo bunch for ten.

Ouisa   Happy days! Oh God!

Paul *returns.*

Paul   Two million dollars?

Ouisa   Figure it out. He doesn't have the price of a dinner but he can cough up two million dollars and the Japs will go ten! Break all those dishes! Two million! Go to ten! And we put up nothing?

Flan   He sold that Hockney print I know he bought for a hundred bucks fifteen years ago for thirty-four thousand dollars. Sotheby took their cut, sure, but still – Two million! Wildest dreams. Paul, I should give you a commission.

Paul   Your kids said you were an art dealer. But you don't have a gallery. I don't understand –

Flan   People want to sell privately. Not go through a gallery.

Ouisa   A divorce. Taxes. Publicity.

Flan   People come to me looking for a certain school of painting.

Ouisa   A modern. Impressionist. Renaissance.

Flan   But don't want museums to know where it is.

Ouisa Japanese.

Flan I've got Japanese looking for a Cézanne. I have a syndicate that will buy the painting. There is a great second-level Cézanne coming up for sale in a very messy divorce.

Ouisa Wife doesn't want hubby to know she owns the Cézanne.

Flan I needed an extra two million. Geoffrey called. Invited him here for dinner.

Ouisa Tonight was a very nervous very casual very big thing.

Paul I couldn't tell –

Ouisa All the better.

Paul I'm glad I helped –

Ouisa You were wonderful!

Paul I'm so pleased I was wonderful. All this *and* a pink shirt.

Ouisa Keep it. Look at the time.

Paul It's going to be time for me to get up.

Flan Then we'll say our good-nights now.

Paul Oh Christ. Regretfully. I'll tiptoe.

Flan *takes out his wallet.*

Flan Take fifty dollars.

Ouisa Give him fifty dollars.

Paul Don't need it.

Ouisa Suppose your father's plane is late?

Flan A strike. Air controllers.

Ouisa Walking-around money. I wouldn't want my kids to be stuck in the street without a nickel.

Flan   And you saved us a fortune. Do you know what our bill would've been at that little Eye-tie store front?

Ouisa   And we picked up two million dollars. One billionth of a percent commission is –

Flan   Fifty dollars.

Flan *hands him the money.* **Paul** *hesitates, then takes it.*

Paul   But I'll get it back to you tomorrow. I want my father to meet you.

Ouisa   We'd love to. Bring him up for dinner.

Paul   Could I?

Flan   You see how easy it is.

Ouisa   Sure. If Paul does the cooking. (*They all laugh.*)

Flan, Ouisa *and* **Paul**   Good night.

Flan *points* **Paul** *to his room.*

Flan   Second door on the right.

Paul *goes.* **Flan** *and* **Ouisa** *get ready for bed, pulling on their robes.*

Flan   I want to get on my knees and thank God – money –

Ouisa   Who said when artists dream they dream of money? I must be such an artist. Bravo. Bravo.

Flan   I don't want to lose our life here. I don't want all the debt to pile up and crush us.

Ouisa   It won't. We're safe.

Flan   For a while. We almost lost it. If I didn't get this money, Ouisa, I would've lost the Cézanne. It would've gone. I had nowhere to get it.

Ouisa   Why don't you tell me how much these things mean? You wait till the last minute –

Flan   I don't want to worry you.

Ouisa   Not worry me? I'm your partner.

They embrace.

Flan   There is a God.

Ouisa   And his name is –

Flan   Geoffrey?

Ouisa   Sidney.

Flan *goes.* **Ouisa** *curls up on the sofa.*

Ouisa *(to us)*   I dreamt of Sidney Poitier and his rise to acclaim. I dreamt that Sidney Poitier sat at the edge of my bed and I asked him what troubled him. Sidney? What troubles you? Is it right to make a movie of *Cats*?

Paul *appears as Sidney Poitier in dinner clothes.*

Paul/Sidney   I'll tell you why I have to make a movie of *Cats*. I know what *Cats* is, Louisa. May I call you Louisa? I have no illusions about the merits of *Cats*. But the world has been too heavy with all the right-to-lifers. Protect the lives of the unborn. Constitutional amendments. Marches! When does life begin? Or the converse. The end of life. The right to die. Why is life at this point in the twentieth century so focused on the very beginning of life and the very end of life? What about the eighty years we have to live between those two inexorable bookends?

Ouisa   And you can get all that into *Cats*?

Paul/Sidney   I'm going to try.

Ouisa   Thank you. Thank you. You shall.

Darkness. Then **Flan** *appears.*

Flan *(to us)*   This is what I dreamt. I didn't dream so much as realize this. I felt so close to the paintings. I wasn't just selling them like pieces of meat. I remembered why I loved paintings in the first place – what had got me into this – and I thought – dreamed – remembered – how easy it is for a painter to *lose* a painting. He can paint and paint – work on a canvas for months and one day he loses it – just loses the structure – loses the sense of it – you lose the painting.

When the kids were little, we went to a parents' meeting at their school and I asked the teacher why all her students were geniuses in the second grade? Look at the first grade. Blotches of green and black. Look at the third grade. Camouflage. But the second grade – your grade. Matisses everyone. You've made my child a Matisse. Let me study with you. Let me into second grade! What is your secret? And this is what she said: 'Secrets? I don't have any secret. I just know when to take their drawings away from them.'

I dreamt of color. I dreamt of our son's pink shirt. I dreamt of pinks and yellows and the new Van Gogh that MOMA got and the *Irises* that sold for 53.9 million and, wishing a Van Gogh was mine, I looked at my English hand-lasted shoes and thought of Van Gogh's tragic shoes. I remembered me as I was. A painter losing a painting. But a South African awaiting revolution came to dinner. We were safe.

Darkness. **Ouisa** *appears.*

Ouisa (*to us*) And it was six a.m. and I woke up so happy looking at my clean kitchen, all the more memorable because the previous evening had left no traces, and the paper was at the front door and I sat in the kitchen happily doing the crossword puzzle in ink. Everybody does it in ink. I never met one person who didn't say they did it in ink. And I'm doing the puzzle and I see the time and it's nearly seven and Paul had to meet his father and I didn't want him to be late and was he healthy after his stabbing?

I went down the hall to the room where we had put him. The hall is eighteen feet long. I stopped in front of the door. Paul? (*She calls into the darkness.*)

Paul's voice (*moaning*) Yes Yes

Ouisa Paul??

Paul's voice (*moaning*)   Yes Yes

Ouisa   Are you all right? (*To us.*) I opened the door and turned on the light. (*Screams.*) Flan!!!

The stage is blindingly bright. **Paul**, *startled, sits up in bed. A naked guy stands up on the bed.*

Hustler   What the fuck is going on here? Who the fuck are you?!

Ouisa   Flan!

Flan   What is it?

Flan *appears from the dark, tying his robe around him. The* **Hustler**, *naked but for white socks, comes into the room.*

Hustler   Hey! How ya doin'?

Flan   Oh my God!

Ouisa (*a scream*)   Ahhh!

The **Hustler** *stretches out on the sofa.*

Hustler   I gotta get some sleep –

Paul *runs into the room pulling on his clothes.*

Paul   I can explain.

Paul *tosses the* **Hustler**'s *clothes onto the sofa.*

Ouisa   You went out after we went to sleep and picked up this thing?

Paul   I am so sorry.

Flan   You brought this thing into our house! Thing! Thing! Get out! Get out of my house!

Flan *tips the sofa, hurling the* **Hustler** *onto the floor. The* **Hustler** *leaps at* **Flan** *threateningly.*

Ouisa   Stop it! He might have a gun!

Hustler   I might have a gun. I might have a knife.

Ouisa   He has a gun! He has a knife!

The **Hustler** *chases* **Ouisa** *around the room.*

Paul   I can explain!

Flan   Give me my fifty dollars.

Paul   I spent it.

Ouisa   Get out!

Flan   Take your clothes. Go back to sleep in the gutter.

He flings the **Hustler**'s *clothes into the hall. The* **Hustler**
viciously grabs **Flan** *by the lapels of his robe.*

Hustler   Fuck you!

The **Hustler** *throws* **Flan** *back, picks up his clothes and leaves.*
Flan *catches his breath.* **Ouisa** *is terrified.*

Paul   Please. Don't tell my father. I don't want him to
know. I haven't told him. He doesn't know. I got so lonely.
I got so afraid. My dad coming. I had the money. I went
out after we went to sleep and I brought him back. I
couldn't be alone. You had so much. I couldn't be alone. I
was so afraid.

Ouisa   Just go.

Paul   I'm so sorry.

Paul *goes.*

Flan *and* **Ouisa**, *at a loss, straighten out the pillows on the sofa.*
They are exhausted.

Ouisa *(to us)*   And that's that.

Flan   I am shaking.

Ouisa   You have to do *something*!

Flan   It's awful.

Ouisa   Is anything gone?

Flan   How can I look? I'm shaking.

Ouisa   Did he take anything?

Flan   Would you concentrate on yourself?

Ouisa   I want to know if anything's gone?

Flan   Calm down.

Ouisa   We could have been killed.

Flan   The silver Victorian inkwell.

Ouisa   How can you think of *things*? We could have been murdered.

An actor appears for a moment holding up an ornate Victorian inkwell capped by a silver beaver.

Flan   There's the inkwell. Silver beaver. Why?

Ouisa   Slashed – our throats slashed.

Another actor appears for a moment holding up a framed portrait of a dog, say, a pug.

Flan   And there's the watercolor. Our dog.

Ouisa   Go to bed at night happy and then murdered. Would we have woken up?

Flan   We're alive.

Ouisa   We called our kids.

Flan   No answer.

The phone rings. They clutch each other.

Ouisa   It's him!

Flan *goes to the phone.*

Ouisa   Don't pick it up!

Flan *does.* **Geoffrey** *appears.*

Geoffrey   Flanders, I'm at the airport. Look, I've been thinking. Those Japs really want the Cézanne. They'll pay. You can depend on me for an additional overcall of two-fifty.

Flan   Two hundred and fifty thousand?

Geoffrey   And I was thinking for South Africa. What about a Black American Film Festival? With this Spike Lee you have now and of course get Poitier down to be the president of the jury and I know Cosby and I love this Eddie Murphy and my wife went fishing in Norway with Diana Ross and her new Norwegian husband. And also they must have some *new* blacks –

Flan   Yes. It sounds a wonderful idea.

Geoffrey   I'll call him at the Sherry –

Flan   No! We'll call!

Geoffrey   They're calling my plane – And again last night –

Flan   No need to thank. See you shortly.

Geoffrey   The banks.

Flan   My lawyer.

Geoffrey   Exactly.

Flan   Safe trip.

Geoffrey *goes.*

Another couple in their forties, **Kitty** *and* **Larkin**, *appear.* **Ouisa** *and* **Flan** *take off their robes and are dressed for day.*

Ouisa   Do we have a story to tell you!

Kitty   Do we have a story to tell *you!*

Ouisa (*to us*)   Our two and their son are at Harvard together.

Kitty *and* **Larkin** *are pleased about this.*

Flan   Let me tell you our story.

Larkin   When did your story happen?

Flan   Last night. We are still zonked.

Kitty   We win. Our story happened Friday night. So we go first.

Larkin   We're going to be in the movies.

Kitty   We are going to be in the movie of *Cats*.

Ouisa *and* **Flan** *look at each other.*

Ouisa   You tell your story first.

Larkin   Friday night we were home, the doorbell rang –

Kitty   I am not impressed but it was the son of –

Ouisa *and* **Flan** (*to us*)   You got it.

Kitty   The kid was mugged. We had to go out. We left him. He was so charming. His father was taking the red eye. He couldn't get into the hotel till seven a.m. He stayed with us.

She is very pleased.

Larkin   In the middle of the night, we heard somebody screaming Burglar! Burglar! We came out in the hall. Paul is chasing this naked blond thief down the corridor. The blond thief runs out, the alarm goes off. The kid saved our lives.

Flan   That was no burglar.

Ouisa   You had another house guest.

Kitty *and* **Larkin** *laugh.*

Larkin   We feel so guilty. Paul could've been killed by that intruder. He was very understanding –

Ouisa   Was anything missing from your house?

Larkin   Nothing.

Flan   Did you give him money?

Kitty   Twenty-five dollars until his father arrived.

Flan (*to us*)   We told them our story.

Kitty *and* **Larkin**   Oh.

Ouisa   Have you talked to your kids?

Kitty   Can't get through.

Ouisa *makes a phone call.*

Ouisa   Sherry Netherlands. I'd like –

Larkin (*to us*)   She gave the name.

Kitty   Sidney Poitier must be registered.

The doorbell rings. **Flan** *goes.*

Ouisa   No! I'm not a fan. This is not a fan call. We know he's there. His son is a friend of –

Click. The Sherry's hung up.

Larkin   He must be there under another name.

Another phone call.

Ouisa   Hi. Celebrity Service? I'm not sure how you work.

Kitty   Greta Garbo used the name Harriet Brown.

Ouisa   You track down celebrities? Am I right?

Larkin   Everybody must have known she was Greta Garbo.

Ouisa   I'm trying to find out how one would get in touch with – No, I'm not a press agent – No, I'm not with anyone – My husband. Flanders Kittredge. (*Click.*) Celebrity Service doesn't give out information over the phone.

Larkin   Try the public library.

Kitty   Try *Who's Who.*

Flan *returns carrying an elaborate arrangement of flowers.* **Flan** *reads the card.*

Flan   'To thank you for a wonderful time. Paul Poitier.'

Flan *reaches into the bouquet. He takes out a pot of jam.*

Flan   A pot of jam?

Larkin   A pot of jam.

They back off as if it might explode.

Kitty   I think we should call the police.

A **Detective** *appears.*

Detective   What are the charges?

Ouisa   He came into our house.

Flan   He cooked us dinner.

Ouisa   He told us the story of *Catcher in the Rye.*

Flan   He said he was the son of Sidney Poitier.

Detective   Was he?

Ouisa   We don't know.

Flan   We gave him fifty dollars.

Kitty   We gave him twenty-five.

Larkin   Shhhh!

Ouisa   He picked up a hustler.

Flan   He left.

Kitty   He chased the burglar out of our house.

Ouisa   He didn't steal anything.

Larkin   We looked and looked.

Kitty   Top to bottom. Nothing gone.

The **Detective** *closes his notebook.*

Ouisa   Granted this does not seem major now.

Detective   Look. We're very busy.

Flan   You can't chuck us out.

Detective   Come up with charges. Then I'll do something.

The **Detective** *goes.*

Ouisa   (*to us*)   Our kids came down from Harvard.

Their children, **Woody** *and* **Tess**, *and* **Kitty** *and* **Larkin**'s *boy,*
Ben, *enter, groaning.*

Flan   – the details he knew – how would he know about
the painting? Although I think it's a very fine Kandinsky.

Ouisa   And none of you know this fellow? He has this
wild quality – yet a real elegance and a real concern and a
real consideration –

Tess   Well, Mom, you should have let him stay. You
should have divorced all your children and just let this
dreamboat stay. Plus he sent you flowers.

Flan   And jam.

The kids   Oooooo.

Ouisa   I wish I knew how to get hold of his father. Just
to see if there is any truth in it.

Larkin   Who knows Sidney Poitier so we could just call
him up and ask him?

Kitty (*eager*)   I have a friend who does theatrical law. I bet
he –

Larkin   What friend?

Kitty   Oh, it's nobody.

Larkin   I want to know.

Kitty (*screams*)   Nobody!

Larkin   Whatever's going on anywhere, I do not want to
know. I don't want to know. I don't want to know . . .

Kitty (*overlapping*)   Nobody. Nobody. Nobody . . .

Ben   Dad. Mom. Please. For once. Please?

Ben, **Kitty**, **Larkin** *go in anguish.*

Flan   Tess, when you see your little sister, don't tell her
that he and the, uh, hustler, used her bed.

Tess   You put him in that bed. I'm not going to get

involved with any conspiracy.

Flan   It's not a conspiracy. It's a *family*.

Tess *and* **Flan** *growl at each other.*

Darkness.

Ouisa, *alone, stretches out on the sofa.* **Paul** *appears wearing the pink shirt.*

Paul   The imagination. That's our out. Our imagination teaches us our limits and then how to grow beyond those limits. The imagination says Listen to me. I am your darkest voice. I am your 4 a.m. voice. I am the voice that wakes you up and says this is what I'm afraid of. Do not listen to me at your peril. The imagination is the noon voice that sees clearly and says yes, this is what I want for my life. It's there to sort out your nightmare, to show you the exit from the maze of your nightmare, to transform the nightmare into dreams that become your bedrock. If we don't listen to that voice, it dies. It shrivels. It vanishes.

Paul *takes out a switchblade and opens it.*

The imagination is not our escape. On the contrary, the imagination is the place we are all trying to get to.

Paul *lifts his shirt and stabs himself.* **Ouisa** *sits up and screams.* **Paul** *is gone. The phone rings. It's the* **Detective**.

Detective   I got a call that might interest you.

Dr Fine *appears, a very earnest professional man in his fifties.*

Dr Fine (*to us*)   I was seeing a patient. I'm an obstetrician at New York Hospital. The nurse opened my office door and said there's a friend of your son's here . . .

Paul *appears.*

Dr Fine (*to us*)   I treated the kid. He was more scared than hurt. A knife wound, a few bruises.

Paul   I don't know how to thank you, sir. My father is coming here.

The four parents appear.

Flan *and* **Ouisa** *and* **Kitty** *and* **Larkin**   He's making a
film of *Cats*.

Dr Fine   And he told me the name of a matinee idol of
my youth. Somebody who had really forged ahead and
made new paths for blacks just by the strength of his own
talent. Strangely, I had identified with him before I started
medical school. I mean, I'm a Jew. My grandparents were
killed in the war. I had this sense of self-hatred, of fear.
And this kid's father – the bravery of his films – had given
me a direction, a confidence. Simple as that. We're always
paying off debts.

Then my beeper went off. A patient in her tenth month of
labor. Her water finally broke. I gave him the keys.

Paul *catches the keys.*

Paul   Doug told me all about your brownstone. How you
got it at a great price because there had been a murder in
it and for a while people thought it had a curse but you
were a scientific man and were courageous!

Dr Fine   Well, yes! Courageous! I ran off to the delivery
room. Twins! Two boys. I thought of my son. I dialed my
boy at Dartmouth. Amazingly, he was in his room. Doing
what I hate to ask.

Doug, *twenty, appears.*

Dr Fine   So you accuse me of having no interest in your
life, not doing for friends, being a rotten father. Well, you
should be very happy.

Doug   The son of who? Dad, I never heard of him. Dad,
as usual, you are a real cretin. You gave him the keys?
You gave a complete stranger who happens to mention my
name the keys to our house? Dad, sometimes it is so
obvious to me why Mom left. I am so embarrassed to
know you. You gave the keys to a stranger who shows up
at your office? Mother told me you beat her! Mom told me
you were a rotten lover and drank so much your body

smelled of cheap white wine. Mom said sleeping with you was like sleeping with a salad made of bad dressing. Why you had to bring me into the world!

Dr Fine   There are two sides to every story –

Doug   You're an idiot! You're an idiot!

Doug *goes into the dark, screaming.*

Dr Fine   I went home – courageously – with a policeman.

A **Policeman** *accompanies* **Dr Fine**. **Paul** *appears wearing a silk robe, carrying a snifter of brandy.*

Dr Fine   Arrest him!

Paul   Pardon?

Dr Fine   Breaking and entering.

Paul   Breaking and entering?

Dr Fine   You're an imposter.

Paul   Officer, your honor, your eminence, Dr Fine *gave* me the keys to his brownstone. Isn't that so?

Dr Fine   My son doesn't know you.

Paul   This man gave me the keys to the house. Isn't that so?

Policeman *(screams)*   Did you give him the key to the house?

Dr Fine   Yes! But under false pretenses. This fucking black kid crack addict came into my office lying –

Paul   I have taken this much brandy but can pour the rest back into the bottle. And I've used electricity listening to the music, but I think you'll find that nothing's taken from the house.

Paul *goes.*

Dr Fine   I want you to arrest this fraud.

The **Policeman** *walks away.*

Doug *returns.*

Doug   A cretin. A creep! No wonder mother left you!

Doug *goes.*

Pause.

Dr Fine   Two sides. Every story.

Ouisa *holds up a book.*

Ouisa   I went down to the Strand. I got Sidney Poitier's autobiography. (*Reads:*) 'Back in New York with Juanita and the children, I began to become aware that our marriage, while working on some levels, was falling apart in other fundamental areas.'

Flan   There's a picture of him and his four -- daughters. No sons. Four daughters. The book's called *This Life.*

Dr Fine   Published by Knopf.

Kitty   1980.

Larkin   Out of print.

Kitty   Oh dear.

Ouisa   This kid bulldozing his way into our lives.

Larkin   We let him in our lives. I run a foundation. You're a dealer. You're a doctor. You'd think we'd be satisfied with our achievements.

Flan   Agatha Christie would ask, what do we all have in common?

Ouisa   It seems the common thread linking us all is an overwhelming need to be in the movie of *Cats.*

Kitty   Our kids. Struggling through their lives.

Larkin   I don't want to know anything about the spillover of their lives.

Ouisa   All we have in common is our children went to

boarding school together.

Flan (to **Dr Fine**)   How come we never met?

Dr Fine   His mother had custody. I lived out West. After he graduated from high school, she moved West. I moved East.

Larkin   I think we should drop it right here.

Kitty   Are you afraid Ben is mixed up in this fraud?

Larkin   I don't want to know too much about my kid.

Kitty   You think Ben is hiding things from us? I tell you, I'm getting to the bottom of this. My son has no involvements with any black frauds. Doctor, you said something about crack?

Larkin   I don't want to know.

Dr Fine   It just leaped out of my mouth. No proof. Oh dear God, no proof.

Flan   We'll take a vote. Do we pursue this to the end no matter what we find out about our kids?

Ouisa   I vote yes.

Dr Fine   I trust Doug. Yes.

Larkin   No.

Kitty   Yes.

Flan   Yes.

Kitty *looks through the Poitier autobiography.*

Kitty   Listen to the last page. '. . . making it better for our children. Protecting them. From what? The truth is what we were protecting those little people from . . . there is a lot to worry about and I'd better start telling the little bastards – start worrying!' The end.

Kitty *closes the book in dismay. All the children,* **Tess**, **Woody**, **Ben**, **Doug**, *enter, groaning.*

Flan It's obvious. It's somebody you went to high school with, since you each go to different colleges.

Ouisa He knows the details about our lives.

Flan Who in your high school, part of your gang, has become homosexual or is deep into drugs?

Tess That's like, about fifteen people.

Larkin I don't want to know.

Tess I find it really insulting that you would assume that it has to be a guy. This movie star's son could have had a relationship with a girl in high school –

Ben That's your problem in a nutshell. You're so limited.

Tess That's why I'm going to Afghanistan. To climb mountains.

Ouisa You are not climbing mountains.

Flan We have not invested all this money in you to scale the face of K-2.

Tess Is that all I am? An investment?

Ouisa All right. Track down everybody in your high school class. Male. Female. Whatever. Not just homosexuals. Drug addicts. The kid might be a drug dealer.

Doug Why do you look at me when you say that? Do you think I'm an addict? A drug pusher? I really resent the accusations.

Dr Fine No one is accusing you of anything.

Larkin I don't want to know. I don't want to know. I don't want to know.

Flan Nobody is accusing anyone of anything. I'm asking you to go on a detective search and find out from your high school class if anyone has met a black kid pretending to be a movie star's son.

Ben   He promised you parts in *Cats*?

Ouisa   It wasn't just that. It was fun.

Tess   You went to *Cats*. You said it was an all-time low in a lifetime of theater-going.

Ouisa   Film is a different medium.

Tess   You said Aeschylus did not invent theater to have it end up a bunch of chorus kids wondering which of them will go to Kitty Kat Heaven.

Ouisa   I don't remember saying that.

Flan   No, I think that was *Starlight Express* –

Tess   Well, maybe he'll make a movie of *Starlight Express* and you can all be on roller skates –

Doug   This is so humiliating.

Ben   This is so pathetic.

Tess   This is so racist.

Ouisa   This is *not* racist!

Doug   How can I get in touch with anybody in high school? I've outgrown them.

Kitty   How can you outgrow them? You graduated a year ago!

Ouisa   Here is a copy of your yearbook. I want you to get the phone numbers of everybody in your class. You all went to the same boarding school. You can phone from here.

Dr Fine   You can charge it to my phone.

Ouisa   Call everyone in your class and ask them if they know –

Doug   Never!

Tess   This is the KGB.

Dr Fine   You're on the phone all the time. Now I ask

you to make calls all over the country and you become reticent.

Tess   This is the entire McCarthy period.

Woody   I just want to get one thing straight.

Flan   Finally, we hear from the peanut gallery

Woody   You gave him my pink shirt? You gave a complete stranger my pink shirt? That pink shirt was a Christmas present from *you*. I treasured that shirt. I loved that shirt. My collar size has grown a full size from weight lifting. And you saw my arms had grown, you saw my neck had grown. And you bought me that shirt for my new body. I loved that shirt. The first shirt for my new body. And you gave that shirt away. I can't believe it. I hate it here. I hate this house. I hate you.

Doug   You never do anything for me.

Tess   You've never done anything but tried to block me.

Ben   I'm only this pathetic extension of your eighth-rate personality.

Doug   Social Darwinism pushed beyond all limits.

Woody   You gave away my pink shirt?

Tess   You want me to be everything you weren't.

Doug   You said drugs and looked at me.

The parents leave, speechless, defeated. The kids look through their high school yearbook. **Tess** *spots a face.*

Tess   Trent Conway.

All the kids   Trent Conway.

Trent Conway *appears.*

Tess   Trent Conway. Look at those beady eyes staring out at me. Trent Conway. He's at MIT.

(*To us.*) So I went to MIT. He was there in his computer room and I just pressed him and pressed him and pressed him. I had a tape recorder strapped to me.

Darkness.

Trent's voice taped Yes, I knew Paul.

Tess's voice taped But what happened between you?

Trent's voice taped It was ... It was ...

The lights come up slowly. **Paul** *and* **Trent** *appear. Rain. Distant thunder. Jazz playing somewhere off.* **Paul** *is dressed in jeans and a tank top, high-top sneakers.*

Trent This is the way you must speak. Hear my accent. Hear my voice. Never say you're going horse-back riding. You say you're going riding. And don't say couch. Say sofa. And you say *bodd*-ill. It's bottle. Say bottle of beer.

Paul Bodd-ill a bee-ya.

Trent Bottle of beer.

Paul *sits on the sofa. He pulls out a thick address book from under him.*

Paul What's this?

Trent My address book.

Paul All these names. Addresses. Tell me about these people.

Trent *sits beside him.*

Trent I want you to come to bed with me.

Paul (*fierce*) Tell me about these people, man!

Trent I just want to look at you. Sorry.

Paul *is hypnotized by the address book.*

Paul Are these all rich people?

Trent No. Hand-to-mouth on a higher plateau.

Paul I think it must be very hard to be with rich people. You have to have money. You have to give them presents.

Trent   Not at all. Rich people do something nice for you, you give them a pot of jam.

Paul   That's what pots of jam are for?

Trent   Orange. Grapefruit. Strawberry. But fancy. They have entire stores filled with fancy pots of jam wrapped in cloth. English. Or French.

Paul   I'll tell you what I'll do. I pick a name. You tell me about them. Where they live. Secrets. And for each name you get a piece of clothing.

Trent   All right.

Paul   Kittredge. Talbot and Woodrow.

Trent   Talbot, called Tess, was anorexic and was in a hospital for a while.

Paul *takes off a shoe and kicks it to* **Trent**.

Paul   Their parents.

Trent   Ouisa and Flan, for Flanders, Kittredge. Rhode Island, I believe. Newport, but not along the ocean. The street behind the ocean. He's an art dealer. They have a Kandinsky.

Paul   A Kan–what–ski?

Trent   Kandinsky. A double-sided Kandinsky.

Paul *kicks off his other shoe.* **Trent** *catches it joyously.*

Trent   I feel like Scheherazade!

He embraces **Paul** *with fierce tenderness.*

I don't want you to leave me, Paul. I'll go through my address book and tell you about family after family. You'll never not fit in again. We'll give you a new identity. I'll make you the most eagerly sought-after young man in the East. And then I'll come into one of these homes one day – and you'll be there and I'll be presented to you. And I'll pretend to meet you for the first time and our friendship will be witnessed by my friends, our parents' friends. If it all happens under their noses, they can't judge me. They can't disparage you. I'll make you a guest in their houses. Ask me another name. I'd like to try for the shirt.

Paul *kisses* **Trent**.

Paul   That's enough for today.

Paul *takes his shoes and the address book and goes.*

Trent *turns to* **Tess**.

Trent   Paul stayed with me for three months. We went through the address book letter by letter. Paul vanished by the L's. He took the address book with him. Well, he's already been in all your houses. Maybe I will meet him again. I sure would like to.

Tess   His past? His real name?

Trent   I don't know anything about him. It was a rainy night in Boston. He was in a doorway. That's all.

Tess   He took stuff from you?

Trent   Besides the address book? He took my stereo and sport jacket and my word processor and my laser printer. And my skis. And my TV.

Tess   Will you press charges?

Trent   No.

Tess   It's a felony.

Trent   Why do they want to find him?

Tess   They say to help him. If there's a crime, the cops will get involved.

Trent   Look, we must keep in touch. We were friends for a brief bit in school. I mean we were really good friends.

Tess   Won't you press charges?

Trent   Please.

They go. **Ouisa** *appears.*

Ouisa (*to us*)   Tess played me the tapes.

Tess's voice taped   Won't you press charges?

Trent's voice taped   Please.

Ouisa (*to us*)   Can you believe it? Paul learned all that in three months. Three months! Who would have thought it? Trent Conway, the Henry Higgins of our time. Paul looked at those names and said I am Columbus. I am Magellan. I will sail into this new world.

I read somewhere that everybody on this planet is separated by only six other people. Six degrees of separation. Between us and everybody else on this planet. The president of the United States. A gondolier in Venice. Fill in the names. I find that A) tremendously comforting that we're so close and B) like Chinese water torture that we're so close. Because you have to find the right six people to make the connection. It's not just big names. It's *anyone*. A native in a rain forest. A Tierra del Fuegan. An Eskimo. I am bound to everyone on this planet by a trail of six people. It's a profound thought. How Paul found us. How to find the man whose son he pretends to be. Or perhaps *is* his son, although I doubt it. How every person is a new door, opening up into other worlds. Six degrees of separation between me and everyone else on this planet. But to find the right six people.

Flan *appears.*

Flan (*to us*)   We didn't hear for a while. We went about our lives.

The **Doorman** *appears.*

Ouisa (*to us*)   And then one day our doorman, whom we tip very well at Christmas and any time he does something nice for us – our doorman spit at my husband, J. Flanders Kittredge. I mean, spit at him.

The **Doorman** *spits at* **Flan**.

Doorman   Your son! I know all about your son.

Flan   What about my son?

Doorman   Not the little shit who lives here. The other son. The secret son. The Negro son you deny.

The **Doorman** *spits at* **Flan** *again.*

Flan   The Negro son?

Doorman   The black son you make live in Central Park.

Ouisa (*to us*)   The next chapter. Rick and Elizabeth and Paul sit on the grass in Central Park.

Rick, **Elizabeth** *and* **Paul** *run on laughing in Central Park.* **Rick**, *a nice young guy in his mid-twenties, plays the guitar energetically. He and* **Paul** *and* **Elizabeth**, *a beautiful girl in her mid-twenties, are having a great time singing a cheery song, say James Taylor's 'Shower The People', until* **Rick** *hits the wrong chord. They try to break down the harmony.* **Rick** *can't for the life of him find the right chord. The three of them laugh.* **Paul** *is wearing the pink shirt.*

Paul   Tell me about yourselves.

Rick   We're here from Utah.

Paul   Do they have any black people in Utah?

Rick   Maybe two. Yes, the Mormons brought in two.

Elizabeth   We came to be actors.

Rick   She won the all-state competition for comedy and drama.

Paul   My gosh!

Elizabeth
   'The quality of mercy is not strained.
   It droppeth like the gentle rain from heaven.'

Rick   And we study and we wait tables.

Elizabeth   Because you have to have technique.

Paul   Like the painters. Cézanne looked for the rules behind the spontaneity of Impressionism.

Rick   Céz – That's a painter?

Elizabeth   We don't know anything about painting.

Paul   My dad loves painting. He has a Kandinsky but he loves Cézanne the most. He lives up there.

Rick   What?

Paul   He lives up there. Count six windows over. John Flanders Kittredge. His chums call him Flan. I was the child of Flan's hippie days. His radical days. He went down South as a freedom marcher, to register black voters – his friends were killed. Met my mother. Registered her and married her in a fit of sentimental righteousness and knocked her up with me and came back here and abandoned her. Went to Harvard. He's now a fancy art dealer. Lives up there. Count six windows over. Won't see me. The new wife – the white wife – The Louisa Kittredge Call Me Ouisa Wife – the mother of the new children wife –

Rick   Your brothers and sisters?

Paul   (*bitter*)   They go to Andover and Exeter and Harvard and Yale. The awful thing is my father started out good. My mother says there is a good man inside J. Flanders Kittredge.

Elizabeth   He'll see you if he was that good. He can't forget you entirely.

Paul   I call him. He hangs up.

Rick   Go to his office –

Paul   He doesn't have an office. He works out of there. They won't even let me in the elevator.

Rick   Dress up as a messenger.

Elizabeth   Say you have a masterpiece for him. 'I got the Mona Lisa waitin' out in the truck.'

Paul   I don't want to embarrass him. Look, this is so fucking tacky. (*Pause.*) You love each other?

Elizabeth   A lot.

Rick *and* **Elizabeth** *touch each other's hands.*

Paul   I hope we can meet again.

Paul *turns to go.*

Rick   Where do you live?

Paul   Live? I'm home.

Elizabeth   You're not out on the streets?

Paul   You're such assholes. Where would I live?

Rick   Stay with us.

Elizabeth   We just have a railroad flat in a tenement –

Rick   It's over a roller disco. The last of the roller discos but it's quiet by five a.m. and a great narrow space –

Elizabeth   A railroad loft and we could give you a corner. The tub's in the kitchen but there's light in the morning –

Rick (*to us*)   And he did!

The light changes to the loft.

Paul   This is the way you must speak. Hear my accent. Hear my voice. Never say you're going horse-back riding. You say you're going riding. And don't say couch. Say sofa. And you say bodd-ill. It's bottle. Say bottle of beer.

Rick   Bodd-ill a bee-ya.

Paul   Bottle of beer. And never be afraid of rich people. You know what they love? A fancy pot of jam. That's all. Get yourself a patron. That's what you need. You shouldn't be waiting tables. You're going to wake up one day and the temporary job you picked up to stay alive is going to be your full-time life.

Elizabeth *embraces* **Paul** *gratefully.*

Paul   You've given me courage. I'm going to try and see him right now.

Paul *goes.* **Rick** *and* **Elizabeth** *lay on their backs and dream.*

Rick   I'll tell you all the parts I want to do. Vanya in *Uncle Vanya.*

Elizabeth   Masha in *Three Sisters.* No, Irina first. The young one who yearns for love. Then Masha who loves. Then the oldest one, Olga, who never knows love.

Rick   I'd like a shot at Laertes. I think it's a much better part.

Elizabeth *gazes in the mirror.*

Elizabeth   Do you think it'll hurt me?

Rick   What'll hurt you?

Elizabeth   My resemblance to Liv Ullmann.

Paul *runs in.*

Paul   HE WROTE ME! I WROTE HIM AND HE WROTE ME BACK!!! He's going to give me a thousand dollars! And that's just for starters! He sold a Cézanne to the Japanese and made millions and he can give me money without her knowing it.

Elizabeth   I knew it!

Paul   I'm moving out of here!

Elizabeth   You can't!

Rick   No!

Paul   But I am going to give you the money to put on a showcase of any play you want and you'll be in it and agents will come see you and you'll be seen and you'll be started. And when you win your Oscars – both of you – you'll look in the camera and thank me –

Elizabeth   I want to thank Paul Kittredge.

Rick   Thanks, Paul!

Paul   One hitch. I'm going to meet him in Maine. He's up there visiting his parents in Dark Harbor. My grandparents whom I've never met. He's finally going to tell my grandparents about me. He's going to make up for lost time. He's going to give me money. I can go back home. Get my momma that beauty parlor she's wanted all her life. One problem. How am I going to get to Maine? The wife checks all the bills. He has to account for the money. She handles the purse strings. Where the hell am I going to get two hundred and fifty dollars to get to Maine?

Elizabeth   How long would you need it for?

Paul   I'll be gone a week. But I could wire it back to you.

Rick (*quiet*)   We could lend it to him for a week.

Elizabeth (*quiet*)   We can't. If something happens –

Rick (*quiet*)   You're like his stepmother. These women holding on to all the purse strings.

Elizabeth   No. We worked too hard to save that. I'm sorry. I'll meet you both after work. If your father loves you, he'll get you the ticket up there.

She goes.

Rick (*to us*)   We stopped by the bank. I withdrew the money. He took it.

Paul   Let's celebrate!

Elizabeth *appears.*

Elizabeth (*to us*)   I went to a money machine to get twenty dollars and I couldn't get anything. The machine devoured my card. I called up the emergency number and the voice said my account was closed. They had withdrawn all the money and closed the account. I went to that apartment on Fifth Avenue. I told the doorman: I want my money. I work tables. I work hard. I saved. I'm here trying to get to meet people. I am stranded. Who do I know to go to? 'The quality of mercy is not strained'? Fuck you, quality of mercy.

She goes. **Rick** *appears.*

Rick (*to us*)   He told me he had some of his own money and he wanted to treat me. We went to a store that rented tuxedos and we dressed to the nines. We went to the Rainbow Room. We danced. High over New York City. I swear. He stood up and held out my chair and we danced and there was a stir. Nothing like this ever happened in Utah. And we danced. And I'll tell you nothing like that must have ever happened at the Rainbow Room because we were asked to leave. I tell you. It was so funny.

And we walked out and walked home and I knew Elizabeth was waiting for me and I would have to explain about the money and calm her down because we'll get it back but I forgot because we took a carriage ride in the park and he asked me if he could fuck me and I had never done anything like that and he did and it was fantastic. It was the greatest night I ever had and before we got home he kissed me on the mouth and he vanished.

Later I realized he had no money of his own. He had spent my money – our money – on that night at the Rainbow Room.

How am I going to face Elizabeth? What have I done? What did I let him do to me? I wanted experience. I came here to have experience. But I didn't come here to do this or lose that or be this or do this to Elizabeth. I didn't come here to be *this*. My father said I was a fool and I can't have him be right. What have I done?

He goes into the dark. **Larkin** *and* **Kitty** *appear.*

Larkin   Kitty and I were at a roller disco two clients opened.

Kitty   And it was Valentine's Day

Larkin   and we came out and we saw a body on the street.

Kitty My legs were still shaky from the roller skating which I have not done in I hate to tell you how many years and we knew the body had just landed there in that clump

Larkin because the blood seeping out had not reached the gutter yet.

Kitty You could see the blood just oozing out slowly towards the curb.

Larkin The boy had jumped from above.

Kitty The next day we walked through the park by Gracie Mansion

Larkin and it was cold and we saw police putting a jacket on a man sitting on a bench.

Kitty Only we got closer and it wasn't a sweater.

Larkin It was a body bag. A homeless person had frozen during the night.

Kitty Was it that cold?

Larkin Sometimes there are periods where you see death everywhere.

Darkness. **Ouisa** *and* **Flan** *appear in their robes with the* **Detective** *and* **Elizabeth**.

Detective This young girl came forward with the story. She told me the black kid was your son, lived here. It all seemed to come into place. What I'm saying is she'll press charges.

Elizabeth I want him dead. He took all our money. He took my life. Rick's dead! You bet your life I'll press charges.

Ouisa We haven't seen him since that night.

Detective Find him. We have a case.

Flan I'll release it to the papers. I have friends. I can call the *Times*.

Ouisa (*to us*)   Which is what happened.

Flan (*to us*)   The paper of note – the *Times* – ran a story on so-called smart, sophisticated, tough New Yorkers being boondoggled by a confidence man now wanted by the police. Who says New Yorkers don't have a heart? They promised it would either run in the Living section or the Home section.

Kitty (*to us*)   The story ran.

Dr Fine (*to us*)   In the B section front page.

Detective (*to us*)   Smart New Yorkers.

Larkin (*to us*)   We never heard from Sidney Poitier.

Ouisa (*to us*)   Six degrees. Six degrees.

They all go except for **Ouisa** *and* **Flan**, *who pull off their robes. They are dressing for the evening. Evening gown. Black tie.*

Ouisa (*to us*)   We are bidding tonight on an Henri Matisse.

Flan (*to us*)   We will go as high as –

Ouisa   Don't tell all the family secrets –

Flan (*to us*)   Well over twenty-five million.

Ouisa (*to us*)   Out of which he will keep –

Flan (*to us*)   I'll have to give most of it away, but the good part is it gives me a credibility in this new market. I mean, a David fucking Hockney print sold for a hundred bucks fifteen years ago went for thirty-four thousand dollars! A print! A flower. You know Geoffrey. Our South African –

Ouisa (*to us*)   – it's a black-tie auction – Sotheby's –

Flan   I know we'll get it.

Ouisa (*noting the time*)   Flan –

Flan   I know the Matisse will be mine – for a few hours. Then off to Tokyo. Or Saudi.

Flan *leaves as* **Ouisa** *phones* **Tess**.

Ouisa (*to* **Tess**) I'm totally dolled up. The black. Have you seen it? I have to tell you the sign I saw today. Cruelty-free cosmetics. A store was selling cruelty-free cosmetics.

Tess Mother, that is such a beautiful thing. Do you realize the agony cosmetic companies put rabbits through to test eye shadow?

Ouisa Dearest, I know that. I'm only talking about the phrase. Cruelty-free cosmetics should take away all evidence of time and cellulite and –

Tess Mother, I'm getting married.

Ouisa I thought you were going to Afghanistan.

Tess I am going to get married and then go to Afghanistan.

Ouisa One country at a time. You are not getting married.

Tess Immediately so deeply negative –

Ouisa I know everyone you know and you are not marrying any of them.

Tess The arrogance that you would assume you know everyone I know. The way you say it: I know everyone you know –

Ouisa Unless you met them in the last two days – you can't hold a secret.

The other line rings.

Wait – I'm putting you on hold –

Tess No one ever calls on that number.

Ouisa Wait. Hold on.

Tess Mother!

Ouisa Hello?

Paul *appears, frightened.*

Paul   Hello.

Ouisa   Paul?

Paul   I saw the story in the paper. I didn't know the boy killed himself. He gave me the money.

Ouisa   Let me put you on hold. I'm talking to my child --

Paul   If you put me on hold, I'll be gone and you'll never hear from me again.

Ouisa *pauses.* **Tess** *fades into black.*

Ouisa   You have to turn yourself in. The boy committed suicide. You stole the money. The girl is pressing charges. They're going to get you. Why not turn yourself in and you can get off easier. You can strike a bargain. Learn when you're trapped. You're so brilliant. You have such promise. You need help.

Paul   Would you help me?

Ouisa   What would you want me to do?

Paul   Stay with you.

Ouisa   That's impossible.

Paul   Why?

Ouisa   My husband feels you betrayed him.

Paul   Do you?

Ouisa   You were lunatic! And picking that drek off the street. Are you suicidal? Do you have AIDS? Are you infected?

Paul   I do not have it. It's a miracle. But I don't. Do you feel I betrayed you? If you do, I'll hang up and never bother you again --

Ouisa   Where have you been?

Paul   Traveling.

Ouisa You're not in trouble? I mean, more trouble?

Paul No, I only visited you. I didn't like the first people so much. They went out and just left me alone. I didn't like the doctor. He was too eager to please. And he left me alone. But you. You and your husband. We all stayed together.

Ouisa What did you want from us?

Paul Everlasting friendship.

Ouisa Nobody has that.

Paul You do.

Ouisa What do you think we are?

Paul You're going to tell me secrets? You're not what you appear to be? You have no secrets. Trent Conway told me what your kids have told him over the years.

Ouisa What have the kids told him about us?

Paul I don't tell that. I save that for blackmail.

Ouisa Then perhaps I'd better hang up.

Paul (*panic*) No! I went to a museum! I liked Toulouse-Lautrec!

Ouisa As well you should.

Paul I read *The Andy Warhol Diaries*.

Ouisa Ahh, you've become an aesthete.

Paul Are you laughing at me?

Ouisa No. I read them too.

Paul I read *The Agony and the Ecstasy*, by Irving Stone, about Michelangelo painting the Sistine Chapel.

Ouisa You're ahead of me there.

Paul Have you seen the Sistine Chapel?

Ouisa Oh yes. Even gone to the top of it in a rickety

elevator to watch the men clean it.

Paul You've been to the top of the Sistine Chapel?

Ouisa Absolutely. Stood right under the hand of God touching the hand of man. The workman said 'Hit it. Hit it. It's only a fresco.' I did. I slapped God's hand.

Paul You did?

Ouisa And you know what they clean it with? All this technology. Q-tips and water.

Paul No!

Ouisa Clean away the years of grime and soot and paint-overs. Q-tips and water changing the history of Western Art. Vivid colors.

Paul Take me to see it?

Ouisa Take you to see it? Paul, they think you might have murdered someone! You stole money!

Flan *appears, needing help with his studs.*

Flan Honey, could you give me a hand with –

Ouisa (*mouths to* **Flan**) It's Paul.

Flan *goes to the other phone.*

Flan I'll call that detective.

The other line rings. **Tess** *appears.*

Tess Dad! We were cut off. I'm getting marr –

Flan Darling, could you call back –

Tess I'm getting married and going to Afghanistan –

Flan We cannot talk about this now –

Tess I'm going to ruin my life and get married and throw away everything you want me to be because it's the only way to hurt you!

Tess *goes. The* **Detective** *appears.*

Flan   I've got that kid on the line.

Detective   Find out where he is.

The **Detective** *goes.*

Flan (*mouths to* **Ouisa**)   Find out where he is???

Paul   Who's there?

Ouisa   Look, why don't you come here. Where are you?

Paul   I come there and you'll have the cops waiting.

Ouisa   You have to trust us.

Paul   Why?

Ouisa   Because – we like you.

Flan (*mouths*)   Where is he?

Paul   Who's there?

Ouisa   It's –

Flan   I'm not here.

Ouisa   It's Flan.

Paul   Are you in tonight? I could come and make a feast for you.

Ouisa   We're going out now. But you could be here when we come back.

Flan   Are you nuts! Tell a crook we're going out. The house is empty.

Paul   Where are you going?

Ouisa   To Sotheby's.

Flan *grabs the phone.*

Flan   The key's under the mat!

Paul   Hi! Can I come to Sotheby's?

Flan *hands the phone back to* **Ouisa**.

Ouisa   Hi.

Paul   I said hi to Flan.

Ouisa   Paul says hi.

Flan   Hi.

Ouisa   Sotheby's.

Paul   That's wonderful! I'll come!

Ouisa   You can't.

Paul   Why? I was helpful last time –

Flan   Thank him – he was very help –

Ouisa *hands* **Flan** *the phone.*

Flan   Paul? You were helpful getting me this contract –

Paul   Really! I was thinking maybe that's what I should do is what you do – in art but making money out of art and meeting people and not working in an office –

Flan   You only see the glam side of it. There's a whole grotty side that –

Paul   I could learn the grotty –

Flan   You have to have art history. You have to have language. You have to have economics –

Paul   I'm fast. I could do it. Do your kids want to –

Flan   No, it's not really a profession you hand down from generation to gen – what the hell am I talking career counselling to you! You embarrassed me in my building! You stole money. There is a warrant out for your arrest!

Ouisa *wrests the phone away.*

Ouisa   Don't hang up! PAUL? Are you there? PAUL? (*To* **Flan**.) You made him hang up –

Paul   I'm here.

Ouisa   You are! Who are you? What's your real name?

Paul If you let me stay with you, I'll tell you. That night was the happiest night I ever had.

Ouisa (*to* **Flan**) It was the happiest night he ever had.

Flan Oh please. I'm not a bullshitter but never bullshit a bullshitter.

Flan *goes.*

Ouisa Why?

Paul You let me use all the parts of myself that night –

Ouisa It was magical. That Salinger stuff –

Paul Graduation speech at Groton two years ago.

Ouisa Your cooking –

Paul Other people's recipes. Did you see Donald Barthelme's obituary? He said collage was the art form of the twentieth century.

Ouisa Everything is somebody else's.

Paul Not your children. Not your life.

Ouisa Yes. You got me there. That is mine. It is no one else's.

Paul You don't sound happy.

Ouisa There's so much you don't know. You are so smart and so stupid –

Paul (*furious*) Never say I'm stupid –

Ouisa Have some flexibility. You're stupid not to recognize what you could be.

Paul What could I be?

Ouisa So much.

Paul With you behind me?

Ouisa Perhaps. You liked that night? I've thought since that you spent all your time laughing at us.

Paul No.

Ouisa That you had brought that awful hustling thing back to show us your contempt –

Paul I was so happy. I wanted to add sex to it. Don't you do that?

Pause.

Ouisa No.

Paul I'll tell you my name.

Ouisa Please?

Paul It's Paul Poitier-Kittredge. It's a hyphenated name.

Pause.

Ouisa Paul, you need help. Go to the police. Turn yourself in. You'll be over it all the sooner. You can start.

Paul Start what?

Ouisa Your life.

Paul Will you help me?

Ouisa *pauses, and makes a decision.*

Ouisa I will help you. But you have to go to the police and go to jail and –

Paul Will you send me books and polaroids of you and cassettes? And letters?

Ouisa Yes.

Paul Will you visit me?

Ouisa I will visit you.

Paul And when you do, you'll wear your best clothes and knock em dead?

Ouisa I'll knock em dead. But you've got to be careful in prison. You have to use condoms.

Paul I won't have sex in prison. I only have sex when

I'm happy.

Ouisa   Go to the police.

Paul   Will you take me?

Ouisa   I'll give you the name of the detective to see –

Paul   I'll be treated with care if you take me to the police. If they don't know you're special, they kill you.

Ouisa   I don't think they kill you.

Paul   Mrs Louisa Kittredge, I am black.

Ouisa   I will deliver you to them with kindness and affection.

Paul   And I'll plead guilty and go to prison and serve a few months.

Ouisa   A few months tops.

Paul   Then I'll come out and work for you and learn –

Ouisa   We'll work that out.

Paul   I want to know now.

Ouisa   Yes. You'll work for us.

Paul   Learn all the trade. Not just the grotty part.

Ouisa   Top to bottom.

Paul   And live with you.

Ouisa   No.

Paul   Your kids are away.

Ouisa   You should have your own place.

Paul   You'll help me find a place?

Ouisa   We'll help you find a place.

Paul   I have no furniture.

Ouisa   We'll help you out.

Paul I made a list of things I liked in the museum. Philadelphia Chippendale.

Ouisa (*bursts out laughing*)   Believe it or not, we have two Philadelphia Chippendale chairs.

Paul I'd rather have one nice piece than a room full of junk.

Ouisa Quality. Always. You'll have all that. Philadelphia Chippendale.

Paul All I have to do is go to the police.

Ouisa Make it all history. Put it behind you.

Paul Tonight.

Ouisa It can't be tonight. I will take you tomorrow. We have an auction tonight at Sotheby's –

Paul Bring me?

Ouisa I can't. It's black tie.

Paul I have black tie from a time I went to the Rainbow Room. Have you ever been to the Rainbow Room?

Ouisa Yes.

Paul What time do you have to be there?

Ouisa Eight o'clock.

Paul It's five-thirty now. You could come get me now and take me to the police tonight and then go to Sotheby's –

Ouisa We're going to drinks before at the Pierre.

Paul Japanese?

Ouisa Germans.

Paul You're just like my father.

Ouisa Which father?

Paul Sidney!

Pause.

Ouisa   Paul. He's not your father. And Flanders is not your father.

Flan *comes in, dressed.*

Flan   Oh fuck. We have drinks with the Japanese at six-fifteen – Get off that fucking phone. Is it that kid? Get him out of our life! Get off that phone or I'll rip it out of the wall!

Ouisa *looks at* **Flan**.

Ouisa (*to* **Paul**)   Paul, I made a mistake. It is not the Germans. We will come right now and get you. Where are you? Tell me? I'll take you to the police. They will treat you with dignity.

Paul   I'm in the lobby of the Waverly movie theater on Sixth Avenue and Third Street.

Ouisa   We'll be there in half an hour.

Paul   I'll give you fifteen minutes' grace time.

Ouisa   We'll be there. Paul. We love you.

Paul   Ouisa. I love you. Ouisa Kittredge. Hey? Bring a pink shirt.

Ouisa   We'll have a wonderful life.

She hangs up. **Paul** *goes into the dark.*

We can skip the shmoozing. Pick the boy up, take him to the police and be at Sotheby's before eight.

The **Detective** *appears.*

Flan   He's at the Waverly Theater. Sixth Avenue and Third Street. The lobby.

Ouisa   We promised we would bring him to you. He's special. Remember that he's special. Honor our promise.

The **Detective** *nods and goes.*

Ouisa (*to us*)   We go. Traffic on the FDR.

Flan (*to us*)   We get there. I run into the theater. No one.

Ouisa   A young man. Black. Have you seen him?

Flan (*to us*)   The girl in the box office said the police were there, had arrested a young man. Dragged him kicking, screaming into a squad car. He was a kid waiting for his family. We could never get through or find out.

Ouisa (*to us*)   We weren't family.

Flan (*to us*)   That detective was transferred.

Ouisa (*to us*)   And we didn't know Paul's name.

We called the precinct.
Another precinct had made the arrest.
Why? Were there other charges?
We couldn't find out.

We weren't family.
We didn't know Paul's name.

We called the District Attorney's office.
We weren't family.
We didn't know Paul's name.

I called the Criminal Courts.
I wasn't family.
I didn't know Paul's name.

Flan   Why does it mean so much to you?

Ouisa   He wanted to be us. Everything we are in the world, this paltry thing – our life – he wanted it. He stabbed himself to get in here. He envied us. We're not enough to be envied.

Flan   Like the papers said. We have hearts.

Ouisa   Having a heart is not the point. We were hardly taken in. We believed him – for a few hours. He did more for us in a few hours than our children ever did. He wanted to be your child. Don't let that go. He sat out in that park and said that man is my father. He's in trouble and we don't know how to help him.

Flan   Help him? He could've killed me. And you.

Ouisa   You were attracted to him –

Flan   Cut me out of that pathology! You are on your own –

Ouisa   Attracted by his youth and his talent and the embarrassing prospect of being in the movie version of *Cats*. Did you put that in your *Times* piece? And we turn him into an anecdote to dine out on. Or dine in on. But it was an experience. I will not turn him into an anecdote. How do we fit what happened to us in life without turning it into an anecdote with no teeth and a punchline you'll mouth over and over for years to come. 'Tell the story about the imposter who came into our lives –' 'That reminds me of the time this boy –'. And we become these human juke boxes spilling out these anecdotes. But it was an experience. How do we *keep* the experience?

Flan (*to us*)   That's why I love paintings. Cézanne. The problems he brought up are the problems painters are still dealing with. Color. Structure. Those are problems.

Ouisa   There is color in my life, but I'm not aware of any structure.

Flan (*to us*)   Cézanne would leave blank spaces in his canvases if he couldn't account for the brush stroke, give a reason for the color.

Ouisa   Then I am a collage of unaccounted-for brush strokes. I am all random. God, Flan, how much of your life can you account for?

Flan   Are you drunk? The Cézanne sale went through. We are rich. Geoffrey's rich. Tonight there's a Matisse we'll get and next month there's a Bonnard and after that –

She considers him.

Ouisa   These are the times I would take a knife and dig out your heart. Answer me? How much of your –

Flan   – life can I account for! *All*! I am a gambler!

Pause.

Ouisa   We're a terrible match.

(*To us.*) Time passes.

I read today that a young man committed suicide in Riker's Island. Tied a shirt around his neck and hanged himself. Was it the pink shirt? This burst of color? The pink shirt. Was it Paul? Who are you? We never found out who you are.

Flan   I'm sure it's not him. He'll be back. We haven't heard the last of him. The imagination. He'll find a way.

(*To us.*) We have to go. An auction.

I'll get the elevator.

Flan *goes.*

Ouisa (*to us*)   But if it was the pink shirt. Pink. A burst of pink. The Sistine Chapel. They've cleaned it and it's all these colors.

Flan's voice   Darling –

Ouisa *starts to go. She looks up.* **Paul** *is there, wearing the pink shirt.*

Paul   The Kandinsky. It's painted on two sides.

He glows for a moment and is gone.

She considers. She smiles. The Kandinsky begins its slow revolve.

Methuen Drama World Classics
include

Lightning Source UK Ltd.
Milton Keynes UK
UKHW011552080420
361503UK00001B/8